D1487130

Many things would come to pass, but the nature of the place would remain a matter of opinion.

Wright Morris, *God's Country and My People*

The Nature of the Place

DIANE DUFVA QUANTIC

A Study of Great Plains Fiction

University of Nebraska Press, Lincoln and London

Portions of chapter 1 originally appeared in "Learning to Live on the Land: Theories of Land and Society in Great Plains Literature," in *Platte Valley Review* 17, no.1 (1989).

Portions of chapter 4 originally appeared in "Frederick Manfred's *The Golden Bowl:* Myth and Reality in the Dust Bowl," in *Western American Literature* 25, no.4 (1991).

Portions of chapter 6 originally appeared in "Ceremonies in Lone Tree: Wright Morris Examines the West," *The Nebraska Humanist: Rereading the Classics of the American West,* vol.11, 1989, published by the Nebraska Humanities Council, Lincoln NE.

Portions of chapter 7 are reprinted from "The Unifying Thread: Connecting Place and Language in Great Plains Literature," *American Studies* 32, no.1, © 1991 Mid-America American Studies Association. Used by permission.

First Bison Books printing: 1997

Library of Congress Cataloging-in-Publication Data. Quantic, Diane Dufva. The nature of the place: a study of Great Plains fiction / Diane Dufva Quantic. p. cm. Includes bibliographical references and index. ISBN 0-8032-3800-2 (cl: alk. paper) ISBN 0-8032-8850-6 (pbk.: alk. paper). 1. American fiction – Great Plains – History and criticism. 2. Great Plains – In literature. 3. Regionalism in literature. 4. Myth in literature. I. Title. PS274.Q36 1995   813.009'03278 – dc20   94-34986 CIP

Cover photograph 1940, © by Wright Morris.

To Bruce, Cathryn, and David for their patience and encouragement
and in Memory of Charles and Hilda Johannson Dufva
and Sylvanus and Margaret McKim Bell
and all the others who came on to the Great Plains and stayed

Contents

Preface

My mother grew up in Lebanon, Kansas, the geographic center of the contiguous forty-eight states. My father's parents arrived in Kansas from Sweden just before the turn of the century. My family tree includes old-stock American Bells, who were in the Ohio valley in 1797 and moved steadily westward, Scottish McKims, who came into Kansas from Canada, and Swedish Dufva grandparents, who paused in Chicago on their way west. All of these people were in Kansas by 1897. I grew up in northeastern Kansas, oblivious to the symbolic significance of my ancestry. I only knew that across the alley that ran along the back of our house was an alfalfa field, and beyond that a wooded hill where we played cowboys and Indians, uninterrupted by the civilized calls of parents. Our neighbors kept a cow that we could "milk." In winter our sleds went two blocks beyond the bottom of the hill on the blocked-off street. The old quarry at the top of the hill yielded fossils and a pleasant view of the river valley where the town nested. In the back seat of a 1948 Nash I rode to my grandfather's farm at the speed of a good horse, which was my grandfather's accustomed pace. With my father, I occasionally went "hunting" on the hill behind my grandmother's tiny farm, and on Sundays we drove to the small town where my uncle had a bank, and the town had a real square. My cousins and I entertained ourselves listening in on telephone party lines. The "Great Plains" I subconsciously experienced was the wooded hills and small towns of the Flint Hills prairie. Today, my grandfather's farm and the small town are submerged beneath the muddy waters of an artificial reservoir, my grandmother's eighty-acre farm has been sold, and the alfalfa field and hillside are beneath the ordered squares of lots and houses.

When I was a child and we traveled outside of Kansas, people would comment, "Oh, it's flat there, isn't it?" I assumed they were right: below the hill we claimed as ours the town stretched out along the old riverbed, curving to fit the bowl of hills that protected us from tornadoes, according to a supposed Indian legend we gladly adopted.

Then, as an adult, I moved to south central Kansas, near a city where Meridian is a street name and where a short drive east pushes one into the high, curved prairie of the southern Flint Hills and an equally short drive west brings one face to face with the limitless horizon of the plains. We hunted for a shady picnic spot for half a day and ended up eating in the shadow of our car before we learned where to find the shade trees (in city parks). Here I began to appreciate the true nature of "flatlands" when our daughter, at age ten, on a trip to her grandparents' home in my hilly hometown, commented that she liked it there "because they didn't take the dirt out and make the streets flat." She was almost grown before she realized that trees do not naturally grow around farmyards.

I wrote much of this manuscript in the mountains of Colorado, on the rim of the Great Plains. On afternoon hikes, I can climb a narrow ridge and look out over the flat patterns that spread east beyond the urban sprawl, sharing a vision with Wright Morris, who recalls his first view of the plains:

In my boyhood my father took me to the Rockies, where he had a cabin in Estes Park. Of all that I recall little or nothing. My memory is blocked by a single vibrant image, of the great plains spreading eastward from the mountains. I saw it from a train window. In a way, it was my first view from space. The plains fell away eastward in a manner that left me dizzy, as if the earth were spinning. (*Fork River Space Project* 17)

In my own mind's eye I see beyond the curve in the earth, the plains slanting across the horizon, dotted with the circles of pivot sprinklers, and orderly patchwork farms, with green-shaded towns and tree-lined creeks hidden in folds of the earth. Dogs sleep in the center of small-town highways. Cattle stand in warm brown ponds. A one-room bar, with a patch of dirt for parking, advertises "warm beer and bad service." At Christmas, Santa's sled is pulled across a farmer's lawn by wooden cutouts of pigs. In our suburban yard a volunteer, cotton-laden cottonwood dominates the shabby trees left behind by the developer. On our summer trips across Kansas I imagine the long journey of the wagons that stretched between the resting places that were close, perhaps, to the shaded rest stops placed strategically along the interstate. The rough outcroppings that the highway ignores meant long detours for the wagons. In winter, on our trips across the high plains, occasionally we have to surrender to the climate and stop for shelter when the unrelenting storms threaten us as they threatened the first settlers.

Perhaps this personal perspective has influenced my point of view in this study of Great Plains fiction. Most of my life has been spent in the center of the country, on the edge of the line between prairie and plains; yet it was not until I began to read about the Great Plains, some fifteen years ago, that I began to think about the place that I had always lived. My childhood perspective – confusing "flat" with "hills" – and the adjustment we made when we moved to the edge of the true plains have made me aware of the effect of place upon point of view. How far one can see and *what* one can see affects more than eyesight. Shapes, sounds, seasons become important in a land with no variation along the horizon.

In a region where there are no natural barriers the great expanses exacerbate the weather's natural violence, and the land's products continue to influence the quality of life, no matter how far removed one imagines oneself to be from the land. The drought, the coming storm, the promised crops are the stuff of daily newscasts and journalists' analyses. Social calendars, sporting plans, conversations, and jokes depend upon the weather and the nature of the land. Water conservation is still one of the region's most volatile issues. The coming death of the last small town, the declining number of farms, and the public or private control of the last vestiges of true prairie persist as apparently insoluble problems. The disparity between life as it is and life as it "should be" is grounded in mythic assumptions about the land itself and the remnants of the democratic utopia assumed to exist in the small town on the Great Plains.

Acknowledgments

I have been thinking about our visions and experiences on the Great Plains for a long time. A number of people have shared their viewpoints with me. The late Wayne Rohrer, a professor of sociology at Kansas State University, prompted my curiosity about the relationship between literature and sociological research when he asked me to assist him in a comparative investigation of Middle Western literature and sociology. That work evolved over a number of years, and when it ended I found myself focusing more and more on the Great Plains, curious about not only the literature but also the history, the ecology, the cultural geography, and the art of the region.

Wichita State University has supported my work in Great Plains literature with a sabbatical, a summer research grant, and, most important, a typist and editor, Fran Majors, whose eagle eye and efficient computer skills made my copy look good and saved my sanity when my own computer's memory collapsed and took my electronic manuscript copy with it.

Richard Etulain of the University of New Mexico, James Shortridge of the University of Kansas, and Robert Thacker of St. Lawrence University read portions of early drafts of this work and provided important suggestions. My sturdy colleague Gerald Hoag read all of an earlier and much longer draft. I thank him for his comments and encouragement.

My colleagues in the Western Literature Association have given me a forum to test my theories in conference sessions over the years and, more important, have helped me to realize that to a growing number of scholars the Great Plains is an exciting scholarly venue.

Finally, I thank Bruce for his unfailing patience, and Cathy and David, who grew to adulthood while their mother thought about the Great Plains and who, nevertheless, expressed their faith in this project, even when they had no idea what I was doing.

Introduction

Since the first settlers arrived on the Great Plains, we have been trying to come to terms with the physical reality and the psychological significance of open space. Our concept of the region is encapsulated in a tangle of phrases and images – the Garden of the World, the Great American Desert, the closed frontier, Manifest Destiny, the safety valve, democratic utopia; wagon trains crawling west; explorers mapping rivers and mountains; Indians attacking, then fleeing, the settlers' encroachment; Cooper's Natty Bumppo, looming larger than life over Ishmael Bush's immigrant train; Cather's plow against the setting sun. Continuing efforts to define the region – the prairies as the ultimate ecological system, the romance or the reality of the plains frontier, the Great Plains wheat acreage as the ideal family farm – provide a kind of litmus test for the nation's state of mind.

Great Plains fiction reflects this often confusing collection of ideas about the character of the nation's center. Wright Morris laments that "the names on the land now turn up as the themes or the titles of books. The dry places and the wet, the forces natural and unnatural, have been catalogued" (*The Territory Ahead*, 1957, 21). On the Great Plains, renaming is a necessary process. Where acts are repeated in the continuing struggle to make the land produce, writers conjure up seemingly endless variations of past experience. The impulse arises not only from nostalgia, as Morris suggests, but also from a need to connect the present with the past. As Stegner points out in *Wolf Willow* (1962), "[H]istory on the Plains took a lot of learning" (254). No matter how often the tale is told, there are those who are doomed to repeat the experience.

In this study I explore the various manifestations of the myths of westward expansion in Great Plains fiction and the transformation of the assumptions implicit in the mythic images that became necessary when the land was claimed, communities were formed, and life began in real time. Four intricately related words – *land, society, myth*, and *reality* – provide one way to describe this experience. The land is the physical reality of tallgrass prairie or short-grass high plains. To be usable, it must be occupied and transformed into identifiable places – farms and towns – by people who come from somewhere else. The first settlers carried with them myths, popular conceptions, that influenced the way they viewed the region. The unfamiliar land before them forced settlers to reevaluate their expectations.

Long before the central prairies and high plains were opened for settlement, Americans had developed fantastical myths about the westering experience that arose from the absence of precise knowledge of the region.[1] As Lee Clark Mitchell points out in *Witnesses to a Vanishing America* (1981), "America had been imagined from the beginning in terms of timeless space as a vacant land awaiting the starter's gun of history" (6). Throughout the nineteenth century, political and economic theories and decisions were based upon the underlying assumptions expressed by these mythic expectations: industry could crowd the East as long as the prairies and plains provided limitless arable land for population expansion. Those who went west would send their agricultural produce to the East. Then, with their accumulated wealth they would buy the East's manufactured goods.

Myth as the term is used here refers, first, to the preconceptions settlers brought with them and, second, to the collective world-view of a society, a composite of the legendary, religious, political, even economic concepts a society shares.[2] On the Great Plains these two points of view were diametrically opposed: the preconceptions did not coincide with the world the settlers left behind or with the world they faced. The dialectical opposition implicit in these mythic concepts contributes to the ambivalence often found in Great Plains fiction.

The nature of the place, the land itself, influences changes in these mythic concepts. As Henry Nash Smith points out in his seminal study, *Virgin Land: The American West as Symbol and Myth* (1950), "one of the most persistent generalizations concerning American life and character is the notion that our society has been shaped by the pull of a vacant continent drawing populations westward" (3).[3] In the late eighteenth century and well into the nineteenth century, proponents of geographical determinism asserted that the land determines the nature of society, the quality of life, and even the form and theme of literature. In some ways, these theorists were right: Life on the plains is determined by the land. Farmers can raise only those crops that weather and soil will tolerate.

An underlying assumption is that the land belongs to those who know best how to use it. Settlement brings change in the land itself, and the land forces adaptation of the societies settlers bring with them. The new arrivals need a place to enclose that represents security, identifiable boundaries, and emotional attachments, but on the plains many new arrivals saw nothing familiar and therefore nothing at all. Nevertheless, the land had been promised and given to them in parcels of one hundred and sixty acres, and they believed that this was enough to make every man his neighbor's equal. Believing in the myth of the garden, thousands settled in to face an unfamiliar landscape. In Great Plains fiction the focus is on the resulting change, the cultivation of the land, and not on preservation of the pristine wilderness or the clash of native and encroaching cultures. Ambivalence arises in part from the necessary destruction of the wilderness, which is gone before its value is acknowledged. Why people were willing to leave the security of their homes and families and travel into unsettled land, why they continue to live in a hostile environment, why they insist that the family farm is to be preserved at all costs – these familiar contradictions reflect both historical tradition and mythic concepts that persist in the fiction and the popular imagination even when experience disproves them.

The earliest myths – El Dorado, the Northwest Passage, the Passage to India – lured French, Spanish, English, and finally American explorers onto the Great Plains. By the end of the nineteenth century the region was the last great expanse of free land, the last hope for the American dream of democratic utopia, the safety valve that would ensure stability in the East, the melting pot that would meld disparate immigrants into Americans. Told and retold, these myths of the westward course of empire became self-fulfilling prophecies. If a new home proved to be less than the expected Edenic garden, the disappointed homesteader imagined the garden to be further west. If the plains seemed to be the Great American Desert, the yeoman farmer assumed that if he worked even harder he could realize the promise of the Garden.

The Great Plains do not end at the northern border, but extend in a crescent into the prairie provinces of Canada – Manitoba, Saskatchewan, and Alberta. Although Canadian prairie literature recounts the same problems of establishing new communities in a demanding land, there are some differences in the myths, if not in the realities (Harrison, esp. xv; Kreisel; Richtik). The Wild West is not a part of the tradition in Canada, where the Mounties' reassuring presence brought law and order at the time of settlement and the displacement of the Indian population was not such a violent confrontation. Nevertheless, Henry Kreisel describes a familiar dichotomy: "man, the giant-conqueror, and man, the insignificant dwarf always threatened by defeat," form the two familiar "polarities of the state of mind produced by the sheer physical facts of the prairie" (173) that are expressed as the Garden and the Desert in American literature. Canadian prairie fiction and Great Plains fiction in the American tradition reveal the same patterns of arrival, confrontation, and transformation of mythic preconceptions.

By the time writers began to tell the stories of the Great Plains, in the 1890s, the great expectations that the westering myths expressed were in the past. The 1890 census asserted that the frontier was closed. The depression that followed several years of severe weather, as well as the shift to the gold standard in 1893, confirmed pessimistic suspicions. Nevertheless, the myths persist and are woven into the fabric of the region's fiction, the source of heroic vision in pioneer tales or ironic points of reference. The myths have been offered as promises, tested against reality, conserved as images of the past, and finally transformed into what Wright Morris, in *The Territory Ahead*, calls the "raw material" of clichés that the artist can transform into new material of metaphor and symbols.

This study focuses primarily on Great Plains fiction. To examine just a few Great Plains novels and stories in any significant context is a large enough task. The journals of Lewis and Clark and autobiographical works of writers such as Washington Irving, Mari Sandoz, Wallace Stegner, and Laura Ingalls Wilder reinforce and complement the region's fiction. In spite of the variety these writers represent, they use common motifs and devices that reflect collective experience on the Great Plains. Their works provide patterns of meaning for the past (however inaccurate) that are part of our way of seeing the Great Plains. The conceptual framework that lured men and women onto the plains and prairies has been codified in Rølvaag's Per Hansa and Cather's Alexandra Bergson and petrified in Morris's Tom Scanlon. Despite the persistence of the myth, the verdant utopia has never been realized, and as hope that it is attainable has dimmed, the myths have been transformed into ironic, sometimes comic, sometimes antipastoral motifs. Without the original conceptual framework the myths create in the communal memory and experience, Great Plains fiction would be a collection of mere tales.

Despite occasional surveys of regional literature, most often labeled "Middle Western," Great Plains literature as a distinct body of works has not been thoroughly explored.[4] In this volume I examine Great Plains fiction in a particular context, arrived at inductively after years of reading a continually expanding list of Great Plains works, in the hope that other scholars will continue to examine the region's literature. In selecting works for this study, I tried to be as inclusive as possible in order to demonstrate the wide use of similar themes and techniques. My purpose here is not to provide a close analysis of particular authors; nor is it to provide a full account of the region's fiction. Rather, I examine ways that these various writers depict the interrelated influences of the various westering myths, the land itself, and the establishment of society. Although chapters follow roughly the region's chronological development, the focus is thematic. To provide a context for an examination of the literature, chapter 1 surveys the theories of land and society that cultural geographers and other scholars use to explain the way people live in a region. Like the writers of Great Plains fiction, these scholars try to determine the "reality." Conversely, Great Plains fiction explores some of the issues studied by scholars in other fields, such as the failure of some to adapt and the struggle of others to create a community.

Chapters 3 through 6 begin with an examination of particular myths that drew men and women on to the Great Plains and offer some illustrations of their appearance in Great Plains fiction. Chapter 6 focuses in particular on the metamorphosis of the original myths into familiar motifs that can be transformed. The final chapter examines the ways in which space and place have influenced the language of Great Plains fiction. What I hope to demonstrate in this study is that the broad concepts of land, society, myth, and reality have come together in a distinct body of fiction. Nevertheless, as Wright Morris has said, it is evident that the nature of the place remains a matter of opinion.

CHAPTER ONE

Theories of Land and Society:
Making the Myths

It is hard to come to terms with a place that can be benign one day, malevolent the next, that produces a bumper crop of wheat one year and dust the
next. In *Space and Place: The Perspective of Experience* Yi-Fu Tuan describes such a contrast as a relationship between space and place: "Place is
security, space is freedom: we are attached to the one and long for the
other" (3). Tuan points out that we attach meaning to space and place; or as
Edward Relph says, "[A] place is not just the 'where' of something; it is the
location plus everything that occupies that location seen as an integrated
and meaningful phenomenon" (3). On the Great Plains, space and place
were at first indistinguishable. On a purely physical level, where there
were no landmarks to delineate direction or distance men and women became disoriented. In Willa Cather's *My Ántonia* (1918), for example, the
narrator, Jim Burden, expresses a fear repeated time and again in Great
Plains fiction:

There was nothing but land . . . I had the feeling that the world was left behind, that we had got over the edge of it, and were outside man's jurisdiction. I had never before looked up at the sky where there was not a familiar mountain ridge against it. But this was the complete dome of heaven, all there was of it. (7–8)

It is difficult to impose a scheme on space when there seems to be nothing there. We measure distance as distinct from self, and on the plains that distance, both physical and psychological, can seem infinite.

On the Great Plains land is not merely ground for crops. For some it is the source of life, while for others it is empty space that symbolizes psychological erasure. For some the land symbolizes unlimited opportunity. Others feel the threat of isolation in a land where they can find nothing to look at. The first minuscule marks that the settlers leave on the land symbolize their struggle to transform it. The devices they construct seem both presumptuous and insignificant. The upright windmill pulls water from the prehistoric depths of the earth, but its height can symbolize the dangers of pride and carelessness. The vertical grain elevator, Wright Morris tells us, signals humans' tenuous presence on the vast prairie.

The creation of a place is not a simple act for the plains pioneer. At first the house, the enclosure that acknowledges the presence of men and women, is hardly distinguishable from empty space. Where to build can be an overwhelming question if there is no physical feature such as a hill or a stream to relate to. Materials must be hauled from miles away or cut from the ground itself. Physical effort and time must be taken from the more important tasks of getting a cash crop into the soil. The sod house that disappears into the wild land symbolizes man's reversion to animalism for Mr. Shimerda in *My Ántonia* (1918), but for Ma in Laura Ingalls Wilder's *On the Banks of Plum Creek* (1937) the whitewashed rooms of the dugout create a solid wall of protection from the cold, the wolves, and the Indians that kept her awake at night in the log cabin in Indian territory (*Plum Creek* 1–16). Rosie in John Ise's *Sod and Stubble* (1936) characteristically sets to work and transforms her new husband's bachelor quarters into a home with flowers, rosebushes, and a garden (7–9).

Framed by sheltering trees, the vertical house replaces the first primitive protection of the sod or log dwellings. It is the center of a cluster of barns, outbuildings, and ordered fields that spread like a fairy ring, evidence that men and women have left an indelible mark on the land. Sometimes, as in Frederick Philip Grove's *Fruits of the Earth* (1933), the promised house is postponed year after year: barns, more land, and equipment take priority when cash is scarce. The farmhouse can symbolize material success that becomes excessive. In Bess Streeter Aldrich's *Spring Came On Forever* (1935) the pioneer bride Amalia lives first in a log cabin; then, after her husband's death, her brother Fritz helps her build a simple frame house. Later, Fritz and her son Emil build a house of native stone, as rooted in the land as Amalia and Fritz themselves. But in the third generation the house becomes the town wife's showpiece. As their land and the good fortune it symbolizes disappear in mortgages and bad investments, Joe's wife Myrtie completes the ironic transformation of the house by having the solid stones covered with fashionable stucco.

Conflicts over the house often symbolize conflicts over the place of men and women on the land. In Cather's novel *One of Ours* (1922) Claude Wheeler, who loves the land if not the dulling work it demands, marries Enid, who gardens but has never farmed (108). To Claude, a house is a practical extension of his solicitous concern for the land. Enid wants to create a spotless ideal, as distinct from the land as lace, linoleum, and her own white dresses and shoes can make it. He wants big, gaudy gourds growing on the lattice; she wants ornamental clematis. Claude lavishes on the house "the solicitude and cherishing care that Enid seemed not to need" (152), but Enid's ascetic presence destroys any link between the house and the land. To regain a sense of balance, Claude slips off to the timber claim. "In the open, grassy spots, shut in by the bushy walls of yellowing ash trees, he felt unmarried and free." By reestablishing his connection with the land he recreates the past. "He went off into the timber claim to meet a young man

Theories of Land and Society 3

more experienced and interesting than himself who had not tied himself up with compromises" (183). When Enid and Claude go their separate ways, Claude looks from the timber claim at their "little house, giving itself up so meekly to solitude" (193), fading back into the land as their marriage becomes a memory.

Stretching down the continent's center, with few natural boundaries, the Great Plains would seem to defy delineation, yet the region fits the definition of a "popular" or "vernacular" region, that is, a definable place perceived by the inhabitants to exist.[1] A region that seems featureless to the casual observer nevertheless seems distinct to its inhabitants, but there is little agreement among scholars concerning the boundaries or even the label of the country's core. For instance, the map developed by cultural geographer Wilbur Zelinsky divides the central plains states – Kansas, Nebraska and the Dakotas – neatly in two, between the Middle West and the West (118–19).

One of the most persistent representations of the region is Walter Prescott Webb's Region I in his study of the Great Plains. Webb cites three distinguishing characteristics of this central region that influence the way people live in this place: it is level, treeless, and semiarid. He points out that after nearly a century of scientific and pseudoscientific debate and attempts at manipulation, "these forces, historically speaking, are constant and eternal; therefore, they make a permanent factor in the interpretation of history. . . . If the Great Plains forced man to make radical changes, sweeping innovations in his ways of living, the cause lies almost wholly in the physical aspects of the land" (10).

Two of Webb's factors are important to Great Plains fiction. First, he asserts that the Great Plains experience will not change. Time and again in the stories, the person who attempts to impose his or her will upon the land is overcome by natural disaster, a blizzard, a prairie fire, or a dust storm, and the person who understands the land's potential reaps bountiful harvests. Second, Webb asserts that the land itself determines the quality of life in the region. The settlers who created houses out of sod where there were no trees acknowledge their debt to the land in the most fundamental sense. They can pull water from the ground when it is there, but when the land refuses to yield water they have only two choices: to leave or to learn to do without.

To describe the Great Plains has proved no easy task. Even before the region was explored by Europeans, mapmakers filled in blank space with fantastic myths: a water passage to the West, cities of gold, dangerous adventures (Boorstin 229).[2] Most of the earliest travelers had no vocabulary to describe the unfamiliar landscape and thus relied upon inept similes and euphuistic clichés. Focusing on the landscape or the exotic Indians or hoping to find wealth in trapping or trading, few of these early visitors recognized the rich fertility of the soil. As early as the 1820s travelers passed through the region on their way to Santa Fe or the mountain fur-trading posts. Between 1840 and 1860 thousands of settlers, bound for Oregon and California, crossed the region with hardly a thought of stopping.

Despite Americans' misgivings, inexorably the farthest edge of the contiguous states moved west to include the Great Plains. In the 1850s Kansas was the focus of the free-state question. Abolitionists settled in the territory to counteract the movement of proslavery Missourians and thereby to secure Kansas's admission to the Union as a free state. The abolitionists' yeoman farmer challenged the Southern plantation system and, in part because of the nature of the land itself, came to dominate agricultural practice and political theory in the latter half of the nineteenth century. After the Civil War, the Homestead Act and the exaggerated claims of boomers and land speculators who wanted settlers and customers near the rails that were stretching across the region drew settlers by the thousands onto the prairies. By the turn of the century only the northern plains remained unsettled.

Thomas Jefferson first turned the nation's attention to the importance of the interior. He sponsored Lewis and Clark's expedition and outlined the size and distribution of the small farms that would enfranchise the most citizens and thereby assure the establishment of a true democracy. Frederick

Jackson Turner, working within the tradition established by Jefferson, first delineated the significance of America's open, available land in scholarly terms. In "The Significance of the Frontier in American History" (in *The Frontier in American History*) and in subsequent works Turner explained the importance of geography in the westward movement and especially in the development of the plains and prairies. Although Turner's theories have been challenged by twentieth-century scholars who criticize him for his broad approach and his lack of careful attention to detail, they have been a part of our national mind-set for almost a century. Some of Turner's themes are evident in Great Plains fiction. For example, he identifies the complex interplay of the attraction of available land and the perceived economic necessity to inhabit it as the driving force in American society. Certainly it provided the tremendous impetus needed to settle the Great Plains. The democratic point of view that he identifies in society and politics pervades the fiction, and his description of the state of flux at the frontier corroborates the underlying conflict between the demands of the land and society that is a major fictional theme.

Scholars continue to examine the Great Plains landscape in their attempts to explain the development of society in the region. Some of their studies help clarify conflicts and ideas in the region's fiction. For example, Walter Kollmorgen traces the assumptions of late-nineteenth-century theorists and settlers who believed that farmers could change the land by rainmaking, irrigation, or dryland farming techniques. He contends that the myths of the safety valve and the democratic yeoman attracted people with limited economic resources to the Western homesteads because settlers and policymakers alike assumed that reality was the small family farm no matter what the land dictated (21). His study corroborates the conflict between expectations and reality that is evident in a wide variety of fictional works about the struggle to preserve a farm on marginal land. Mari Sandoz's *Old Jules* (1935), Frederick Manfred's *Golden Bowl* (1944), Lois Philips Hudson's *Bones of Plenty* (1962), Wallace Stegner's *Wolf Willow* (1962), Douglas Unger's *Leaving the Land* (1984), and Dan O'Brien's *In the Center of the*

Nation (1991) recount conflicts that arise from differences between political myths of the safety valve and the sacredness of the small farm, on the one hand, and the economic dictates of the land, on the other.

Archer Butler Hulbert, in his study of soil, confirms a familiar scene in Great Plains fiction, the selection of a homestead. Hulbert contends that settlers were attracted to one region or another by reports that the soils in that region were familiar (78). Great Plains authors confirm his primary observation. Sandoz's Old Jules bases his decision on careful observation, knowledge of botany, and a study of government bulletins: he selects land that will grow sunflowers (*Old Jules* 19). In Wilder's series, Pa, in selecting sites for his family's successive homes, always looks for prairie grass, some slight rise, and a nearby creek bottom, all characteristics of their original Wisconsin home (*Little House on the Prairie*, 1935, 53; *Plum Creek* 1–2).[3] He describes his last Dakota claim in familiar terms:

It lies south of where the lake joins Big Slough, and the slough curves around to the west of it. There's a rise in the prairie to the south of the slough that will make a nice place to build. A little hill just west of it crowds the slough back on that side. On the quarter section there's upland hay and plow land lying to the south; and good grazing on all of it, everything a farmer could ask for. (*By the Shores of Silver Lake*, 1939, 173)

A novel that illustrates Hulbert's theory is *The Homesteaders* (1916), by Canadian author Robert J. C. Stead. John Harris accompanies land locator Alec McCrae on a search for land. The particular McCrae presses on far beyond the settlements. "Here McCrae began paying more minute attention to the soil, examining the diggings around badger holes, watching out for clumps of 'wolf willow,' with always a keen eye for stones and low-lying alkali patches and the general topography of the quarter" (49). He urges Harris to select land suitable for both wheat and grazing. The care that Pa Ingalls and John Harris take in their selection of a homestead reflects a broader awareness of the quality of the land that is evident in Great Plains fiction.

Some settlers reluctantly ventured onto the open prairies. In a chapter titled "Hesitation along the Ninety-eighth Meridian," Carl Kraenzel points out that for several decades before 1880, westward settlement came to a near halt at the 98th meridian. He asserts that this was because there were no trees for buildings or fencing, little water, and few railroads. Space itself "was something of a threat" (125). This reluctance is a frequent fictional theme. As they drive through the dark on an unmarked trail toward their next new home, Laura knows that Ma Ingalls "had never wanted to leave Plum Creek and did not like to be here now; she did not like traveling in that lonely country" (*By the Shores of Silver Lake* 66). Even Rosie, in Ise's *Sod and Stubble*, who proves to be stronger than her husband Henry, finds it difficult to share his enthusiasm for the treeless landscape and the barely visible sod houses despite his assertion that he has turned up only black soil (2–4).

The nation of small farmers envisioned by Jefferson and established by the definition of a homestead as a section of only 160 acres was difficult to establish and maintain in this semiarid region. Arable land, thought to be infinite when the law was conceived, soon disappeared. What remained was located in the semiarid regions or was controlled by railroad developers and land promoters, who lost sight of Jefferson's vision: land became a commodity, something that could be used up. Homesteads were distributed like food rations, in equal portions regardless of the land's quality or configuration. The Homestead Act itself was not entirely successful. Between the establishment of the act in 1862 and 1890 only 372,659 claims were proved, benefiting at most two million people during a period when the population of the Western states increased by more than ten million (Smith 221).

Despite these limitations, those who stayed to farm the high plains created a distinct culture. The settlement patterns predicated by the terms of the Homestead Act and the railroads resulted in scattered farm homes, at least a mile apart, connected by marginal roads to the small trading villages spread out along the railroad tracks. For a family to be successful, every member had to be committed to working the land. Hired help was scarce and expensive. Time was a commodity, more valuable than money. Women were workers, not companions. School and cultural amenities were low priorities. Growing up was a time for more work than play, and religion reinforced duty to work and to family.

Great Plains writers often focus on the complex interplay of place and society that arises from the dichotomy of attraction and repulsion. The fiction is rife with examples of people transformed by their encounter with the land. Often they go mad. Anthropomorphism signals this extreme deterministic point of view. O. E. Rølvaag titles the last chapter of *Giants in the Earth* (1927) "The Great Plain Drinks the Blood of Christian Men and Is Satisfied." The fiction abounds with portraits of women worn out by the land: William Allen White's silent, isolated and soon dead Mrs. Burkholder in "A Story of the Highlands" in *The Real Issue* (1897); Old Jules's gnarled and toothless wife Mary in Sandoz's biography of her father; Ada shrinking as her children grow in Kent Haruf's novel *The Tie That Binds* (1984). All young and vigorous women at one time, their transformation results from a combination of circumstances dictated by the land: the elements, hard manual labor, and isolation.

The land that defeats some ennobles others. In a number of works the overburdened woman becomes a symbol of endurance and strength. Bess Streeter Aldrich's enduring matriarchs Abbie Deal in *A Lantern in Her Hand* (1928) and Amalia Holmsdorfer in *Spring Came On Forever* retain their physical and emotional strength. Rosie bears fifteen children and manages the farm as Henry's health declines in Ise's *Sod and Stubble*. In Cather's *My Ántonia*, Ántonia survives to achieve mythical status as the archetypal prairie woman. Her comment to Jim is the quintessence of endurance: "We'd never got through if I hadn't been so strong. . . . I belong on a farm. I'm never lonesome here like I used to be in town. . . . And I don't mind work a bit" (342–43).

Some scholars have attempted to demonstrate scientifically that the nature of a place plays a large part in determining the kind of society that will develop there. For example, Hulbert claims that settlers migrated into regions for which they were naturally fit (22, 66–67). Although this theory can be taken to an unlikely extreme, in Great Plains fiction settlers who survive and succeed *are* experienced farmers, and as we have seen, they select their homesites with care. Those who lack some knowledge of the land often succumb to discouragement, suicide, or murderous frustration. The city-dwelling Kinkaiders in Sandoz's *Old Jules* soon abandon their claims. Mr. Shimerda commits suicide in Cather's *My Ántonia*, and Frank Shabata murders his wife Marie and Alexandra's brother Emil in *O Pioneers!* (1913).

Most scholars modify or reject the most deterministic geographic theories. And yet, in *The Grassland of North America* James C. Malin points out that the type of farming that can be done in a region is determined by soil and climate and that disaster can follow the attempt to farm in ways that do not conform to them. Malin uses the term *forest complex* to refer to the views of those Anglo-Americans who persisted in regarding forestland as productive and grassland as deficient even as they moved on to the prairies and high plains.[4] This attitude is often evident in the fiction. As early as 1896 William Allen White recognized distinct geographic divisions and the varying degrees of uncertainty on the Great Plains. In the opening of "The Story of Aqua Pura" he writes:

People who write about Kansas, as a rule, write ignorantly, and speak of the state as a finished product. Kansas, like Gaul of old, is divided into three parts, differing as widely each from the other, as any three countries in the same latitude upon the globe. . . . Eastern Kansas is a finished community like New York or Pennsylvania. Central Kansas is finished, but not quite paid for; and Western Kansas, the only place where there is any suffering from drouth or crop failures, is a new country – old only in pluck which is slowly conquering the desert. (*The Real Issue* 2)

In this passage, White acknowledges the differences between the prairies of the eastern section of the region, settled before the Civil War, and the arid high plains, still being homesteaded by settlers who are discouraged by the dry summers and harsh winters and still ignorant of the land's potential. The literary record asserts repeatedly that the land itself – soil, weather, and landscape – largely determines the quality of life on the plains and the prairies.

The Great American Desert barrier broke down under the onslaught of homesteaders who were forced onto the short-grass prairie when more familiar-looking homesteads were taken up. Three theories ran through the period of settlement: that settlement would change the climate; that irrigation would neutralize the climate; and that man would have to adapt to regional differences and complexities (Emmons; Kollmorgen 218–36). All of these theories appear to some degree in Great Plains fiction and scientific studies.

The first theory implies that the land and the climate can be changed by force of will. Josiah Gregg contemplated the salubrious effect of civilization on the high plains:

The high plains seem too dry and lifeless to produce timber; yet might not the vicissitudes of nature operate a change likewise upon the seasons? Why may we not suppose that the genial influences of civilization – that extensive cultivation of the earth – might contribute to the multiplication of showers, as it certainly does of fountains? Or that shady groves, as they advance upon the prairies, may have some effect upon the seasons? At least, many old settlers maintain that the droughts are becoming less oppressive in the West. . . . Then may we not hope that these sterile regions might yet be thus revived and fertilized, and their surface covered one day by flourishing settlements to the Rocky Mountains? (135)

The theory Gregg reports as merely an observation had scholarly support. G. P. Marsh, in his 1864 study *Man and Nature, or Physical Geography as Modified by Human Actions*, after a careful survey of evidence concluded somewhat reluctantly that "forests . . . promote the frequency of showers, and, if they do not augment the amount of precipitation, they equalize its distribution through the different seasons" (quoted in Kollmorgen 219).

His judicious study became "the bible of the rainmakers of the West" (Kollmorgen 219). The government, clinging to the "forest mentality," encouraged the planting of trees, usually cottonwood, ash, elm, or hackberry, by allowing a homesteader to file a claim for an additional 160 acres if he planted forty acres of the claim in trees and kept them alive for eight years (Dick 130). Few homesteaders were able to fulfill the condition. It was simply impossible to grow trees in soil and climate that nourished long-rooted prairie grasses. The failure of their timber claim contributes to the first discouraged years of marriage for Laura and Almanzo Wilder (*First Four Years*, 1971, 122–23).

Still, throughout the boomer years, 1870–90, the belief that "rain follows the plow" persisted. Settlers, scientists, and shysters contended that the plains would be blessed by rain if only the clods were turned up to the sun so that the entrapped moisture would evaporate and fall again as rain. Samuel Aughey, a professor of natural history at the University of Nebraska, studied the moisture content of plowed and unplowed ground and concluded that the plowed surface absorbed eight to twelve times more moisture (Kollmorgen 225). As the promoter Charles Dana Wilber rather illogically put it, "[N]ot by any magic or enchantment, nor by incantations or offerings but instead by the sweat of his face, toiling with his hands, man can persuade the heavens to yield their treasures of dew and rain upon the land he has chosen for a dwelling place" (quoted in Emmons 140–41).

The second theory is closely associated with the first: producing water artificially will neutralize the need for rain. The idea, again, is to farm as one would in a wetter, "forest" climate, to grow crops that require more moisture than the semiarid plains are willing to provide. Advocates of this theory pointed out that with a well and a windmill there is no excuse for losing a crop to drought. They proposed a Great Western American Canal that would make every foot of the Great American Desert "susceptible to irrigation" (Kollmorgen 230). The assumption was that there was a limitless layer of water underneath the land. According to this irrigating logic, cultivation would increase rainfall, which would provide adequate flow in streams and aquifers, so that irrigation would be possible.

Rølvaag includes one of the most compelling portraits of such theoretical excesses in his third novel, *Their Fathers' God* (1931). Peder Victorious challenges the rainmaker's rhetoric, which reflects scientific theory prevalent in the late nineteenth century and which has mesmerized the community. According to the promoter, "Everyone knew that the rain was drifting about in the upper regions of the atmosphere. Why should man not draw some of it down whenever he stood in need of moisture?" (38). Peder attacks this logic by appealing to the community's ironic sense of pride in its ignorance: "Until to-day," he tells his fellow farmers, "we didn't know about the 'empty rooms' drifting in the air and waiting for rain to come along and fill them" (41). Peder's argument, sprinkled with references to the rainmaker's seven-hundred-dollar fee, convinces the conservative County Board to reject the "scientific" offer (47).

Most writers of Great Plains fiction agree with scientific theorists who advocate the third option and insist that man must adapt to the region's complex ecology. As Malin explains, "It is agreed that the prairie soils are unique, that no other substantial area of similar soils exist anywhere in the world. . . . They were the richest of all soils in plant nutrients, the only limiting factor to their productivity being rainfall which was sometimes deficient" (54–55). Malin describes the subtle shifts in the continuums of temperature, moisture, and soil from southeastern Kansas to the northwestern Dakotas. The 98th and 100th meridians, though unseen, are solid barriers: between them farmers can grow sorghums and wheat without irrigating, but beyond the 100th meridian farming techniques must change.

The barrier of the 100th meridian was well established by the end of the nineteenth century. John Wesley Powell, in his 1878 *Report on the Lands of the Arid Regions*, warned against the expansion of the Homestead Act, with its small-farm requirement, into the arid West, a region more suited to grazing than to farming. As Wallace Stegner has pointed out, Powell was willing "to look at what was, rather than at what fantasy, hope or private

Theories of Land and Society 13

interest said there should be" (Stegner, *Beyond the Hundredth Meridian* xi). A century of experience and failure has brought some improvement in knowledge and land use. Nevertheless, on the high plains most farmers realize that the land dictates their crops and their methods. In the fiction this lesson is not confined to stories of settlement. The recurring wanderer character in Wright Morris's novels, such as Will Brady in *The Works of Love* (1949), moves from farm to town to city, a symbol of failed adaptation that becomes displacement.

Great Plains writers share a conviction that one must first come to terms with this vast stretch of space that leaves no place to hide from the physical emptiness or psychological horrors that trick one with mirages of water or ghosts from the past. The man or woman who is afraid to come to terms with this open space, who exploits the land or cannot endure the storms and drought, will be defeated.

One example of this conflict will suffice. In *Fruits of the Earth* Canadian writer Frederick Grove's Abe Spalding is comparable to O. E. Rølvaag's Per Hansa and Cather's Alexandra Bergson in *O Pioneers!*⁵ All three believe in the land and the wealth it will yield. They seem larger than life, capable of imposing their dreams upon the land. The evening of his arrival on his claim, Abe begins to work the land even before he unloads his wagons: "He was here to conquer. Conquer he would! . . . he had the peculiar feeling as though he were ploughing over an appreciable fraction of the curvature of the globe; for whenever he turned at the north end of his furrow, he could no longer see his wagon, as though it were hidden behind the shoulder of the earth" (14–15). Abe likes the feel of the plow, but although he dimly senses a power within the landscape, the key word is *conquer*. What he wants, Abe tells himself, is "a piece of land capable of being tilled from line to line, without waste areas, without rocky stretches, without deep-cut gullies which denied his horses a foothold. He wanted land, not landscape" (12). When he wants trees, he plants them "where he wanted them" (36). To accomplish this, he abandons the ideal of the self-sufficient homestead and relies instead on machines, not men, to work his land. But as his neighbor

Nicoll has warned, the land does not always yield proportionately: more land means more work. It does not enfranchise, but enslaves.

In the end Abe is left to till his hundreds of acres alone, and his wife Ruth sits by herself in their huge house, an empty mausoleum that Abe admits he has surrounded with windbreaks on all sides as "a rampart which, without knowing it, he had erected to keep out a hostile world" (165). Abe sees the futility of his dominance of the land. He notes that the bricks of his new house are starting to weather and crumble. The trees in his windbreak will die and decay, or else they will spread and conquer his fields. "And so with everything, with his machines, his fields, his pool; they were all on the way of being leveled to the soil again" (160). The land is not a static commodity to use up but a source of change, not merely the means to obtain annual crops but something that must be respected and understood in itself.

A frequent symbol that reveals yet another attitude toward the land is the earth as fertile mother.[6] The grass, symbol of natural order, is plowed under (an act often depicted as a violation) and forced into reordered fields that promise limitless fertility. The land as earth mother is both abused and revered. In Martha Ostenso's *Wild Geese* (1920) Caleb Gare regards the land as his true mistress, caressing his flax with the affection he denies his wife. Other Great Plains novelists note this attraction and abuse. Old Jules nurtures the land and abuses his wives and children. In *Slogum House* (1937) Sandoz separates and inverts this symbolic relationship: Gulla Slogum exploits the land and abuses her family and the community, while her husband Ruedy nurtures his fertile retreat and nurses those Gulla has wounded and cast aside. In Rølvaag's *Giants in the Earth* Per Hansa regards the land as a fertile goddess, even as his wife Beret cowers in terror at the land's isolation and dreads the birth of her child, symbol of Per's violation both of her and of the wild land. In *O Pioneers!* Alexandra has a recurring dream in which she is borne across the land by a strong man and immersed in cold water. While readers and critics continue to discuss the dream's significance, most agree that it is clearly an echo of ancient fertility rituals, symbolizing Alexandra's deep commitment to the land.[7]

Theories of Land and Society 15

Land is central to Wright Morris's works, but he invokes it in quite a different way: its psychological power is manifested in minutiae. The same details, the same incidents, recur in novel after novel, until they accumulate metaphorical meaning. Clichés reflect the few monotonous truths that people cling to when the choices are few. The sky looms oppressively over all. The grain elevator and the false storefront are tiny signs of man's presence in the "sea of grass." The railroad symbolizes the intrusion of the mechanical world – capable of tossing men and horses off its path in the wink of an eye but capable as well of bringing goods in and providing a way out for the discontented. Everything in this landscape is on the move: the very soil itself blows away, just as men and women blow in and out.

If the land influences the way people live on the Great Plains, society exerts equal and sometimes opposing pressure on the landscape. The mark of a single wagon leaves a wake of broken grass. The first arrival leaves a trail, builds a shelter, makes paths to the nearest neighbor, leaves deepening ruts on return trips to the nearest town. The plow moving across the brown square of sod pulls up the grass's deep roots. False fronts announce a town's bravura. The railroad cuts the landscape into arrow-straight lines aimed west. The land transformed into ordered squares begins to produce. One man's mark may be ephemeral, but the town leaves a wider mark and becomes a permanent feature of the landscape.

The struggle to establish a society was repeated endlessly across the Great Plains as the myths of the democratic utopia and the safety valve, the political question of free and slave states, and above all the lure of free land pushed the frontier's boundary west. Progress was the watchword of the nineteenth century, with little thought given to its effect upon the land. As Wallace Stegner put it in *Wolf Willow*, "[I]t is impossible not to believe in progress in a frontier town. Every possibility is open, every opportunity still untested" (251). But as Stegner relates in this chronicle of his boyhood, optimism in East End, Saskatchewan (here called Whitemud), was often short-lived: "The lesson that the plains settler could not learn, short of living it out, was that no system of farming, no matter how strenuously applied, could produce crops in that country during one of the irregular and unpredictable periods of drought and that the consequences of trying to force the issue could be disastrous to both people and land" (254).

Reading Stegner's account, one might think that the plains and prairies were void of communities. But for every Whitemud there is a story of Germans or Mennonites or Yankees who founded towns that have endured. Nostalgia for the pristine wilderness often exists in Great Plains fiction as an important, often ironic counterpoint to the drive for progress, but writers do not deny the need to use the land and build communities.

Theorists who are interested in cultural patterns rather than geological factors have advanced often confusing explanations for the diversity that characterizes the middle region of the United States. Their studies focus on the habits people accumulate and carry with them when they settle a region. They assume that a culture is gradually modified when it enters a different physical environment. In the early twentieth century, however, some cultural geographers theorized that society was the primary cultural determiner and discounted the influence of place. This idea is reflected in the "Doctrine of First Settlement," the theory that the activities of a few hundred or even a few score initial colonizers play a larger part in determining the character of a place than does the contribution of tens of thousands of new immigrants a generation later (Zelinsky 13–14). The "proof" of this theory is evident across the Great Plains in the farming districts and small towns that are still identified as Czech, Swedish, Catholic, Lutheran, or African-American.[8]

If one considers the nature of both the land and the developing society in the Great Plains, the region's character become infinitely complex. For example, Donald Worster attributes the Dust Bowl disaster to the greed of farmers who stripped the land. According to Worster, it was capitalism that brought people to a region where they "encountered a volatile, marginal land" and brought destruction to the "delicate ecological balance that had evolved there" (*Dust Bowl* 5). Obviously, regional variations do not arise from only one cause, but from the region's geography and from the complex interplay of past patterns of behavior and present conditions. Stegner's portrait of Whitemud, in which time, geography, people, and weather combined to defeat its grandiose ambitions, illustrates this. More specifically, the absence of a deeply rooted attraction to the land and the lack of the technological expertise necessary to farm in a semiarid region doomed the town.

This complex relationship between place and culture is the focus of the conflict in Rudy Wiebe's novel *Peace Shall Destroy Many* (1962). Pastor Block and his followers assume that they can continue their tightly closed Russian Mennonite community upon their arrival in the Canadian wilderness. Their settlement, Wapiti, is isolated by distance, hills, and trees, as well as by Pastor Block's iron-willed determination to discourage outside contact. But others in the community are curious about the land and the people around them. The weakening of the pastor's authority over his congregation as the people become involved with the local Métis children and the tragic death of his own daughter in childbirth indicate that other forces at work even on the edge of the wilderness will inexorably doom one person's attempt to impose his or her own will on society.

Despite the continued appeal of rural life, Great Plains society is determined not by the farms that derive their character from the land but by the towns.[9] If the image of the Great Plains as a social and cultural desert persists, it is due in large measure to the character of the small trading towns that have atrophied into trading centers only, often resented by the farmers (Hudson, "Towns of the Western Railroads" 49). The failure of small-town society to develop a mature culture arises from several causes. The rush to settle the plains and prairies was so rapid that towns did not have an opportunity to establish the traditions that nurture culture and a vibrant society. Towns sprang up within an easy day's journey of each other, only to die when people back-trailed during the drought and depression of the 1890s or when the railroad passed them by. Portraits of the inequities farmers suffer in the narrow prairie towns are rife in Great Plains novels and short stories. Sophus Keith Winther's novel *Take All to Nebraska* (1936) chronicles the natural, human, and economic hardships the Grimsens endure. Peter Grimsen risks his own money to make improvements on his rented farm, hoping to buy it eventually. Plagued by multiple disasters and forced to borrow from his neighbor Paulsen, Peter falls into a trap that catches many Great Plains farmers: Paulsen, in collusion with Peter's lawyer, greedily buys the farm from under him (137–40). In Hudson's *The Bones of Plenty* George Custer, embittered by years of failure, loses his temper when he faces his landlord, Vick, for their annual rent renegotiation. The showdown takes place in Vick's dry goods store. George is forced to walk through the "jammed aisles under the busy little funiculars flying money up to Vick" (406). When George points out that his improvements have increased the farm's value, Vick replies that none of the work was done at his request. Vick tells George, "'You *know* you're going to wind up signing this paper here, because you always do, don't you? There's no place else for you to go, is there?' " (410–11). George refuses to sign, and the novel ends with the Custers' departure.

For farm women the town can be a mixed blessing. Meta Grimsen finds relief in town from her own barren farmyard. Like the lonely housewife Delia Markham in Garland's story "A Day's Pleasure," in *Main-Travelled Roads*, Meta enjoys seeing "all the pretty houses, especially the banker's place. . . . The yard was almost a quarter of an acre and all in grass and flowers. There were cool vines growing on the side of the house and large elm trees on the lawn," a contrast to her own yard, where, despite her efforts to plant flower seeds around the house, bare ground persists (Winther, *Take All to Nebraska* 259–60).

But the small town is hardly adequate socially or culturally. It offers little beyond an occasional respite from physical isolation and a rare hint of the rich cultural life that exists beyond its banal expectations. Long before Carl Van Doren coined the term "Revolt from the Village" in 1920, writers were telling tales of repulsion and revolt.[10] In some accounts townspeople consciously repress behavior that does not conform to the community's models. Schoolteachers deride the language and inexperience of immigrant children in the novels of Rølvaag and Winther. In Winther's novels the town children are hostile and cruel to Grimsen's children. Merchants are indifferent to Garland's lonely farm wife in "A Day's Pleasure." They belittle the artistic ambitions of the young in Cather's novels and short stories.[11] Jim Laird's scathing denunciation of the small town of Sand City in Cather's "The Sculptor's Funeral" is perhaps the grimmest in Great Plains fiction: "You [elders] drummed nothing but money and knavery into [the young men's] ears from the time they wore knickerbockers; . . . Now that we've fought and lied and sweated and stolen, and hated as only the disappointed strugglers in a bitter, dead little Western town know how to do, what have we got to show for it?" (*Youth and the Bright Medusa*, 1920, 247–50). Only in sentimental novels such as Aldrich's *The Rim of the Prairie* (1925) or White's *In the Heart of a Fool* (1918), where towns are populated with natives and imported Easterners who are enlightened (but often patronizing), does the town offer islands of culture, and then only to those of unusual abilities or the right social class.

The railroads played an important part in these isolating patterns of settlement on the plains, but they were also the link to the rest of the world.[12] To encourage the railroads to reach across the Great American Desert and thereby join the country from coast to coast, the government granted them twenty to forty sections of land per mile of railroad constructed. The railroad companies built their lines near the best of the land that the government had ceded to them. As they gained control of more and more territory, they mapped out routes that would attract maximum business with minimum miles of track (Hudson, *Plains Country Towns*, chap. 5). At regular intervals they established supply points that became the towns and cities of the plains. Excursion and immigrant trains brought settlers, who spread out over the railroad land grants, repaying the railroads for the cheap land by shipping their goods on those very same lines. The rampant speculation that followed the railroads enabled individuals with money to avoid the restrictions of the Homestead Act and accumulate large areas of choice land.

In the fiction the railroad is an ambivalent symbol. It can mean economic success or ruin. Comings and goings by train mean both connection with and separation from the wider world. Old Jules's mail-order wives arrive by train, and some also depart by train when they see Jules and the rough frontier town. The Ingalls family rides the train almost all the way to their new railroad-camp home in Wilder's *By the Shores of Silver Lake*, and they spend their first winter in a surveyor's shack in the deserted camp. In *The Long Winter* (1940) they almost perish when the trains are blocked by successive blizzards. In Mela Meisner Lindsay's *Shukar Balan: The White Lamb* (1976) Evaliz's first view of her prairie home is from the window of the train at the end of their long journey from the Russian Volga.

Scholars acknowledge the complex relationship between the society and culture that settlers brought with them and their need to adapt to a new environment. Advocates of possibilism believe that people must recognize the environment's limiting factors. Thus, when farmers had to contend with wind and drought on the high plains, they built windmills. When they were challenged by the thick roots of prairie grasses, they developed a new steel plow. James Malin, whose theories of the interrelatedness of history and geography have drawn sharp debate, points out that when farmers abandoned corn to grow wheat they began to enjoy the success that had eluded them as long as they persisted in raising a crop unsuited to the land. In fact, he attributes the Populist movement, and the familiar admonition of Mary Elizabeth Lease to the farmers to raise less corn and more hell, to the new aggressiveness of farmers in the central part of Kansas who were beginning to accumulate some wealth from wheat (238). In this instance the land forced a radical change in the political and economic nature of society in the region.

Most settlers took up land on the open prairies only when all the other land was occupied. Some observers followed this line of thought to an illogical deterministic conclusion, assuming that less desirable people – dull, unimaginative, poor stragglers who came at the end of the homestead era – settled upon this treeless and therefore less desirable land. Ironically, however, some who seem the most unsuited to life on the high plains learn how to make the land productive. The focus of Sandoz's *Old Jules* is her father's faith in the fruitfulness of the Nebraska Sandhills. It is a classic study of adaptability and persistence. Unlike those who are satisfied with the land's remnants, Old Jules' envisions not only the land itself but also the society that he will create: "[O]n the hard land that must be black and fertile, where corn and fruit trees would surely grow well, Jules saw his home and around him a community of his countrymen and other homeseekers, refugees from oppression and poverty, intermingled in peace and contentment" (19). Jules's vision is borne out: his farm is even designated a horticulture experiment station (248). What is more important, Jules realizes his dream to create a community.

That cultural and social changes must occur for society to survive is an important theme in Great Plains fiction. What can be abandoned? What must be preserved? Repeatedly the struggle to establish a new society is reduced to the barest essentials. The focus is on the ironic struggle to establish society – a place – in a barren land. Left to their own devices in such a place, people might assume that they are free to establish any culture that they please. But the issue is not so simple: people left in such an apparently nonexistent place have to confront placelessness. Physical escape from the land may be possible, but to give up the community that has been established at great cost, no matter how stultifying it may be, can be tragic. The struggle with the land is often a metaphor for the individual's inner conflict, his or her quest for a place in a society that offers only a rudimentary identity.

In novels and stories of the Great Plains some find that they cannot live exposed on the open plain, cut off from familiar places and traditions. In Cather's *My Ántonia*, Ántonia's father is such a man. His suffering arises from his disorientation. Nothing around him resembles the warm Bohemian village society he abandoned at his wife's insistence. Reduced to living in the earth itself, he feels degraded and displaced. During a spring blizzard, Mr. Shimerda goes to bed in the barn, puts a gun in his mouth, and pulls the trigger with his toe. "I knew it was homesickness that had killed Mr. Shimerda," the narrator, Jim Burden, comments, "and I wondered whether his released spirit would not eventually find its way back to his own country" (101). Because he is Catholic and dies a suicide without a priest, there is no cemetery for Mr. Shimerda. His wife buries him in the corner of their farm, but Mr. Shimerda's grave is not forgotten by the community: "Years afterward ... Mr. Shimerda's grave was still there. ... The road from the north curved a little to the east just there, and the road from the west swung out a little to the south; so that the grave, with its tall red grass that was never mowed, was like a little island" (118–19).

It is not only foreign immigrants who feel displaced on the plains. In Scarborough's novel *The Wind* (1925) Virginian Letty Mason arrives on the Texas high plains because her childhood home has been sold, the household goods scattered, her place in the world erased (33). To Letty, the effort to adapt is not worth the price. The sand that sifts into her clothing symbolizes a country that literally gets under her skin. She changes physically and emotionally, worn down by her hard and isolated life on the land. The land, which should be the solid footing for a home, is not a place but merely sand, moved about by the ephemeral force of air.

Madness is a frequent motif in Great Plains fiction. The flat landscape and the storms and droughts underline the cultural isolation. "Insanity and suicide are very common things on the Divide," Cather explains. "They come on like an epidemic in the hot wind season. Those scorching dusty winds that blow up over the bluffs from Kansas seem to dry up the blood in men's veins as they do the sap in the corn leaves" ("On the Divide" [1896], *Collected Short Fiction* 495). In Johan Bojer's novel *The Emigrants* (1925) Per Föll makes a mound of earth to remind him of his "old friend, the fir-clad knoll" at home in Norway. "For when his fits of depression came on, when the prairie overwhelmed him with its muggy, stifling gloom ... he found relief in looking at this mound" (179). In Cather's *O Pioneers!* when Frank Shabata moves from the city to take up farming he changes from a dashing young dandy into a jealous and finally murderous man. On the

Theories of Land and Society 23

plains his yellow cane stands unused at the back of his closet, the symbol of a way of life that is not only foreign but useless on the high plains.

In *Old Jules* Sandoz chronicles madness and suicide in the Nebraska Sandhills. Most often it is the women who go mad. Sometimes they kill their children as well as themselves. "They had only the wind and the cold and the problems of clothing, shelter, food and fuel" (82–83). "If she could a had even a geranium," comments one mourner at the funeral of a woman suicide. "There'll be more killing themselves before long unless they get back to God's country" (83).

Even if isolation does not lead to suicide or madness, a sense of alienation often persists. The pull of the original home results in a sense of longing that can last for years. In Cather's story "A Wagner Matinee" the narrator hosts his Aunt Georgiana on her first visit to the East after thirty years on an isolated Nebraska farm. Their afternoon at a concert stirs emotions in the former music teacher, and the narrator realizes that "it never really died, then – the soul which can suffer so excruciatingly and so interminably; it withers to the outward eye only" (*Youth and the Bright Medusa* 223). In most stories the sense of displacement diminishes over time. White includes "The Home-coming of Colonel Hucks" in *The Real Issue*. Colonel Hucks and his wife "conquered the wilderness," but they grow old without ever visiting their old Ohio home. "Their children had been brought up to believe that [Ohio] was little less than heaven" (150). But when they return to Ohio after years on their Kansas farm, the colonel notes that it seems "kind of dwarfed here. . . . Seems to me like it 's all shriveled, and worn out, and old." When the colonel says the hills "do n't seem so big as our bluff back – back home," he means Kansas (159).

Writers who adopt a more cynical attitude focus on the restrictive small-town society that is the social norm in Great Plains fiction. Some observers are appalled at the conditions they see around them. In the opening chapter of his bitter novel *The Story of a Country Town* (1883) Edgar Watson Howe finds the people unpleasant, their character reflected in an unattractive place: "I became early impressed with the fact that our people seemed to be miserable and discontented, and frequently wondered that they did not load their effects on wagons again, and move away from a place which made all the men surly and rough, and the women pale and fretful" (8). In his preface to the 1922 edition of *Main-Travelled Roads*, Garland explains his trip West after a six-year absence in the East and his repulsion by the life his mother has been subjected to on the Dakota plains: "The farther I got from Chicago the more depressing the landscape became. . . . The houses, bare as boxes, dropped on the treeless plains, the barbed-wire fences running at right angles, and the towns mere assemblages of flimsy wooden sheds with painted-pine battlement, produced on me the effect of almost helpless and sterile poverty" (xi).

A society founded on endurance and work lacks the amenities that make life bearable, especially for the second and third generations. Without a strong attraction to the land and a fierce loyalty to the tasks of establishing a civilization in the wilderness, children are torn between their loyalty to the family, the only real community they know, and their urge to find a more rewarding life somewhere else. The family, isolated and not subject to community controls, becomes a close and sometimes repressive bond.

After the first generation of settlers come two kinds of children. The strong ones inherit the imagination and creativity of their parents or find creative resources deep inside themselves. Their strength is not physical endurance but a determination to express themselves in something besides deadening farm labor. What they want is not material success but the opportunity to use their full potential. For many, education is a way out of the drudgery and into a broader world. To go beyond the rudimentary rural education, young people go to the small-town school, if they can get their parents to release them from the heavy workload on the farm, which in many cases must be shared by the entire family. The children of Abbie Deal in Aldrich's *Lantern in Her Hand* and of Rosie and Henry in Ise's *Sod and Stubble* pursue careers beyond the farm with their parents' blessings. But some parents feel that education merely takes valuable time from more important labors. If parents do concede that education is important, they still

Theories of Land and Society 25

demand that it be delayed until the work is done. Sometimes the chance for an education slips away. In Hope Williams Sykes's *Second Hoeing* (1935) Hannah cannot escape her obligations to the fields and the family long enough to go beyond the rural school's eighth grade. She longs for an education, denied her by her immigrant father, who declares, "All she do is get married und there goes alla that money for nothers!" (33).

The children do not reject their parents' commitment, although they may reject the deadening effects of the work ethic. The pull of family and the land persists. In Morris's *The Home Place* (1948) Clyde Muncy returns to Nebraska, searching for a place to raise his family. Elof Lofblum in Manfred's *The Chokecherry Tree* (1948) returns to Chokecherry Corner, despite his dislike for his father and the town itself, because it is a safe haven after failure. As Ginny says in Jane Smiley's *A Thousand Acres* (1991), "[L]odged in my every cell, along with DNA, are molecules of topsoil" (369).

The second kind of children are the weaker ones. They debase the pioneer values rather than affirm them. Unlike their more imaginative siblings, they have no understanding or appreciation of their parents' sacrifices. That their parents should have struggled to make their lives comfortable seems only proper to them. They focus on the creature comforts that their parents' hard work has brought to them. They want to escape not the physical farm itself but the past. They reject their parents' values and accept instead the shallow conformity of small-town society. In some cases they even try to change their parents, forcing them to conform to their hedonistic standards. Alexandra Bergson's brother will not let his mother-in-law, Mrs. Lee, speak Swedish, sleep in her nightcap, or bathe in the old tub. Peder Holm denies more than his mother's religion when he rejects the ministry and marries an Irish Catholic girl. Ironically, when the children realize material success, it often proves a chimera. Without an appreciation of the sheer strength of will that accomplished the task, the dream of the garden can quickly fade.

The complexity of social and personal relationships on the plains is an integral part of Morris's novel *Plains Song* (1980).[13] The matriarch Cora, a silently suffering farm wife, raises her daughter Madge and her husband's niece, Sharon Rose. While Madge is content to marry and stay on the farm, Sharon Rose consciously rejects that life. "However much Sharon Rose disliked farmers, her scorn for farmers' wives was greater. She pitied Cora, who seemed to lack the sense to pity herself" (76). The physical alienation that earlier writers represented through metaphors of open spaces and wind, Morris reveals as a deeply personal separation. Cora evokes emotions in Sharon Rose that she cannot deny: "It was not lost on Sharon in how many ways they were alike" (88). Sharon Rose flees to Chicago, where the feelings she cannot express in Cora's farmhouse can be channeled into music. Through her music, rather than through relations with other people, Sharon Rose learns to feel, but these emotions are not a satisfactory substitute for a place or family. Unenlightened and determined "not to be beholden," as Cora often warned, she still cannot escape her past. When letters come from home, "the emotion Sharon Rose had in such abundance to lavish on her music would gather like a knot of pain in her soul" (89).

On a visit home after years away, Sharon Rose feels once again the oppression "so habitual she had hardly suspected its existence," and yet she senses that Madge, plain and pregnant, might have gained something she has not acknowledged: "[D]id this partially conscious life offer comforts she would live to miss? Half consciously she sensed that" (102). The trip home has left her confused. What she has tried to reject, and what Madge has embraced, is the place, the past that they shared with Cora. Dull, even animal-like, it is nevertheless a permanent part of her life. On her next visit Sharon watches Madge, pregnant once again, move "around like a grazing cow. . . . She oozed creature comfort" (130). But this time Sharon Rose recognizes that Cora is a "piece of nature, closely related to cows and chickens" (135). While that diminishes some people, it is right for Cora, literally a woman of the soil. This time Sharon Rose leaves with a feeling of release and guilty remorse. The young man who sits next to her on the departing train breathes a sigh of relief as his own hometown fades into the distance, "happy in his freedom, in his expectations that whatever life held for him in the future, it would henceforth be his own life, it would not be the life of Battle Creek or Colby, . . . which would recede into the past, into the darkness – wouldn't it?" (137). Sharon Rose knows, of course, that the past will not diminish into nothing, that like the railroad tracks, it will create a link to a place; no matter how independent the young man might become, he will always be "beholden" to that place, his past.

The novel ends with Sharon Rose's trip west to attend Cora's funeral thirty-three years later. Cora's farmhouse and its trees are gone, but Sharon Rose feels Cora's presence, fast fading even from the minds of her own family. The past that she tries to avoid and finally acknowledges keeps her from drifting into the void of no past.

Great Plains fiction traces the paths across the unmarked land. It records the intersections of land and people. As Stegner says in *Wolf Willow*, it is our own trails, however faint, that matter most. Great Plains writers agree that no matter how diminished a path seems, one must accept it. The alternative is loss of identity. Even the dust between the teeth, the dull, animal-like nature of the farm people, the stagnant, dying trading towns are better than no past at all.

CHAPTER TWO

The Lure of the West:
Searching for the Myths

As the farming frontier spread westward, settlers east of the Mississippi proved time and again that the Indians could be subdued or moved, that the forest soil was rich, and that the waterways were a simple means of transportation and marketing. But after the Civil War the rise of industry and increasingly crowded cities marred the dream of a true democracy. The prairies and plains were the last hope for the establishment of a democratic utopia. Underlying this ideal was the rising belief in the economic potential of the West. The optimistic myths of the effortless garden were replaced by a more complex vision of the region's role in American life. During the early nineteenth century, as explorers returned and settlements spread into the interior, the early myths – wild, imaginative tales – were displaced by shifting concepts of the nation's interior: it was a garden; a desert; a desert that could become a garden. As population spread onto the prairies and plains in the years immediately before and after the Civil War, the contradictions persisted, some to prove more true than anyone wanted to believe, some to reveal their derivation in fear or wishful thinking. But even those myths that have proven false persist, a part of the region's collective consciousness. For example, in the early 1980s the plight of the family farm, home of the original yeoman farmers' grandsons, the backbone of the democratic utopia that blossomed on the barren prairie, was threatened by one of the inevitable periods of economic instability and attracted national attention in Congress and on the movie screens.[1]

As explorers and settlers drifted across the plains, they searched for images adequate to encompass the vast expanse. At first, as Thacker points out, they drew on standard metaphors to describe what the landscape was *like*, not what it *was* (14).[2] Later authors wrote from experience, creating images that dwarfed man: the sky as a bowl, the grasses as sea. In works that emphasize the overwhelming power of the land, nature is personified as a force that resists man's efforts to control it. As settlements were established, writers raised questions about political and economic control of this new land; to some it was important not as a natural phenomenon but as something to be exploited. This experience is not unique to the Great Plains, but the sheer size of the open spaces focuses attention upon the land in distinct ways.

The first Europeans to step into the American wilderness expected to create a utopia, a righteous community, or a pastoral paradise. They brought with them ideas of what this place should be, a priori combinations of Virgil's pastorals, Europe's carefully cultivated gardens, God's kingdom, More's *Utopia*, and the Edenic garden. These first arrivals viewed the wilderness immediately before them as a source of evil. In biblical tradition the wilderness was a curse to Adam, the scene of the Israelites' wanderings and Christ's temptations (13–14). In Canadian prairie literature this biblical view is a frequent motif.[3] The garden, these first arrivals believed, was further west, beyond the line of settlement, but there, nonetheless, to be pursued by adventurers and hopeful pioneers. No one questioned its existence; the problem was to find it. Jefferson promoted this myth, and his believers, the yeoman farmers, cultivated the garden, thereby destroying its Edenic quality. Daniel Boone led the way further and further west, across the first mountain barriers into Kentucky and finally Missouri.[4] By the mid-nineteenth century, literary ideas of the land began to take form. Emerson and Thoreau reshaped the raw image of the wilderness, once a place of imagined terror, the refuge of savages and their captives, into a safe haven, a source of inspiration rather than fear. The myth of the garden, kept alive by the fertile imagination of the land promoters, paralleled the wilderness-desert myth throughout the eighteenth and nineteenth centuries. Not until the end of the nineteenth century, when the wilderness had been taken up and drought and economic decline had depressed the Great Plains farm economy, did America begin to abandon the preconceived image of a garden paradise and replace it with a darker but more realistic image.

The myths that first lured explorers and adventurers into the interior West were based on European concepts. At the start, the explorers believed that there must be a water passage through the vast land mass by which they would reach the riches of the Orient without a perilous ocean voyage. A natural outgrowth of this search was the myth of the Course of Empire, or Manifest Destiny: that the lands stretching beyond the settlements were empty and wasted, used only by roaming native tribes, and that they were destined to be settled and cultivated by civilized (i.e., European) people. Those who were not drawn west by the promise of trade or land were looking for treasure. Tales of fortunes in gold and riches in Indian villages or rich natural lodes persisted from the time of Coronado to the California and Colorado gold rushes.

In a land where history did not exist, where myth could not derive slowly from tradition, people were quick to adapt their expectations to new information. Although much of the exploration undertaken by Spanish and French explorers was motivated by the European myths of the Fountain of Youth and the lost cities of El Dorado or by the desire to spread their religion and thereby their political influence into new lands, returning explorers described lush, fertile fields full of potential for settlement (Dondore 34–38). The French, exploring the great Mississippi valley, at the eastern edge of the Great Plains, laid the "factual" foundations for the myths of the Garden of the World and the passage to India (Allen 2). They assumed that a land so lush and varied must be connected to the riches of the Far East. Occasionally, they overstated their discoveries; nevertheless, their concept of the interior persisted until the journey of Lewis and Clark (Allen; Thacker 18).

British and Spanish explorers reported on a region not quite as sublime as that created by the French reports. Experiencing the cold winds further north, in the continental interior, the British thought that the soil and climate of the Missouri country was insufficient to support European agriculture (Allen 18). Most Canadians assumed that the West was fit only for fur traders and explorers (Owram, chap. 1). As Spanish traders ventured onto the truly arid high plains, they reported a mixture of barren and sterile soil (Allen 39). The early explorers de Vaca and Coronado were discouraged and confused by the flat, endless land (Thacker 14–15). As these reports reached Europe, they reinforced both the virginal myths of the Edenic garden and the visions of the diabolical wilderness.

As factual reports were published and distributed in America and Europe, the process of mythmaking shifted from refining imported European myths to selecting, misconstruing, and misunderstanding the explorers' quite accurate reports so that they fit the mythic expectations and, more important, the political and economic purposes of the missions. Slowly, myth and reality began to coalesce. In the late nineteenth century, immigrants from the steppes of Russia recognized in the rich grasslands of the Great Plains soil similar to the soil on their farms in Russia, where they grew hard winter wheat. The practical knowledge and expectations regarding the land's potential that these settlers brought with them changed the mythic conception of the region, and it became the breadbasket of the world. The ability to recognize the potential of the plains and prairies to grow particular crops was an important element in the mythic development of the region and is a recurring motif in the fiction. Those who see the hidden secrets of the sleeping land – the Mennonite settlers, Cather's Alexandra Bergson, Rølvaag's Per Hansa, Sandoz's Old Jules, Grove's Abe Spalding – become heroes and heroines as they transform the land.

Like the myth of the garden, Manifest Destiny was part of the "intellectual baggage" settlers brought from Europe. The idea of empire drew the Dutch, the Swedes, the Spaniards, the French, and the English to North America in search of ways to expand their territories without encroaching on their neighbors in Europe itself. In England and northern Europe, religious dissension was added to this political rivalry. The myth of empire, when it was transferred to America itself, was gradually transformed by the reality of wilderness and apparently limitless space. The traditional assumption, based on the northern European Puritan interpretation of the Bible that the earth was created for humankind's use (Genesis 1:26–28) but only if they worked for it, seemed especially appropriate in the New World. Stewardship meant working to transform the wilderness into cultivated land. As Lee Clark Mitchell points out, this exploitive myth preceded settlers as they spread across the continent (4) and merged with the vision of the garden: to prove their worth, men and women must reestablish the garden, and to do that they must prove the wealth of the land by tilling it.

Meriwether Lewis and William Clark proved themselves to be up to the wilderness challenge. Commissioned by President Jefferson in 1804 to explore the area recently purchased from France, their two-year expedition established for Jefferson and the new nation the actual boundaries of the empire and laid to rest, for all practical purposes, the myth of the passage to India. Their role in shaping this American political and economic policy was primary: without their report of the geography, Indians, flora, and fauna of this unknown interior, Americans might have conceived the nation's development in quite different terms. As he planned the expedition, Jefferson had before him written and oral reports of fifty years of exploration and contact with the plains Indians (Ronda 7). But in size and scope, the Lewis and Clark expedition surpassed any other that had been sent into the American interior.

Jefferson did not act on simple curiosity.[5] To him, America's course of empire dictated an orderly distribution of lands from the nation, and not from states or local governments. The country was to be a nation, a closely united political entity, rather than a loose collection of regions. Jefferson believed that in order for this national vision to be achieved, the land must be settled by yeomen farming individual, self-sustaining units. In Jefferson's vision, the course of empire was linked to the myths of democratic utopia, the government's pursuit of the people's happiness, and the safety valve, the idea that the West provided economic and political release for excess population.

Before the myth could become reality, Jefferson had to know what was there. Still searching for the passage to India but spurred more immediately by Alexander Mackenzie's 1793 journey that resulted in British control of the rich fur trade, as well as by the need to establish the boundaries of the newly acquired territory and inform the native population of American possession of the land, Jefferson commissioned his personal secretary, Meriwether Lewis, and William Clark, an experienced wilderness scout, to lead an expedition up the Missouri River in 1804.[6] The men were uniquely qualified to carry out Jefferson's commission. Their careful observations of weather, geography, geology, flora, and fauna fulfilled his desire for scientific information. Their judicious dealings with the Indians assured, for a time at least, the cooperation of the natives and the orderly progression of settlement westward. But above all, Lewis and Clark shared Jefferson's vision of the new region as "a garden of wealth and beauty." Time and again, they refer to a "Butifull open Prarie" and describe the land as good. The report they submitted upon their return signaled the acknowledgment of Jefferson's vision: in the West, America could realize an agrarian democratic utopia. The published accounts of Lewis and Clark's travels, even heavily edited versions, became the reference for Americans' sense of the West in the mid-nineteenth century. Their journey gave substance to the old myths and was a rich wellspring of new images. Henry Nash Smith points out that "the importance of the Lewis and Clark expedition lay on the level of the imagination: it was drama, it was the enactment of myth that embodied the future. It . . . established the image of a highway across the continent so firmly in the minds of Americans that repeated failures could not shake it" (16–17).

Although there were obvious political and economic reasons for the expedition, Jefferson specifically asked the leaders as well as other members of the party to observe and identify the flowers and animals of the region. For the first time, men trained to notice the particular looked at the plains and prairies. In his study *Lewis and Clark: Pioneering Naturalists*, Paul Russell Cutright lists 178 plants first described by Lewis and Clark, including sagebrush, the mariposa lily, the scarlet gilia, the gaillardia, Engelmann's spruce, and the plains cottonwood, and 122 animals, including the prairie rattler, the bull snake, the western meadowlark, the pronghorn antelope, the coyote, the cougar, the pack rat, the raccoon, and the grizzly bear (423, 425–47). The men observed, measured, and weighed the unfamiliar animals and plants they encountered and compared them with familiar species. Here, for example, is their description of the "Prarie Dog":

Those Animals are about the Size of a Small Squrel shorter [x:or *larger longer*] & thicker, the head much resembling a Squirel in every respect, except the ears which is Shorter, his tail like a ground Squirel which thy Shake & whistle when. alarmd. the toe nails long, they have fine fur & the longer hair is gray, it is Said that a kind of Lizard also a Snake reside with those animals. (Lewis and Clark 3:53)[7]

As the expedition's reports appeared, the myth of plenitude in the garden of the West was proved a reality. The course of empire was assured.[8]

In works ranging from those of Lewis and Clark to those of Wright Morris, the mythic image of the Great Plains is grounded in specific images; in unlimited space the smallest detail can be noted. For example, Clark describes the Council Bluffs like this:

Capt. Lewis and my Self walked in the Prarie on the top of the Bluff and observed the most butifull prospects imagionable, this Prarie is Covered with grass about 10 or 12 Inch high, (Land rich) rises about 1/2 a mile back Something higher and is a Plain as fur as Can be Seen, under those high Lands next the river is butifull Bottom interspersed with Groves of timber, the River may be Seen for a great Distance both above & below meandering thro: the plains between two ranges of High land which appear to be from 4 to 20 ms. apart, each bend of the river forming a point which Contains tall timber, principally Willow Cotton wood some Mulberry elm Syucamore & ash. the groves Contain walnut coffeenut & Oake in addition & Hickory & Lynn [linden]. (2:428–29)

Clark first establishes a panoramic point of view: the top of a bluff, which provides the men with a three-and-a-half-mile view, carefully calculated and recorded in the day's notes. Yet he is not satisfied with a general description; he estimates how high the grass is and how far away the highlands appear to be, and he accurately names the trees he sees below. The remainder of this paragraph is a careful description of a badger, with an assurance that if anyone wanted further information, "We have this animale Skined and Stuffed" (2:429).

In a June 1805 entry, Lewis describes encounters with a bear and then buffalo near Great Falls. On foot and admiring the "magnificent and sublime" falls, he kills a buffalo, then turns to face "a large white or reather brown bear" on "an open level plain, not a bush within miles nor a tree within less than three hundred yards" (4:294). When the bear retreats (an action Lewis carefully describes), Lewis continues his walk, "determined not to be thwarted in my design of visiting medicine river." Following "the direction which the bear had run," he sees "a handsome stream, about 200 yurds. wide with a gentle current, apparently deep, it's waters clear, and banks which were formed principally of darkbrown and blue clay." They are "about the hight of those of the Missouri or from 3 to 5 feet." Then he speculates: "[Y]et they had not the appearance of ever being overflown a circumstance, which I did not expect so immediately in the neighbourhood of the mountains, from whence I should have supposed, that sudden and immence torrants would issue at certain seasons of the year; but the reverse is absolutely the case." He draws a conclusion: "I am therefore compelled to believe that the snowey mountains yeald their warters slowly" (4:295).

Lewis begins to walk the twelve miles to camp, when he encounters "three bull buffaloe" that run "full speed towards me," but they retreat when he veers off course to face them. "It now seemed to me that all the beasts of the neighbourhood had made league to destroy me" (4:294). The pragmatic Lewis is almost convinced that "the succession of curious adventures wore the impression on my mind of inchantment." But he resists this hint of the power of imagination: "[T]he prickly pear which pierced my feet very severely once in a while . . . convinced me that I was really awake and that it was necessary to make the best of my way to camp" (4:294). On the plains and prairies, the prickly pear and the long walk back pull one into reality when bears, dreams, or the immensity of space are about to carry one off.

In their journals, the explorers do not speculate about the Northwest Passage or Manifest Destiny; rather, they focus on the effort, from day to day, to record the nature of the place: buffalo numbers, the Osage plums, polecats and prairie dogs, the wind and rain and cold, the live green of the spring, the changing colors of fall. The journals of Lewis and Clark provided Jefferson the scholar with the careful detail he wanted, and they confirmed his decision to purchase the Mississippi watershed lands.

Americans, however, were not interested in the scientific report when they heard of the return of Lewis and Clark. "Nature" was of little interest before the rise of Romanticism. The first editor of the expedition journals, an Easterner named Biddle, omitted the "scientific" part. Americans wanted a "romantic adventure," the affirmation of the myths (Moulton, Introduction 38). The trek put to rest the myth of the passage to India for commercial purposes, even though explorers continued to search for it and half a century later Whitman celebrated it in his poetry. It was the myth of

Manifest Destiny that Biddle's 1814 edition of the journals affirmed. Now, instead of being coupled with the idea of trade beyond the nation's natural borders, Manifest Destiny would be justified by the myth of progress. Expansion and development across the continent would become the primary aim of American society.

It was not long before other Americans followed Lewis and Clark. Not all the explorers viewed the region as benignly as Lewis and Clark did. Zebulon Pike, who published the account of his exploration of the central plains in 1810, did not see the rich promise of the land. In fact, most explorers' accounts were indifferent and sometimes explicitly discouraging. Most damning was the report of Stephen Long's expedition that appeared in 1823. Poorly equipped and not as capably led as the Lewis and Clark expedition, Long's group encountered frustration and hardship. Moreover, they traveled across the southern plains in the heat of August. Because he had not been instructed to assess the region for possible settlement or trails, Long had no reason to withhold his assessment of the region as uninhabitable. Long asserted that the region was "almost wholly unfit for cultivation, and, of course, uninhabitable by a people depending upon agriculture for subsistence." When Long wrote "Great Desert" across his map, the ambivalent dichotomy of garden and desert embedded in ancient tradition acquired a factual base on the Great Plains. Many historians, including Daniel Boorstin and Henry Nash Smith, believe that Long's report delayed settlement by several decades (Boorstin 229–30; Smith 202–4).

It is not surprising that these myths being acted upon by explorers and settlers moving west should draw the attention of American writers and artists. The first writer of national stature to consider the Great Plains imaginatively was James Fenimore Cooper. Long's account of his expedition was published in 1823. Cooper used it as the factual basis for his third Leatherstocking novel, *The Prairie* (1827) (Elliott, sec. 2). However, Cooper's novel is not set during the time of Long's expedition, but during the time of Lewis and Clark's earlier expedition, when the region was still far beyond the boundaries of civilization. Cooper focuses on the true frontier, the point of violent confrontation between wilderness and civilization. He finds the prairie lacking: the land is a barren desert, and the people are not capable of establishing and sustaining a society. Nothing comes of man's encroachments. Yet, it is clear that civilization will inevitably spread across this barren space: the death of Natty Bumppo, avatar of the wilderness man, presages it.

In the opening chapters, Cooper clearly sets out to establish the desert quality of the Great Plains.[9] Natty Bumppo, over eighty years old, has ventured far beyond the great water barrier onto the prairie, the last remaining impediment to the uninterrupted spread of American settlement across the continent, in order to escape the multitudes that his own success has drawn around him. The Bush party has also pushed far beyond the usual limits of civilized habitation. They seem strangely appropriate to the "bleak and solitary place" that offers so little to ordinary settlers of the land (11). Their wagon train, significantly, makes no "deeper impression, than to mark that bruised and withered grass, which the cattle plucked, from time to time, and as often rejected, as food too sour, for even hunger to render palatable" (11). To emphasize that the prairie is a useless barrier, Cooper has Bumppo once more repeat Long's theory: "I often think the Lord has placed this barren belt of Prairie, behind the States, to warn men to what their folly may yet bring the land!" (24). Later Bush asks Bumppo if this is the only land available to a man like him, who avoids the law and the county clerk. Bumppo replies that although there is river soil in the bottoms, "you have journeyed hundreds of miles too far, or as many leagues too little." In the nation's center the land is barren. It is clear that Bush and his sons do not have the ability or the initiative to make the desert bloom. "To make a right good crop even on the richest bottom, there must be hard labor," Bush observes, and then he abandons the idea (86–87).

Bumppo cannot escape the encroachments of civilization, nor does he want to. When he first encounters Bush's party, he is glad to see them eating their daily bread, the picture of simple domesticity (21). Bumppo's attempt to balance his solitary life in the wilderness and his civilized heritage distin-

The Lure of the West 39

guishes him from Bush, the lowest common denominator in American society, who is drawn toward the frontier, not to preserve his integrity, transform the desert, or establish a new society, but to escape society's legal and moral impediments.

Cooper's distrust of civilization's destructive power is encapsulated in Bush's first act in the wilderness. He destroys the very trees that could serve as landmarks or shelter (chap. 2). Asa, Bush's eldest son, "with listless and incurious eyes" steps forward with the contempt of a giant for the puny resistance of a dwarf and buries his axe in the soft body of a cottonwood tree. Quickly severed, the tall tree crashes to the earth "in submission to his prowess" (18–19). There is no intention to use the trees once the livestock have been fed. This violation of mother earth occurs even before settlement.

The encroachment of society onto the land is a central theme in *The Prairie*. In Bush and his companions, Cooper presents a number of alternatives. Closest to Bumppo himself is the bee hunter Paul Hover, who shares Bumppo's simple habits and values the land enough to take only what he needs. But Paul must be close to the settlements to trade his honey, and he commits himself to Ellen Wade, who, as Esther Bush admits, "is not gifted for a frontier wife" (144). Inez and Middleton are even less suited to the barren prairie. Middleton derives his livelihood and identification from his military service. Inez is a product of the Creole world of leisure, if not lethargy. Both are merely passive symbols of a culture unsuited to the plains. Battius provides comic relief as an educated fool and a foil for Bumppo's practical observations on nature and his attacks on the excesses of civilization, especially ideas and objects derived from the Old World (237–40).

Cooper's observations about the potential connection of land and society center on Ishmael Bush. Repeated descriptions of the bleak, meager, decaying, undulating landscape compliment Cooper's description of Bush as indolent and listless. His lineaments are inferior, and he is dressed in motley attire from various frontier classes – a gaudy sash, an ornate knife, a fine fur cap, Mexican buttons and a soiled blanket-coat, a fine gun and three worthless watches. Even so arrayed, Bush appears "unfettered in limb and free from incumbrances" (12). Cooper explicitly links the appearance of Bush with the El Dorado myth: "The vehicle, loaded with household goods and implements of husbandry, the few straggling sheep and cattle that were herded in the rear, and the rugged appearance and careless mien of the sturdy men who loitered at the sides of the lingering teams united to announce a band of emigrants seeking for the Eldorado of the West" (4–5). Ishmael Bush and his party could be called the first literary illustration of the safety-valve theory. Cooper has serious reservations about the future of the Great Plains if refuse like Bush is the vanguard of Jefferson's democratic utopia.

The threat to the wilderness is only one of Cooper's concerns in *The Prairie*. The proper balance of law and society is ultimately more important. It is clear that the approaching settlers can change the desert barrier into a cultivated garden if they are willing to work once they clear the land. The more important problem Cooper explores here and in other novels is the nature of the society that settlers will establish. [10]

Ishmael Bush is an example of an ideal gone mad: he has taken freedom to a literal extreme. As Bush explains, "I have come . . . into these districts, because I found the law sitting too tight upon me" (61). If Bush has little use for the law of the settlement, he has even less regard for Indian law, choosing to espouse a belief in his own version of Manifest Destiny by claiming as his own the ground he happens to occupy. His cattle have been stolen by the Sioux, but he refuses to acknowledge the Indians' rights. Bumppo points out to Bush, "Your beasts are stolen by them who claim to be masters of all they find in the deserts" (61). Bush, adhering to his own interpretation of the Old Testament idea of an eye for an eye, declares that he will retrieve his horses from the Sioux and that he would be a fool if he did not "pay himself, something in the way of commission" (88). He denies the Indians' rights and asserts his own anarchic view of the law: "[T]he air, the water and the ground are free gifts to man, and no one has the power to portion them out in parcels. Man must drink, breathe, and walk – and therefore each has a right to his share of 'arth" (78). But Bush does not accept the Indians' right to a share of the earth if that share is his own stock.

Bush's most crucial test of his own moral and legal sense comes when he is forced to become a judge and impose his own version of the law upon his small society in order to rectify the wrongs he believes he has suffered. Bush proceeds with the help of his wife Esther to right the wrongs he himself has perpetrated, but when he openly accuses the trapper of murder and, in the presence of witnesses, hears the story of the murder of Asa by Abiram, Bush is caught in his own law.[11] Ironically, Bush becomes the harbinger of society's order, which he has tried so hard to avoid.

Cooper does not hold much hope for Manifest Destiny or the democratic utopia. When Battius asserts that man is destined to spread across the continent because "nature did not make so vast a region to lie in uninhabited waste so many ages," Bumppo reminds his companion that he has spent most of his time "looking natur' steadily in the face, and in reasoning on what I've seen, rather than on what I've heard in traditions," and the nature of man, he has concluded, is "the same, be he born in the wilderness, or be he born in the towns. To my weak judgment it hath ever seemed that his gifts are not equal to his wishes" (278).

The novel ends with Natty Bumppo's death. Although thirteen years later Cooper wrote two more Leatherstocking tales, it is clear that in 1827 he believed that the death of Bumppo signaled the end of an era. Significantly, Bumppo dies as Lewis and Clark are returning from their expedition. To Cooper, that mission, while necessary and inevitable, signified the approaching end of the wilderness. A new authority appears in the appropriately named Middleton, not an official part of Lewis's party but a soldier nonetheless, a mediator and the precursor of society's ordered institutions that would come into the wilderness. Manifest Destiny may be inevitable, but it means destruction and anarchy if the vanguard is led by men such as Ishmael Bush, pushing beyond civilization to escape the very forces that make society possible. Middleton's presence modifies the pessimism that Bush suggests.

For Cooper, only the natives and the heroic few could survive on the prairie frontier; everyone else should go back to society. Later writers developed Cooper's idea that the Great Plains must be settled by men and women who shared Leatherstocking's superhuman qualities of endurance, honesty, and an appreciation for the cycle of nature.

In the fall of 1832, five years after Cooper published *The Prairie*, Washington Irving toured the prairies of Oklahoma, traveling from the Arkansas River almost to present-day Oklahoma City (Irving, *The Crayon Miscellany* 2–3). At the invitation of Commissioner Henry Leavitt Ellsworth, Irving and two friends, the young Count Albert-Alexander de Pourtales and his companion Charles Joseph Latrobe, joined a company of Rangers on a month-long expedition among the Osage and Pawnee Indians.[12] For seventeen years Irving had been living abroad. His literary reputation had preceded him home, and he found himself a celebrity, but like Rip van Winkle, he was uncertain of his place in the new Jacksonian order. His trip west was a part of his effort to become reacquainted with his country and his countrymen. In a letter to his brother Peter, Irving explained his purpose. He found Ellsworth's offer to accompany him west

too tempting to be resisted: I should have an opportunity of seeing the remnants of those great Indian tribes, which are now about to disappear as independent nations, or to be amalgamated under some new form of government. I should see those fine countries of the "far west," while still in a state of pristine wilderness, and behold the herds of buffaloes scouring their native prairies, before they are driven beyond the reach of a civilized tourist. (*Letters*, 2:733–34)

This comment reveals much about Irving's purpose and technique. Like Cooper, Irving believed that the West would soon be gone, or that it would be too far removed to be accessible.

Irving was the first professional writer to travel over the prairies. As Anthony Bukoski has pointed out, Irving's trip was a "trying out of the prairies, a cautious advance upon the chaos of space" (7), and, as such, a microcosm of the approaching westward movement. A careful reading of *A Tour on the Prairies* reveals Irving's developing ability to perceive the land. The change comes about gradually. In an early description of the land the party is traversing, Irving uses general adjectives to carry his description – *bright, sunny, transparent, alluvial, redundant, gigantic, sluggish, glassy, fine* (36). [13] To sum up a scene, he often relies on a Romantic or European reference. The travel party reminds him of "bands of buccaneers penetrating the wilds of South America" (36). The sun on the stately column of trees, tinted with autumnal colors, reminds him of the "effect of sunshine among the stained windows and clustering columns of a Gothic cathedral" (25). As the tour continues, Irving's descriptions become more realistic. His description of the party's struggle in the Cross Timbers is especially vivid. Traveling through the region of oak forests, deep ravines, mire and water, fire-blackened grasses, sharp roots and branches, "was like struggling through forests of cast iron" (72). An indifferent camp in the Cross Timbers "was in a grove of scrub oaks, on the borders of a deep ravine, at the bottom of which were a few scanty pools of water" (73). [14]

These descriptions do not arise only from the land's surface. Gradually Irving begins to acknowledge the feelings that prairie space arouses in him. When he compares the scene before him to a Gothic cathedral, he makes an emotional connection: "There is a grandeur and solemnity . . . [in] the West that awakens in one the same feeling I have experienced" in Europe's cathedrals (25). He begins to note changes in the land itself: the "poor hungry soil" (54), oak barrens (57), a thunderstorm (58). At length, he acknowledges the feeling that arises from "the Great Prairie" itself. Emerging from the dense forests of the Cross Timbers, he describes the "expansion of feeling in looking upon these boundless and fertile wastes" (97).

Unlike Bush's immigrant band, the Rangers and their party of half-breeds and Creole guides represent true frontier society. Irving does not fully appreciate the mythic potential of some of the party, especially Tonish (Antoine Descette), who is a frontier braggart in the tradition of Davy Crockett. His wild exaggeration and tall tales set up mythic expectations in the reader as well, but later his boasts about his hunting skills become merely a running joke, akin to the boy crying wolf. Irving seems incapable of fully appreciating what came to be known as Southwestern humor.

One of the most realistic passages in the tale is Irving's report of the guide Beatte's search for the lost Count de Pourtales. It is clear that here Irving is describing in careful detail an event he witnessed. The narrative is unusually direct:

Sometimes [Beatte] would pull up and walk his horse slowly, regarding the ground intensely, where, to my eye nothing was apparent. Then he would dismount, lead his horse by the bridle and advance cautiously, step by step, with his face bent towards the earth, just catching here and there, a casual indication of the vaguest kind to guide him onward. In some places where the soil was hard and the grass withered, he would lose the track entirely and wander backwards and forwards and right and left in search of it. (106–7)

Pierre Beatte is a real-life Natty Bumppo, a representative frontiersman, who inherited French Catholicism from his father but through his mother remained "more of an Indian in his tastes." In their conversations, Irving hears tales of Indian battles, learns of the "wrongs and insults" the Indians have suffered, and gains some insight into Indian superstition and religion. Beatte, a part of civilization and the wilderness, becomes a true frontier guide for Irving and his readers.

Even in this early account, Irving acknowledges the powerful force of the land through the guides' Indian tales of the weather's eccentricities, accounts of the uncontrollable power of nature that surrounds not only the Indians but those white intruders listening to the tales as well. One tale tells of an Indian astride a lightning bolt, who was "whisked away over prairies, and forests, and streams, and deserts until he was flung senseless at the foot of the Rocky Mountains," so far from home that it took him months to return. Beatte's account of his encounter with a bear is framed with a campfire anecdote similar to the Hugh Glass legend (90–91). The interjected story enhances Beatte's own tale, pointing up the potential danger of prairie life and his own strength in battle with the bear.

Irving uses stories and legends as cautionary tales. When the troop's surgeon expresses an interest in acquiring some Indian skulls, Beatte responds angrily, and to heighten the significance of his reaction, Irving recounts Beatte's Indian beliefs and "superstitious forebodings" regarding the body and the afterlife. When the scouts return to camp with the first evidence of the anticipated buffalo herd, Tonish heightens the Rangers' enthusiasm for the approaching hunt by recounting an Osage legend, this time with himself as the hero. An invincible white deer can be killed only by particular bullets. When he uses one, he brings down a fine buck, but the herd vanishes (96). In these tales, Irving implicitly acknowledges the danger to the fragile balance in the wilderness that the intrusion of this party represents. Nature itself controls the prairie's lightning, the grizzly's power, the hunter's aim. Man is a victim, punished for his presumption by being carried off, left to die, or deprived of game. It is clear that Irving regards his account of these tales both as an act of preservation and as a warning.

To heighten the importance of this roaming society, Irving recounts several separations and reunions of the party. Some members fall behind, and others remain behind to wait for them. Some leave to hunt food for a day or two. The count and his companion leave the party briefly at the journey's beginning, but they soon rejoin the troop. "A short experiment had convinced them of the toil and difficulty of inexperienced travellers like themselves making their way through the wilderness" (23). Irving himself is separated from the party during a buffalo hunt: in the excitement of the chase, he loses sight of the rest of the party. Isolated, Irving contemplates his place in the prairie's scheme of things:

I now found myself in the midst of a lonely waste in which the prospect was bounded by undulating swells of land, naked and uniform, where, from the deficiency of land marks and distinct features an inexperienced man may become bewildered and lose his way as readily as in the wastes of the ocean. . . .

To one unaccustomed to it there is something inexpressibly lonely in the solitude of a prairie. The loneliness of a forest seems nothing to it. There the view is shut in by trees, and the imagination is left free to picture some livelier scene beyond. But here we have an immense extent of landscape without a sign of human existence. We have the consciousness of being far, far beyond the bounds of human habitation; we feel as if moving in the midst of a desert world. (100)

It is not only the physical isolation from his companions but the "silence of the waste," the open prairie, that threatens to overwhelm him. It is a fear that Rølvaag's Beret and many other prairie dwellers feel and cannot articulate.

Like Cooper, Irving believes that with the coming of community the wilderness will disappear. This is especially evident in his account of a buffalo hunt. With the count and Latrobe, Irving participates in a hunt as wildly exciting as any Romantic could imagine. At a full gallop, he brings down a buffalo. But when he dismounts and the heat of the chase subsides, he faces the wounded animal and is overwhelmed by the implications of his act: "It seemed as if I had inflicted pain in proportion to the bulk of my victim, and as if there were a hundred fold greater waste of life than there would have been in the destruction of an animal of inferior size" (102). Irving finds firing the bullet to give the dying animal "quietus" to be "a totally different thing from firing in the heat of the chase" (102). Latrobe carves out the tongue, which Irving carries to camp as a trophy – reluctantly, he implies. This entire incident, including the separations and reunions between Irving and the count and the rest of the party, reduces to a personal, emotional level the whole question of the survival of civilized man and wild animal in the wilderness. The incident foreshadows the physical and psychological isolation, the waste, and the destruction that persist as settlers invade the prairies and plains.

A Tour on the Prairies is a realistic work, despite Irving's Romantic embellishments. If Irving sometimes cannot "see" the prairie landscape, he is careful to record his own experiences. Undoubtedly, early readers overlooked the darker implications in these early accounts of the Great Plains. They were searching for the myths. In the discoveries of Lewis and Clark, the quiet heroism of Natty Bumppo, and the bucolic woodland frolic of Irving, Latrobe, and the count, readers could for a time affirm the garden, Manifest Destiny, the democratic utopia, and the safety valve if they ignored the thorn of the prickly pear, the felled trees, and the buffalo carcass.

CHAPTER THREE

Learning to Live on the Land:
Testing the Myths

By the time Whitman published the first edition of *Leaves of Grass*, in 1855, the myths of the howling wilderness and the contradictory Edenic paradise had been replaced by the expansionist vision of Manifest Destiny, the promise of a cultivated garden, the relief of the safety valve, and the lingering fear of the Great American Desert. Americans were eager to move on to the Great Plains to discover the viability of these westering myths. Whitman, the champion of the American landscape, celebrates this westward movement:

All the past we leave behind,

We debouch upon a newer mightier world, varied world,

Fresh and strong the world we seize, world of labor and the march,

Pioneers! O pioneers!

We detachments steady throwing,

Down the edges, through the passes, up the mountains steep,

Conquering, holding, daring, venturing as we go the unknown ways,

Pioneers! O pioneers!

We primeval forests felling,

We the rivers stemming, vexing we and piercing deep the mines within,

We the surface broad surveying, we the virgin soil upheaving,

Pioneers! O pioneers!

("Birds of Passage")

From the start, Americans revealed ambivalent feelings about this process. Their insistence on the westward march of progress was mixed with the romantic attraction of the untrammeled wilderness. Lieutenant Colonel Richard Irving Dodge, who was one of the men responsible for subduing the Indians and encouraging entrepreneurs like his wealthy English friend William Blackmore, could, nevertheless, write in 1876: "Now all is changed. There is no longer an unknown. Rail Roads have bared the silent mysteries of the plains to the inspection of every shop boy. Civilization, like a huge cuttle fish, has passed its arms of settlements up almost every stream, grasping the land, killing the game, driving out the Indian, crushing the romance, the poetry, the very life and soul of the 'plains,' leaving only the bare and monotonous carcass" (126).

In the Western tradition, Leatherstocking's progeny reappear in tales of trappers, mountain men, and loners who live on the fringes of society, sometimes succumbing to marriage and society but more often drifting into lonely oblivion, or dying, as Leatherstocking did, looking westward. When the frontiersman puts down roots in the prairie soil and establishes a home, he becomes a settler, and the wilderness becomes a test of his ability to endure long enough to either reestablish the society that he left in the East or establish a new social order.[1] Great Plains writers record this change. Laura Ingalls Wilder chronicled her father's search for a home on the fringes of the frontier in Wisconsin, Kansas, Iowa, and the Dakotas. Hamlin Garland's parents, looking for a better life on the edge of the wilderness, moved from Wisconsin to Iowa and finally to a Dakota homestead.

Away from established society, settlers had the freedom to behave in a savage, bestial manner – to become barbarians. This is a danger that threatens Bush in *The Prairie*. To these first arrivals, the wilderness is not a simple home, as it is to Natty Bumppo, nor a source of spiritual renewal, as it is to Thoreau, whose retreat is only a short walk from town; rather, it is a dangerous power to be reckoned with (see Slotkin). As Nash points out in his study of wilderness, the pioneers used military metaphors to describe their experiences: they were out to conquer the wilderness (27). Success would be their reward for the inevitable sacrifice the wilderness extracted from them (24).

There can be no doubt that the settlers who crossed the continent for California and Oregon as early as 1840 believed that they were participating in the mythic promise of Manifest Destiny. Diaries and journals reveal that people believed it was their duty to establish civilization in the howling wilderness. John Unruh explains that "most pre– and post–gold rush overlanders had become convinced that their projected Far West destination was a veritable utopia or Eden in which their long-cherished dreams would be realized more quickly and more easily than if they remained where they were" (59). As Unruh points out, travelers believed that in the West they would find not only instant riches but a fruitful land and upward mobility. It was not a possibility but a certainty, fed by the myth of the garden, which promised the individual riches and success, and the myth of Manifest Destiny, which promised wealth and prosperity to the nation that spread from sea to sea.

Almost as soon as Jefferson's purchase made the Missouri basin part of the territory of the new United States, new arrivals began to transform the region into something useful. That the lands were already occupied by Indian inhabitants seemed a minor inconvenience to those who believed that Manifest Destiny gave the United States rights to the entire continent. The Indians, who did not cultivate the land or establish permanent towns, obviously were not using the land as God intended. Through drought, dust storms, locust plagues, blizzards, economic and psychological attrition, and Indian troubles, settlers on the Great Plains persisted in their belief that America was "divinely intended for the white man's occupancy" (Meyer 28). To the end of the nineteenth century, settlers continued to arrive, even as thousands back-trailed during the drought and economic depression in the 1890s. This persistence attests to the strength of the myth, grounded in the northern European Reformation tradition of progress and wealth as God's reward for those who suffer and yet remain steadfast and faithful.

Even when they encountered seemingly impossible circumstances, settlers persisted in their belief that the plains and prairies were a part of God's plan and therefore must be useful. The utilitarian justification for settlement continued even when the biblical mandate began to fade. As Nash points out, those who pushed west did so because they viewed it as a challenge, not out of a love for wilderness. They "conceived of themselves as agents in the regenerating process that turned the ungodly and useless into a beneficent civilization" (43). Some, like Pastor Block in Wiebe's *Peace Shall Destroy Many*, regarded the wilderness as a refuge: the challenge was not merely to create a community but to maintain the barrier of the surrounding wilderness. Wiebe focuses on Pastor Block's attempt to preserve the separate status that Block presumes God has bestowed on him and on the struggle of his antithesis, young Thom Wiens, to understand his obligation to the pacifist Mennonite society and to the wider community in a time of war.

When the settlers encroached on the wilderness, its power was diminished, but the inherent threat persisted in the terrifying possibility of disaster – storms, droughts, grasshopper plagues, winds – threats that men and women on the Great Plains continue to face. Dust, the land itself suspended in air and moving as if it had conscious purpose, signifies not only the malevolent force of nature but also the land's stubborn refusal to provide crops and the barren lives of people who live on it. In her story "Water Witch" (1965) Lois Phillips Hudson makes clear the futility of man's attempts to control nature's forces:

There was, after all, nothing anybody could barter for water – not seed wheat or labor or even money. . . . People who had lived for three generations under the homesteaders' law of unconditional hospitality to those in need now began to live under another law – the law of the desert. . . . None dared to ask for more than enough to water their animals and themselves. . . . If Benjamin could not find new wells for them, there was nothing left for them to do but slaughter their bony milch cows, take the proceeds from their lugubrious auctions, and go West. (*Reapers in the Dust* 78–79)

When their new well fails in the face of a temperature of 112 degrees, even the birds die. It is the death of nature itself. The clumsy irony of a cloudburst destroys the last vestiges of the family's farm. The narrator speculates about causes: "I know I was not clear, at the time, as to whether the drought made the depression or the depression made the drought. . . . I do know that a lone man trying to wrest consistency out of the prairies can be tragically out of scale. Only nomads can live in the wastelands of seas, sand, ice or dust, where the figures of men are forever out of scale" (81).

A blizzard often symbolizes nature's malevolence. In *The Long Winter* Wilder recounts the Ingalles' life during a winter of endless blizzards on the Dakota frontier. Cut off from supplies and civilization when the trains are blocked by snowdrifts, the desperate family is reduced to grinding wheat in a coffee mill to make bread (194) and twisting hay to use as fuel (185–86). Nor has the threat of the blizzard's cold diminished. In the opening story of Louise Erdrich's *Love Medicine* (1984) June Kashpaw, drunk and alone, heads home across the snowy fields. "The heavy winds couldn't blow her off course," but it begins to snow and she is gone, "not only dead but suddenly buried, vanished off the land like that sudden snow" (6–7).

Manifest Destiny reflects the American belief that the wilderness could be conquered and that unlimited growth would naturally follow settlement. Lee Clark Mitchell calls Manifest Destiny the myth of unlimited space, a "formalistic text of the 'official faith' " that was so strong that those who questioned this drive did so only hesitatingly in the introductions and conclusions of their books and then, when they were driven from making public statements, in private letters and journals (6). The myth was self-renewing: as the frontier advanced, Americans experienced a perennial resurgence of the original mandate to transform the wilderness.

In Great Plains fiction, Manifest Destiny becomes an individual mandate. It is clearly evoked in Rølvaag's *Giants in the Earth* through Per Hansa. To Per Hansa and his neighbors, two things are of paramount importance: to turn the prairie into farmland and to establish a true community. To heighten this mythic element, Rølvaag recounts the story in fairy-tale terms, drawing especially from Norse legends of trolls and the Ash-lad, a male Cinderella who embodies the promise of success implicit in the westering myth (Eckstein; Moseley, *Ole Edvart Rølvaag;* Ruud). In the opening scene of the novel, as their wagon creeps alone and lost across the featureless prairie, Per Hansa knows his task: "He was going to do something remarkable out there, which should become known far and wide. No lack of opportunity in that country, he had been told!" (5). There is no doubt in Per Hansa's mind that his is a Manifest Destiny. He envisions not just a farm but an estate "more magnificent than that of many a king of old" (108). Even as his family huddles in a barren sod house, he dreams of land, livestock, and "the royal mansion which he had already erected in his mind. There would be houses for both chickens and pigs, roomy stables, a magnificent store-house and barn . . . and then the splendid palace itself! The royal mansion would shine in the sun – it would stand out far and wide!" This faith in his destiny and his own strength sustains Per Hansa as he faces the inevitable adversities and the hard work that he must do to wrest his kingdom from the prairie. Like Cather's Alexandra in *O Pioneers!* Per Hansa is not passive: he schemes and plans his attack on the nascent land. Rølvaag's description of Per Hansa's first plowing is one of the most memorable in Great Plains fiction for the rich mix of realistic detail and allusion:

That first furrow turned out very crooked for Per Hansa; he made a long one of it, too. When he thought he had gone far enough and halted the oxen, the furrow came winding up behind him like a snake. [. . .] When he had made another round he let the oxen stand awhile; taking the spade which he had brought out, he began to cut the sod on one side of the breaking into strips that could be handled. This was to be his building material. . . . Field for planting on the one hand, sods for a house on the other – that was the way to plow! . . . Leave it to Per Hansa – he was the fellow to have everything figured out beforehand! (46–47)[2]

But there are opposing forces at work. Rølvaag sees the world as the setting for a Manichean struggle between God and the devil. The land is a malevolent force, a giant *in* the earth, reluctantly acquiescing to man's plow.[3] Per knows that his destiny will not be accomplished without adversity. When his wheat appears to be frozen and moldering in the ground, Per Hansa falters in his faith, and when the new shoots appear, he regards it as a miracle (295).

Later, plagues of locusts descend and persist for years, destroying crops capriciously. The people cannot believe that the plague is not of supernatural origin. "To these wandering Norsemen, the old adage that all evil dwells below and springs from the north was proving true again" (340). There is no way to evade the hoard. The prairie is again playing with man: "That night the Great Prairie stretched herself voluptuously; giant-like and full of cunning, she laughed softly into the reddish moon. 'Now we will see what human might may avail against us!' " (339).

The people endure these disasters because they are too poor to move on or to back-trail. "And where would they have gone?" (339). Even in the midst of the locust plague, new settlers arrive, attracted, ironically, by the beauty of the prairie. "[T]he finest soil you ever dreamed of – a veritable Land of Canaan! [. . .] the new Promised Land into which the Lord was leading His poor people from all the corners of the earth!" (339–40). For four years they pray for deliverance from pestilence and famine: "[T]he soil out here is first class; if we hang on, we're sure to make a clean sweep!" (343). The persistent belief in Manifest Destiny helps them to overcome failure and despair.

By 1880 there are neighbors, a town, and farms. It seems that Manifest Destiny has been realized, the kingdom established:

It was as if nothing affected people in those days. They threw themselves blindly into the Impossible, and accomplished the Unbelievable. If anyone succumbed in the struggle – and that happened often – another would come and take his place. . . . Of course it was possible – everything was possible out here. There was no such thing as the Impossible anymore. The human race has not known such faith and such self-confidence since history began. (414–15)

Ironically, Per Hansa, one of the strongest and best, is one of those who succumbs to the prairie. He believes that the fairy-tale ending is assured. But on the plains other forces are at work. Nature itself, the power of the past, even the force of the Lord's judgment must be respected. Even though he has acknowledged these forces, his pride has led him to believe that he can overcome them all. He shares this hubris with his community and with the entire nation.

While Per Hansa pursues his manifest destiny, Beret lives in fear of the vast solitude. To her, this is not God's Promised Land but the land of Satan, a place of punishment. Their opposing visions are the focus of the novel's climax. When their dying friend Hans Olsa asks for a minister, Beret insists that Per Hansa risk the freezing storm to find one. Able to overcome the plagues of nature, he cannot avoid the mandate of his wife, even though he fears that she is mad and that her request means certain death. Harold Simonson, in *Prairies Within: The Tragic Trilogy of Ole Rølvaag*, points out that it is not Beret's religious imperative but Per Hansa's own attempt to achieve the myth in reality that leads to tragic consequences (45–46). Per Hansa knows that to refuse to go into the storm would be to deny both his faith in his manifest destiny and Beret's deep psychological need. However, unlike the mythical hero, he fails to find the needed aid. His heroic act is merely suicidal.

It seems clear that Rølvaag thought of his novel as a story of mythic proportions. The race that would realize the nation's Manifest Destiny must be dragon-slayers, superhuman in strength and in intelligence and willing to sacrifice themselves to the demands of the land. Such men and women are rare, usually found in the first generation. When the task is accomplished, the dragon-slayers become expendable, a sacrifice to the folly and fears of their more pragmatic or fearful progeny.

The sweeping vision of Manifest Destiny is reflected in the vast landscapes of romantic painters, in the works of those who painted the Indian, and, ultimately, in the Wild West of Western literature. Broad vistas, towering mountains, and colorful Indians fill the canvases of Bierstadt, Moran, Russell, Remington, and others (see, e.g., Goetzman and Goetzman; Opie; and Thacker).

Great Plains authors have had to contend with this romantic ideal, at least implicitly, as they explored the more prosaic agrarian world. The garden myth, with its central images of growth and fecundity, was changed by political and economic realities into a commodity rather than a romantic vision. The pastoral garden of leisure became a literal garden, the product of man's intensive labor. After the Civil War the desire to settle the plains and prairies led to heavy promotion by land speculators and railroad officials, who had a vested interest in their settlement. To lure settlers into these open spaces, they presented the potential immigrant with a staggering assortment of crop statistics, personal testimonials, and lyrical promises.

This rather naive faith in the land is reflected in "Among the Corn

Rows," one of Garland's rosier stories in *Main-Travelled Roads*. In this courtship tale, the Dakota prairie, so menacing in Rølvaag (and in other Garland stories), is appropriately benign, a willing partner in the effort to wrest the garden from the land: "It was about five o'clock in a day in late June, and the level plain was green and yellow, and infinite in reach as a sea; the lowering sun was casting over its distant swells a faint impalpable mist, through which the breaking teams on the neighboring claims ploughed noiselessly, as figures in a dream" (86). Clearly, Garland's prairie is not a place where heroes are tested or retreat to die. Rather, this is the setting for a tale of romance tinged with practicality. The bachelor Rob Rodemaker is not of heroic proportion, yet he is equal to the task of breaking the prairie sod: "Middle-sized, cheery, wide-awake, good looking young fellow – a typical claim holder. He was always confident, jovial, and full of plans for the future. . . . He could do anything, and do it well" (88). Lack of opportunity and an oppressive class consciousness sent Rob west looking for land (89). The only thing he lacks to complete his own garden is a wife, and so he returns to Wisconsin, where he finds Julia Peterson, a Norwegian farm girl. Rob, the practical settler, seeks not a romantic, Cooperesque heroine but a hard worker.

Julia dreams of someone who can release her from her drab home and sullen family, to whom she is merely cheap labor. She is ashamed of her family's Norwegian habits and acutely aware of the social gap that separates her even from Rob. Rob's offer of a frugal existence seems preferable to continuing to live at home "ploughin' corn and milkin' cows till the day of judgment" (105), so Julia transfers her dreams of escape to Rob. "She was already living that free life in a far-off wonderful country. . . . She'd work, of course, but it would be because she wanted to, and not because she was forced to" (107). For his part, Rob chooses a plain immigrant over a more sociably acceptable Yankee girl because he knows that acceptance will be based upon success that comes from hard work, not from one's social origins.

Garland makes it clear that Rob is no knight, Julia no princess. The land is not an anthropomorphic adversary but a stand of wheat – one man's garden. The tale ends before the hard work takes its toll. Garland tells that grim story in other stories and novels, most notably in "A Day's Pleasure," "A Branch Road," *The Moccasin Ranch* (1909), and *Jason Edwards* (1892). Still, "Among the Corn Rows" is one of the earliest and most realistic evocations of the garden myth that lured so many onto the plains and prairies.[4]

In O *Pioneers!* Cather presents a more complex vision of the garden. The novel opens in 1888 in Hanover, a small Nebraska town on the 100th meridian, that dividing line between the prairies and the high, dry plains. When Alexandra's father dies, he passes the responsibility for the failing family farm on to his daughter, in whom he sees a strength of will and a passionate commitment to the land. His faith is not misplaced. When a dry year comes and their neighbors are selling their high prairie lands, her trip to the river-bottom farms confirms her faith in the land: "Down there they have a little certainty, but up with us there is a big chance" (64). Instinctively, Alexandra understands her relationship to the land: she cannot control it, but she can gradually transform it. Cather uses the garden myth not as an image but as a metaphor for the emotional union that the land demands. Her happiest days are ones "when she was close to the flat, fallow world about her, and felt, as it were, in her own body the joyous germination in the soil" (204). Susan Rosowski describes the relationship as that between "Beauty and the Beast" ("Willa Cather and the Fatality of Place" 84–86). Just as God demanded the total obedience of Adam and Eve in exchange for perpetual paradise, the land demands total commitment before it will fulfill its promise of fertility. Alexandra realizes a relationship with the land that Per Hansa, for all his physical and emotional efforts, never does.[5]

Cather does not dwell on the years of discovery. Part 2, "Neighboring Fields," begins with a view of the prairie that Alexandra and her neighbors have awakened:

From the Norwegian graveyard one looks out over a vast checker-board, marked off in squares of wheat and corn; light and dark; dark and light. Telephone wires hum along the white roads, which always run at right angles. From the graveyard gate one can count a dozen gayly painted farmhouses; the gilded weather-vanes on the big red barns wink at each other across green and brown and yellow fields. The light steel windmills tremble throughout their frames and tug at their moorings. (75)

Not only has the garden been realized but those who tend it have created the necessary community: roads and telephone wires indicate a network. The graveyard reveals the past. Windmills lessen labor; the weather vane hints at some superfluous spending. Alexandra's success is the result of her intense preoccupation with the land itself, but the awakening of the land has not occurred in isolation. "Neighboring Fields" chronicles life in the community: Alexandra's great farm and her Swedish girls; her concern for her brother, Emil, Crazy Ivar, and Mrs. Lee; her friendship with her neighbor Marie. It is a portrait of a prosperous rural neighborhood.

If *O Pioneers!* ended with this initial success, it would confirm the mythic garden the promoters promised. But this is not a bucolic novel. A counterpoint to Alexandra's love of the land is her love for her friend Marie and her brother Emil. Focused as she is on the land, she cannot see the coming tragedy. Parts 3 and 4, "Winter Memories" and "The Mulberry Tree," recount the tragic death of Emil and Marie. The darker side of the garden is symbolized by the orchard that lies between Alexandra's fields and those of Marie's husband, Frank Shabata. When the friends sit together in the orchard, it becomes not a commodity to be tended but a pastoral bower, a place to find renewal and leisure. Carl, Alexandra, and Marie make "a pretty picture in the strong sunlight, the leafy pattern surrounding them like a net" (134–35). But a leafy net is not impregnable. It is here that Marie's husband, Frank Shabata, murders Emil and Marie.

The price that the land exacts is not the sacrifice of the dragon-slayer or diminished expectations but the denial of ecstasy. Marie, full of life, is a symbol of excessive human nature. Alexandra, who has denied herself any emotion while her vision has been focused on the sleeping land, is discomfited by Marie's energy. "There are women who spread ruin around them through no fault of theirs, just by being too beautiful, too full of life and love," she says. Self-indulgence cannot survive on the prairie: the land demands everyone's full physical and emotional attention to arouse it from its sleep. To underscore this point, Cather includes the account of Emil's friend Amédée, who will not stop work to attend to his pain and dies of appendicitis.

Other, less optimistic myths developed as counterpoints to the myths of Manifest Destiny and the garden. The safety-valve myth is essentially a negative image. It was directed at orphans, destitute children, members of lower social classes, and foreign immigrants. The appeal was supported by Eastern philanthropists and businessmen, perhaps from different motives but ultimately to encourage the poor and the less desirable to move west: "That the emigrant might find more misery and poverty on the Plains than he had known in the urban areas was unthinkable. Such an idea was contrary to tradition and faith, contrary as well to the expressed mission of American democracy after the [Civil] War" (Emmons 80).[6] Like the myths of Manifest Destiny and the garden, the myth of the safety valve assumes that free land will remain available indefinitely. The contradictions implicit in this assumption are obvious: the people who were being urged to emigrate – the Ishmael Bushes of the East – were more apt to squander and exploit that land than they were to tend a fruitful garden.

This explains, in part, the Easterners' early contempt for those who settled the West. The works usually cited as the earliest examples of Middle Western or prairie literature are by Timothy Flint, James Hall, and Caroline Kirkland, all well-bred Easterners who traveled through the prairie regions east of the Mississippi and who reported on their extensive journeys in stories.[7] These early "Western" writers reflect the Eastern attitude that only the East could provide the West with education, religion, and the institutions to support them. Implicit in the myth of the safety valve is the companion myth of the West as lawless, cut off from civilization, closer to the chaos of the wilderness than to the order of society.

In her early stories, Cather reflects this view of the plains as a brutalizing force. In two stories from her college days, "Peter" and "Lou, the Prophet," men are driven to suicide or religious fanaticism by the physical demands and cultural isolation of the land. In "On the Divide" the giant Canute is part of society's refuse. He lives a bestial existence, drinking himself into a stupor after each day of endless work. The carvings he etches into the window sills of his shack reveal a strange, menacing world: "There were men plowing with little horned imps sitting on their shoulders and on their horses' heads. . . . There were men fighting with big serpents, and skeletons dancing together. It would sometimes have been hard to distinguish the men from their evil geniuses but for one fact, the men were always grave and were either toiling or praying, while the devils were always smiling and dancing" (*Collected Short Fiction* 494).[8] When Canute decides to break the spell of isolation, he remains true to his bestial nature, carrying his neighbor's daughter Lena off to his hut. But Cather ameliorates Canute's barbarianism by employing fairy-tale imagery: Canute is a clumsy but simple-hearted giant who sleeps in an eight-foot bed and has a chair, a bench, and shoes of colossal proportions. Like someone under an evil spell, he seems locked away in this ironic garden. Lena, the kidnapped "princess," sees the drawings on his window sill and deplores Canute's existence in his filthy hut. Her recognition that he needs her and her loneliness when he leaves her alone pave the way for Canute's entry into society.

The safety-valve myth is implicit in many other stories that chronicle the first generation of settlers. In "Among the Corn Rows" Rob has gone west because "we fellers workin' out back there got more 'n' more like *hands*, an' less like human beings. Y' know, Waupac is a kind of a summer resort, and the people that use' t' come in summers looked down on us cusses in the fields an' shops . . . so I come West, just like a thousand other fellers, to get a start where the cussed European aristocracy hadn't got a holt on the people" (89–90). Julia views Rob as her own very real safety valve.

Garland's story points up the irony of the myth of the safety valve. The term was conceived by those in established society who wanted to rid themselves of the dregs and misfits, but those who went west regarded their immigration as an escape from social oppression and economic discrimination. Rob is an accepted member of society in Boomtown, glad to be rid of the "Eastern aristocracy." Confident of his own abilities, he does not regard himself as a social outcast, but as an equal member of a new democratic society.

For the immigrant, the West proved to be a problematic safety valve. Acceptance was based on wealth, not social class, but barriers of language and custom cut the new arrival off from familiar community and culture. In "Home-founding," the second chapter of Giants in the Earth, Rølvaag contrasts the buoyant optimism of Per Hansa with the fear of Beret as they venture onto a landscape that to her is featureless. The Norwegians' homesteads are clustered together, but Beret is terrified. Secretly agonizing over her premarital sins with Per and her isolation from all things familiar, she suffers more than the others in the empty space. For Beret, the land is not merely a physical fact beneath her feet but a malevolent presence that threatens psychic, not physical, danger. Bereft of familiar cultural surroundings, especially the church, Beret is vulnerable to what Harold Simonson has called the "ineffable," a region words cannot describe and previous experience cannot explain ("Beret's Ineffable West").[9]

In Villelm Moberg's Unto a Good Land (1954) Karl Oskar and his compatriots arrive in 1850 in Minnesota, where Karl "would begin to rise, rise up to full stature; on his own land he could rise" (236), something he had no right to aspire to in Sweden. Here all of the families establish prosperous farms, and here, in the virgin wilderness, Ulrika, the town whore, can marry a preacher.

Although many of these immigrants find success in the West, for some the separation from familiar landscapes and communities is acute. Morton Kvidal, in Johan Bojer's The Emigrants, is torn between his recognition of the rich potential of his American homestead and his desire to return to

Norway. "He seemed to have drifted so far away . . . from that which had once been great and good in himself. . . . What if he had been as humble as his father and had stayed on the little farm at home? Would n't he have been a better man than he was now?" (221). But when he makes a visit to Norway, the landscape seems "unrestful – shooting up and plunging down. It made him so dizzy that he wanted to hold on to something. Was it because he was so used to the prairie now?" (267). He realizes that even with the wealth he has accumulated in America, the potential for the Norwegian farm he has envisioned for years is still beyond his grasp (274–75). His life would be unbearably limited in a country where government restrictions on the amount of land one could purchase would allow him to accumulate only thirty acres in twenty years.

These Scandinavian writers focus particular attention on the oppression in late-nineteenth-century Sweden and Norway that sent so many abroad and the parallel depression that grew out of their cultural isolation in the new land. Both Bojer and Moberg wrote from their Scandinavian homes of the emigration that had decimated the populations of their countries. Per Hansa's enthusiasm and Beret's depression are rooted in Rølvaag's own experience. He fled Norway in 1896 because he saw as his future the grueling life of a small-boat fisherman, in a place where his family had been for six generations (Reigstad, chap. 1). Bojer's Morten Kvidal remains torn between America and Norway all his life: his struggle for wealth in America never meets his expectations (which continue to expand).

Immigrants must adapt not only to the land, which is often more familiar to them than it is to Americans used to the forests of the East, but also to the language, the customs, the religion, and the prejudice of pretentious Yankees. The conflicts that arise from the insistence upon preserving the old customs in a new society are among the most intense in Great Plains fiction. The finality of cultural isolation heightens the tension in immigrant communities. In Rølvaag's *Peder Victorious* (1929) the conflict is between Beret Holm, who clings to her Norwegian language and her Lutheran church, and her son Peder, who eagerly seeks to become a part of American culture. In Mela Meisner Lindsay's novel *Shukar Balan*, World War I heightens tensions between the narrator's German-Russian family and the town that represents the standards they aspire to. Isolated by language, Evaliz's husband David paints a picture of George Washington on the dining-room wall. "Even some town people, having heard of such a patriotic picture in a foreigner's house come and ask to see it." Evaliz, utilizing another universal symbol of community, feeds the visitors. "Ach, how good it is to be accepted!" (201), she says. Evaliz bridges the gulf between private values and public expectations with paintings and food, but others, like Beret, discover, painfully, that they cannot preserve a culture that does not conform to the new society.

Although the safety valve never closes, it does constrict. By the early twentieth century the new arrivals found only marginal land or rented farms available. In Winther's *Take All to Nebraska* the Danish Grimsens are relegated to renting run-down farms: when they arrive in Nebraska after three years in the East, all the good land has been taken up (4–5). Sandoz chronicles the arrival of the bedraggled city-dwellers, the Kinkaiders, in the years before and after World War I in *Old Jules*, *Slogum House*, and *The Tom Walker* (1947). "The dispossessed were taking [up land] without horse or cow or pig. Sometimes they had to borrow a spade to dig into the earth for shelter, grateful for the roofs of willow and slough hay oldtimers helped them make" (*Slogum House* 293). Poverty, war, and the threat of military service lure German Russians Evaliz and David and their children (in Lindsay's *Shukar Balan*) and Pastor Block and his followers (in Wiebe's *Peace Shall Destroy Many*) from Russia at the turn of the century. Evaliz and David eke out an existence on rented farms, helped by David's skill as a carpenter. Block leads his flock into the bleak wilderness of northern Saskatchewan.

The Great American Desert is another myth that persisted even as the prairies were being claimed by homesteaders. As population pressure pushed the edge of the frontier onto the high plains, farming became more and more precarious. At almost the same time, the slave-free controversy brought the conflict between garden and desert into the political arena. To promote a free Kansas, advocates had to combat the notion of sterility. "Logic and destiny demanded that Kansas be fertile: fertile she became" (Emmons 15). Free Staters pushed for passage of the Homestead Act because they knew that small-acreage farms would be settled by farmers who opposed slavery and the Southern plantation system. Settlers were lured to Kansas and the other states of the high plains by pamphlets and reports in which elaborate promises increased in direct proportion to the desolation of the land they were promoting. Many were unprepared for the work it would take to establish farms or businesses on the high plains. For them, the promised garden soon faded back into desert.

These discouraging years appear in the early stories of the boomers and their unsuspecting victims by White and Cather. White's stories "A Story of the Highlands" and "The Story of Aqua Pura" recount the fate of those lured by promoters onto the arid high plains in the unusually wet years of the mid-1880s. In "A Story of the Highlands" the educated, cultured, and successful Burkholders are worn down by years of drought, winds, mortgages, and crop failures. It is the wife who suffers the most: "The great gray dome seemed to be holding her its prisoner. She felt chained under it. She shut her eyes and strove to get away from it in fancy, to think of green hills and woodland; but her eyes tore themselves open, and with a hypnotic terror she went to the window, where the prairie thrall bound her again in its chains" (81). When their resources are gone, her husband goes east looking for work, leaving his wife behind. She watches the wagons file past, "a huge dust-colored serpent" headed east, and by the end of the summer there is "one more vacant house . . . one more mound in the bleak country graveyard" (86).

White's other Fountain County story is the tale of an entire town founded by Harvard men, cultured Eastern capitalists who, like the Burkholders, intend to establish a cultural as well as an agricultural outpost on the high plains. When the drought "with its furnace-like breath singed the town and the farms in Fountain county," the banker Barringer "leads the majority which proudly claimed that the country was all right" and refused the governor's offer of aid (26). But optimism cannot prevent disaster. "Then came the hot winds of July, blowing out of the southwest, scorching the grass, shrivelling the grain, and drying up the streams that had filled in the spring" (27). Barringer's bank fails, but he stays behind. Finally, he is the only one left, an unkempt remnant of the prosperous, cultured young man who arrived full of hope and confidence in the wet boom years. White counters these grim tales with other stories in *The Real Issue* that are simplistically optimistic, but they are set in eastern Kansas, a very different landscape to White's way of thinking. Geographers would probably agree.

Cather's tale "El Dorado: A Kansas Recessional," published in 1901, is another story of a man lured west by the glowing promises of the promoters to a land that obviously does not offer milk and honey: "Although it was late in the autumn, the corn was not three feet high. The leaves were seared and yellow, and as for tassels, there were none. Nature always dispenses with superfluous appendages; and what use had Solomon Valley corn for tassels? Ears were only a tradition there" (*Collected Short Fiction* 294). This glum scene opens the story of Colonel Josiah Bywaters, whose name ironically reflects the fact that he follows the boom west and is left high and dry, stranded on a Kansas bluff. "He was living where the rattlesnakes and sunflowers found it hard to exist" (295). But it is not the land that defeats the citizens of El Dorado. Cather's piece has villains, the Gump brothers, land promoters who lure Bywaters and many others to El Dorado. Unlike the promoters in White's story, who arrive intending to establish an outpost of Eastern civilization on the prairie, the Gumps simply intend to bilk money from unsuspecting investors.

When the inevitable collapse comes and the Gumps abscond with the town's cash, the townspeople realize that "the land was worth nothing, a desert which the fertile imagination of the Gumps had made to blossom as the rose" (303). When everyone else is gone, Colonel Bywaters remains in his deserted store because "he had sunk his money in this wilderness and he had determined to wait until he had got it out. . . . He had come West, worse than that, he had come to western Kansas, even to the Solomon Valley, and he must abide the consequences" (295). In Cather's story the desert is not merely a physical reality but a symbolic punishment. Bywaters was a fool "to quit a country of honest men for a desert like this" (295), and so he must pay. And yet Cather, like White, seems to regard the high plains as bleak but alluring. Joseph "hated western Kansas; and yet in a way he pitied this poor brown country, which seemed as lonely as himself and as unhappy" (303). Cather cannot sustain the tragedy in this early story. Bywaters's timid faith in the land and his persistent belief that he will be rewarded for his vigil are realized when one of the Gump brothers returns, is bitten by a rattlesnake, and dies. On the dead man's body Bywaters finds a pouch containing ten thousand dollars. "Next day, having got his money out of the place, the Colonel set fire to his old store and urged his horse eastward, never once casting back a look at the last smoking ruins of El Dorado" (310).

In a more realistic version of the desert myth, Haskins, in Garland's story "Under the Lion's Paw," is beaten back by the land before he is beaten down by his landlord, Butler. Haskins travels from northern Indiana to western Kansas searching for affordable land. The frontier is gone, the homesteads taken up. Haskins must find land he can afford to buy, but he does not like western Kansas: "I didn't like the looks o' that dry prairie" (*Main Travelled Roads* 130). When the grasshoppers attack four years in a row, Haskins back-trails to Iowa, where he is cornered by the greedy landlord Butler. Jim Butler offers to sell his farm to his tenants, but he adds to the selling price the value of the improvements that Haskins himself has made to the run-down property. To buy the farm that he has put so much time and effort into, Haskins must accede to the usurer's terms. No matter what he does, Haskins is under the lion's paw. One of those for whom the safety valve was intended, lured west to the barren, cheap lands of the high plains, he has been eaten up by grasshoppers and taken in by a land speculator. For Haskins, the West is no safety valve, but a desert indeed.

This contrast between mythic promise and stark reality remains a part of

Great Plains fiction. In Morris's *Field of Vision* (1956) Lois Scanlon McKee remembers her mother facing the window, gazing out at a town that would never materialize from the prairie mirage:

Rows of maples and elms, lights that would swing over the corners and trap the June bugs, and concrete sidewalks down which she would never walk. . . . Across the tracks big houses, spacious lawns, young women to bear and wash the children, old women to watch and love them, and a man to shovel snow from the walk, mow the lawns. Out in back would be grapes, growing over an arbor, a lawn swing stained with mulberries, and a woman like herself cutting flowers with a pair of shears.

That was what she saw, sitting in the rocker, but the view from the kitchen window showed a road where the tracks were tangled like mop strings, and never went anywhere. (223–24)

These stories illustrate the close relationship of the westering myths. If Manifest Destiny mandated movements of population westward to assure growth and progress, then the promise of the garden must be attainable, at least for those willing to work. But that goal requires superhuman strength. If the West is also a safety valve for the undesirable of the East, and an escape valve for the disillusioned and desperately poor immigrants, then some who are too weak, who lack vision, or who are pushed by poverty onto the marginal lands of the high plains will find the myth an illusion and the land a desert.

The passage onto the plains was more than even Whitman could imagine. For fifty years Americans pushed west, testing the myths of promise and progress. By the 1890s they were beginning to discover the painful limitations of the countermyths of social expendability and the limits of the land itself. Gradually the myths have blended with reality, until they are a part of Great Plains fiction – and history.

CHAPTER FOUR

The Dream Deferred:
Acting on the Myths

As the plains and prairies filled with settlers in the years after the Civil War, scholars and writers began to reexamine the myths and the assumptions that had drawn people westward. The romantic West would be recreated in Owen Wister's story of the Virginian and his successors, but only on paper. In some parts of the Great Plains the garden myth was being reevaluated. The homestead of 160 acres would not support a family on the high plains of western Dakota Territory, Nebraska, or Kansas. Farmers could not keep 40 acres of trees alive for ten years in order to "prove up" another 160 acres as a tree claim. As Walter Prescott Webb said, it is "impossible to legislate forests onto the Plains" (412; see also 411–28). The unusually wet years of settlement in the 1880s were followed in the 1890s by severe drought and grasshopper plagues that led thousands of settlers to give up and back-trail. Between 1888 and 1895, for example, 184,054 people left

Kansas (Davis 127). Those who stayed were creating a distinct society: the safety-valve myth would have to be reevaluated too.

At the Chicago Exposition, in 1893, Frederick Jackson Turner declared that the frontier was the most significant feature of the American character and that it was gone. The importance of Turner's manifesto lies not so much in his declaration of the end of the frontier as in his insistence on the significance of the frontier myth as a generating force in American society. Like earlier forces in the push westward – Manifest Destiny, the garden, the safety valve – the theory that the edge of the frontier was gone now became an idea to be evaluated and debated. Most Americans were not naive enough to believe that the regenerative power of the frontier could be sustained in reality. As Harold Simonson has pointed out, we know from the youthful optimism and subsequent disillusionment of Per Hansa, Huckleberry Finn, Jay Gatsby, Jake Barnes, George Willard, and Joe Christmas that the open frontier is an illusion (*Beyond the Frontier* 59). Turner's declaration was merely a public admission of a fact that Mark Twain and Hamlin Garland, among others, had already surmised. Twain published his tale about Huck's search for an escape chute along the Mississippi and his flight west eight years before Turner read his essay in Chicago.

Those who lived on the plains knew that their conception of the West would have to change. The marginal lands still available and the transformation of the homesteads and farms into profitable enterprises would require yet another kind of settlers, not dragon-slayers, dreamers, or social outcasts, but strong men and women determined to establish not only farms but communities on the plains and prairies. The new myth, derived from Emerson and echoed by Whitman, was of democratic vistas in the West. It would be a utopia, with yeoman farmers committed to creating a society based on the equality of land and work.

This concept is evident in Turner's essays "The Significance of the Frontier" and "Democracy." The frontier, Turner says in his first essay, promotes democracy, because patterns of settlement emphasize individualism. He describes the Western democrat as "coarseness and strength combined with acuteness and inquisitiveness, a practical, inventive turn of mind, quick to find expedients," someone with a "masterful grasp of material things," abundant "restless nervous energy," and "buoyance and exuberance which comes with freedom" (*The Frontier in American History* 37). The democratic utopia, Turner insists, can be realized only on the farms of the plains and prairies, where, at least theoretically, families can farm enough land to exist independently, free of corporate and government control.

But in 1893 many of the conditions necessary to nurture Turner's concept were already disappearing. The Populist movement was at its height. The shift to the gold standard that year resulted in an economic depression that was especially hard on Western farmers. The captains of industry who arose along the railroads and in the markets of Chicago monopolized routes, markets, and currency. For a time, farmers, no longer satisfied with proving a claim and replacing a sod hut with a modest frame house, turned their attention to politics and elected an array of state officers across the Great Plains. But in the final analysis, the Populist movement was like a fly on an elephant, that is, pesky but no threat. The frontier, closed and tamed, no longer enjoyed the nation's attention. Nevertheless, the myth of the democratic utopia persists in political rhetoric, economic planning, and policies on the Great Plains. For example, the Center for the New West advocates a "People-Centered Approach" to economic planning on the Great Plains (14–18).

The democratic utopia has none of the wilderness nostalgia about it. The overriding symbol is the plow against the sunset, not the lone hunter. In the homesteading period from the 1880s until World War I, the task was to establish order on the plains and prairies. Settlers had to learn how to turn this apparently barren land into profitable enterprises. Many farms were marginal hardscrabble, or the farmers had not adopted techniques of dryland farming. Once the wilderness was transformed, residents focused on the democratic community that Rob Rodemaker so enthusiastically espouses in Garland's story "Among the Corn Rows." The schools educate children in the fundamentals they need in order to be members of an equal society. The churches inculcate communal values. The family teaches farming techniques. But the myth soon becomes cluttered with selfish opportunism, economic reversals, religious and cultural differences, and class consciousness, which threaten to destroy any hope for a new order.

Nor is the effort to transform the new towns of the prairies into models of democracy successful. Carol Kennicott in Sinclair Lewis's *Main Street* (1921) tries most valiantly to reconcile her own prosaic, middle-class ideals with the equally unimaginative standards of Gopher Prairie. The occasional pioneers she encounters have settled into a dull routine in a town dominated by a class-conscious social elite with no real class. They look upon Carol's efforts to bring change to their lives with indifference or outright hostility. If the original settlers of Gopher Prairie felt their own psychological strength as they founded the town and established the surrounding farms, they have lost that sense of identity in their rush to find comfort in mediocrity.

Not everyone assumed that democracy on the Great Plains was assured or even desirable. In the early nineteenth century, the alignment of South and West against North and East seemed to promise the westward spread of the plantation system. However, the development of railroads instead of the waterways Southerners preferred, the increasing tension in North-South relations, and the passage of the Homestead Act in 1862, among other factors, deflected the expansion of the Southern model into the plains and prairies. Communities based on the Southern or English model of the leisure-class manorial estate were founded on the high plains, but they were short-lived. Promoters lured wealthy Englishmen and others to the West, promising adventure and leisure to pursue it, but none of their settlements lasted more than a few years, and individuals usually stayed an even shorter time. For example, Victoria, Kansas, was established in 1873 by wealthy Englishmen who were attempting to sustain English social customs in the West. By 1878 the English had abandoned Victoria. The German Catholic immigrants who succeeded them knew how to farm the land.

72 *The Dream Deferred*

Frederick Manfred describes an English settlement in Siouxland in his 1992 novel, *Of Lizards and Angels*.

Settlers who arrived expecting to realize the myth stayed only if they were able to work. According to the Puritan work ethic, an important component of the democratic utopian myth, the necessary sacrifices would be rewarded with God's blessings of ownership and security, if not with equality. Emmons points out that promoters emphasized the hard work that faced settlers in the West: disillusioned emigrants writing home could do more harm than even the railroads could afford. An 1876 Santa Fe statement warned: "If hard work doesn't agree with you or you can't get on without luxuries, stay where you are. If you don't have enough capital to equip or stock a farm, if you are susceptible to homesickness, if you do not have pluck and perseverance, stay where you are. . . . Wealth is won here only by work" (quoted in Emmons 33). Although there is a hint of flattery in this passage, the appeal is not to the poor or the disadvantaged who were encouraged to escape through the safety valve. Railroad promoters obviously wanted settlers along the tracks who could hang on long enough to produce crops to ship on the railroad and buy the goods the rails would carry west.

In Great Plains fiction the accounts that follow the settlers and their families through the inevitable hard times portray work as the grim reality and the promise of material wealth and social advancement as a dimly remembered dream deferred. In Bess Streeter Aldrich's *A Lantern in Her Hand*, the Reinmullers' narrow vision of the land as merely a commodity, and their emphasis on work to accumulate more of it, deadens them to the pleasures of life. The family lives in a dugout so that every bit of cash can be used to buy land. Eventually, the children obtain farms of their own, but to do so, they forgo beauty in their lives. Kal Skaret in Bojer's *Emigrants* has a similar obsession with land; after he inherits his daughter's land, he assuages his grief over her death by going after even more land (322).

For some, the burden of work is alleviated by sharing. In Ise's *Sod and Stubble* Henry regards Rosie as his partner, and she willingly works beside him. But for many others, especially for the women and children, commitment to unending toil is difficult. Per Hansa desperately wants Beret to share his commitment, but the land is a punishment to her; that it should be a source of rewarding work for him only exacerbates her isolation. Old Jules expects his wife Mary and his children to work, and they know that he is capable of cruel physical abuse if they do not. Mary works in silence, bearing his children, picking up after the slovenly man. The farm is her responsibility when Jules is locating settlers or tending to community affairs. Jules's daughter Marie flees home at the first opportunity.

In Sykes's *Second Hoeing*, Hannah's life is an unending chore, hoeing beets in the fields or helping with her brothers and sisters in the house. Her confirmation, a symbol of the end of childhood, leads to more adult responsibilities at home rather than to high school as her father had promised. "School, he is done! *Done*, I say. Sixteen you got. Confirmed you is. Tomorrow, the field you work him" (33). After her mother dies of complications in childbirth brought on by overwork, Hannah takes over. She gains enough control over her father to stop him from beating her, and some of her younger brothers and sisters go to high school and leave home, but Hannah remains trapped by those who depend upon her. When Jim Boswell takes her to the mountain hogback, where she can look out over the beet fields, she realizes that her whole vision has been on work: "My hands have been in the dirt, grubbing out the extra plants so that one beet could grow. Everything for one beet – the strongest, the finest. It hasn't been a game. It's been hard back-breaking work" (283). Jim offers her a life away from work, responsibility, and her family, but Hannah realizes that she cannot leave the life that has kept her confined for so long (chap. 10). Hannah knows that Jim comes from a different class, that his values are not hers. In the best democratic tradition, Hannah marries Fred, the widower of her old friend and "her best friend" (308).

For some, work only exacerbates bitter feelings. In Lois Phillips Hudson's story of the 1930s, *The Bones of Plenty*, George Custer focuses all of his angry energy on work. He is jealous of his wife's father, Will Shepherd, who worked during the boom years after World War I and in the midst of the Depression owns a section free and clear and has money in the bank. "Work had rewarded him" (12). But to George work brings only grief. His angry abuse of his wife and daughter arises from his frustration over drought and economic inequalities. The cows stampede while his young daughter Lucy is herding them, and he beats her. "If a man can't count on his family for help," he says, "I don't see how he can be expected to make a go of it. If he has to fight every fat middleman in the country and then his family too, what in Sam Hill is he going to do?" (188). Drought, Depression, and his own blind anger incapacitate George and cause him to lose the farm. "His operating margin had narrowed into a wedge that was threatening to pinch him to death. Everything and everybody had a hold on him, and *he* had a hold on nothing" (61). For the Custers, even more than for Hannah, work is not its own reward.

The grimmest portrait of work without a hint of reward is Kent Haruf's portrait of Roy Goodnough in *The Tie That Binds*. Roy is so independent that, like George Custer, he is cruelly indifferent to everyone, including his wife and children. His Iowa wife "sinks down" and dies on their barren eastern Colorado homestead (28). He spends money only on land (25). In one of the grizzliest and most ironic instances in Great Plains fiction, Roy's fingers are cut off by the sharp blades of a header, a result of his own vicious anger, which spooks his team. The narrator comments that "he lived for another thirty-seven years with those cruel, raw-looking hands. . . . but he couldn't milk a cow or work a fence pliers or drive a tractor. He couldn't do any of those things that mattered. So he was snookered all right. He was fixed. Now he was dependent on other people, and he hated it" (50–51). Roy forces his children, Edith and Lyman, to do the work he can no longer do. When the narrator, Sunny (Sanders Roscoe), a neighbor boy who becomes Edith's only true friend, complains that her life is not fair, his father voices a Great Plains motto: "Course it's not fair. There ain't none of it that's fair. Life ain't. And all our thinking it should be don't seem to make one simple damn" (126).

A cruelty born of frustration makes these tales as grim as they are. Work is merely work. Roy Goodnough, George Custer, and Hannah's father, Adam Schreissmiller, rarely muse about their dreams for the land; their focus is only on who will do the immediate task.

For some, the land is not merely something to work but a source of wealth – an attitude that can be even more destructive. Two Canadian authors have explored the effect of this greed for land. In *The Homesteaders*, Robert J. C. Stead tells the melodramatic story of John Harris, whose drive for land and wealth becomes an obsession that alienates his faithful wife Mary and his daughter Beulah and eventually makes him vulnerable to a complicated scam. In the beginning he has an idyllic vision of the land's possibilities. With work, their homestead in Manitoba becomes a garden, a reflection of the biblical view that work is necessary to faith (63). His first harvest, six hundred bushels of wheat and seven hundred bushels of oats, seems proof of his good faith. But work gradually inures him to the pleasures of life that are supposed to be his reward.

When greed has obliterated his earlier satisfaction in working the land, he is lured further west by the promise of "wealth to be had without corresponding effort" (165). His belief in the old El Dorado myth makes him a suitable victim for his neighbor, the aptly named Riles, and the bad element Riles falls in with in Calgary. The polemical discussion he has with Mary sets out, in rather obvious terms, one of the great questions in Great Plains fiction: just what is the goal of all this toil?

"There's a great opportunity right now to get land for nothin'. . . . We can be independently rich in five years, if we just stand together."

"Independent of what?" she asked.

"Why, independent of – of everything. Nothin' more to worry about and plenty laid up for old age. Ain't that worth a sacrifice?"

"John . . . Answer me a straight question. What was the happiest time in your life? Wasn't it when we lived in the one-roomed sod shanty, with scarcely a cent to bless ourselves? We worked hard then, too, but we had time for long walks together across the prairies." (169)

The Harrises' decline is contrasted with the success of their friends and former neighbors, the Arthurs, who have established a successful ranch in the West where they can enjoy the good life that Stead believes should be the ultimate reward for one's work on the land, an ideal that Beulah describes in a letter to her mother: "[T]hey seem to live for the pure happiness they find in life, and only to think of their property as a secondary consideration" (162).

When Harris arrives in Alberta, he encounters another West, one that Beulah describes as a "motley crowd. . . . up here they're out for money – the long green, they call it" (159). The plot becomes hopelessly convoluted as Riles and his shady partners contrive to part Harris from his wealth, an easy task, since Harris is convinced that in the West he can gain wealth without work. In the climax, their son Allen is seriously wounded, John's money is lost, and he sees the error of his ways. The Harrises find themselves back on their original homestead, poor but happy. Despite the overstated moral in *The Homesteaders*, Stead sums up a basic tenet of Great Plains fiction: work and commitment to the land bring emotional and financial rewards; work for its own end brings only financial rewards; wealth without work brings personal and financial ruin.

In *Wild Geese*, Martha Ostenso creates the quintessential portrait of an isolated man obsessed by land and work. Caleb Gare's need for control over people and the land isolates him from his family and the community. He blackmails those whose land he covets, and his indifference to the welfare of others has earned him the eternal hatred of the community: he once refused shelter to a man who died in a storm. His greed for the land counterbalances the physical and spiritual sparseness of his life. He wants his entire family to be isolated from all contact with the community.

Caleb controls his wife Amelia with blackmail, threatening to ruin her and her illegitimate son, Mark Jordan, who is ignorant of his true parents.

He effectively controls his children with direct threats and his cruelty to their mother. His son Martin understands only one thing, work. Martin sees them all as pea pods "that had ripened brittle, but could not burst open" (206). Ellen, weak and unimaginative, is trapped by her own vague awareness of the guilty conspiracy that surrounds her: "Rebellion would be the open admission of the consciousness of a wrong. Caleb was her father, and any wrong that he had committed must, necessarily, reflect upon herself" (191–92). Only Judith is physically strong and openly defiant. For her, the land and its attending work is an escape from Caleb's cruelty and Amelia's suffering (66–67). But when she throws an ax at her father, the act gives him the same kind of power over her that he has over Amelia: ignorant of the law, she believes that the ax – a physical symbol of her defiance – which remains buried in the barn wall, can send her to prison (240). As a result, she is imprisoned on the farm.

The Gares "all have a monstrously exaggerated conception of their duty to the land – or rather to Caleb, who is nothing but a symbol of the land" (105). Ironically, Caleb tries to convince himself that his interest in the land is merely a diversion –"It was a challenge to Caleb himself to force from the soil all that it would withhold" (250) – but it is really an obsession. His flax field becomes a perverse substitute for the affection of a wife whom he has tortured into loveless submission:

> While he was raptly considering the tender field of flax – now in blue flower – Amelia did not exist to him. There was a transcendent power in this blue field of flax that lifted a man above the petty artifices of birth, life and death. . . .
> Caleb would stand for long moments outside the fence beside the flax. Then he would turn quickly to see that no one was looking. He would creep between the wires and run his hand across the flowering, gentle tops of the growth. A stealthy caress – more intimate than any he had ever given to woman. (171)

Caleb's narrow vision contributes to his fiery death. When he rushes toward his burning flax field, the marshy land sucks at his boots and traps him (351).[1] The schoolteacher, Lind, thinks of him as a man "who could not be characterized in the terms of human virtue or human vice – a spiritual counterpart of the land, as harsh, as demanding, as tyrannical as the very soil from which he drew his existence" (35–36).[2] Gare is the extreme, but Ostenso makes it clear, through conversations of Amelia's son, Mark Jordan, and the schoolteacher Lind Archer, that "the imbalance of the earth seemed to have crept into the very souls" of the community (147). The harsh land drains more than physical energy from the people.

The most compelling portrait of avarice in American Great Plains fiction is Gulla Slogum, Sandoz's will-to-power individual in *Slogum House*.[3] Alienated from her gentle husband Ruedy, Gulla sets about establishing a kingdom on the marginal land of western Nebraska. She bribes and attacks members of the community and intimidates members of her own family who threaten to inhibit her illegal activities or leave Slogum House.

Gulla's house is a fortress of deception, a sprawling mass of rooms and secret passages. Her hospitality attracts innocent travelers, drawn in by her daughter Libby's good cooking. To those she deems worthy – men with power or position – Gulla offers her twins, Annette and Cellie. Gulla's careless, exploitive house parallels her attitude toward the land. She believes that land – especially free land and lots of it, even if it is unproductive desert – is power. She illegally fences the open range with stolen posts and wire and reroutes old wagon roads past Slogum House (45). Her greed extends beyond mere possession: she ignores the land's potential and uses it up without renewing it. Denying its fertility, Gulla does not plant trees as her husband Ruedy does: "[S]hould they show other, later comers what would grow here?" (44). Her source of water is not, like Ruedy's, a natural spring but underground water, found with a witching stick where others swore she could never find water, suggesting her dependence on sinister, magical forces. The pipe, the windmill, and the water tank are, of course, all nighttime "Slogum purchases" made by sons Hab and Cash (44).

Gulla creates a community based on the sandy soil of greed and corruption. She has no use for anyone who cannot serve her selfish needs. Like

Caleb Gare, she believes that wealth will bring independence from people: "By good management she might get to owning most of Dumur County and tell all that trash that stood against her where to get off at" (171). Like the con men in Stead's novel, Gulla Slogum represents the destructive power of the lawless West: unchecked, those who came west to get rich would turn the promised garden into a desert and build a society based upon deception and corruption. To Sandoz, Stead, Ostenso, and other Great Plains authors, these latter-day incarnations of Ishmael Bush are dangerous. Their power derives from their drive to acquire, not from a respect for nature or a willingness to work. The land is to be stripped bare, and animals are to be used or sold: trees and pets are superfluous.

Ironically, the steps Gulla takes to protect her ill-gotten holdings lead to her decline. Society changes: law gains control of public officials, and community opinion turns against her. Gulla abandons physical force and resorts to bribery and intimidation until these methods too prove ineffective. Her greed has isolated her from community as surely as the hogback and the streams isolate Slogum House. She destroys not only any possibility for a community but her family as well.

Gulla has castrated the land. Even eagles and coyotes, nature's scavengers, have deserted Slogum House (313). Gulla is alive and therefore still a threat, able to disenfranchise farmers with foreclosures of their farm loans, at just the time when the country is paralyzed by the Depression. But the novel does not end in this negative key. Even as Slogum House gradually sinks into decay, Gulla's husband Ruedy is building a solid house in Spring Branch Canyon, a true home for his little community of refugees from Gulla's cruelty, a place as natural as Slogum House is artificial (270–80).

Work is an isolating activity. The physical effort itself leaves little energy or time to cultivate family or community relationships. Those who commit themselves to the land often ignore or actively reject their roles in the larger society. But community is necessary for continuation, and those who remain isolated usually discover, as Ishmael Bush did, that they must turn back to community or face, not economic, but psychological defeat.

In Cather's *O Pioneers!* the struggle to establish a peaceful community is centered around intrafamily conflict between Alexandra and her brothers Lou and Oscar. Envious of Alexandra's success and critical of her indifference to community standards of behavior, they walk a fine line between criticism and coveting. Echoing community opinion, Lou tries to force Alexandra to send the simple old man Iver away, but Lou's wife Annie tempers his sharpness. Alexandra is generous to her brothers' children: they hope she will leave them her land, and it is because of this that her brothers object to her continuing friendship with Carl. The independent Alexandra refuses to consider communal or familial responsibilities that are forced upon her. However, the murder of Emil and Marie destroys Alexandra's illusions about the future. Without her brother to benefit from her labor, she will leave her land to her brothers' children. The land will survive the greed and mismanagement of the weak and the inept. But the myth is left unfulfilled: without heirs and community, the democratic utopia is an illusion.

Cather's late story "Neighbour Rosicky" (*Obscure Destinies*, 1932), an elegy to the myth of the yeoman farmer and the democratic utopia, is the story of the myth's fulfillment.[4] Rosicky spends the months before his death reviewing his life and evaluating his hopes and dreams for his family. As a young immigrant in New York City, he read of Czech farming communities in the West and determined to "go out there as a farm hand; it was hardly possible that he could ever have land of his own. . . . Nobody in his family had ever owned any land, – that belonged to a different station of life altogether" (31). At sixty-five he owns his farm. More than anything, he wants to pass it on to his sons, to keep them on the land. "To be a landless man was to be a wage-earner, a slave all your life; to have nothing, to be nothing" (40). For Anton Rosicky, as for like Alexandra Bergson, the land itself is ample reward for his labor. His task now is to be certain that his sons will continue his work. The farm is not only security but protection from the dishonesty and cruelty of urban life – a persistent countermyth in Great Plains fiction. "There were mean people everywhere, to be sure, even in their own country town here. But they weren't tempered, hardened, sharpened, like the treacherous people in cities" (59).

Rosicky dies satisfied with his life and confident of the future. Hard work has brought a semblance of security, but more important, it has brought freedom from economic domination. Rosicky is the embodiment of the yeoman farmer, a steady, strong man who has faith in himself, in his modest abilities, and, most of all, in the future of the land.

"Neighbour Rosicky" evokes a time and place long past in 1932. Like other myths that receded into memory even as they were being acted upon, the idea that a community of immigrants and Americans who were content with the simple life they earned from the soil could arise on the prairie had receded into nostalgia. Cather knew that: she had written *One of Ours* in 1922; nevertheless, in this story she sought to recreate the mythic ideal not of a dragon-slayer or a fertility goddess but of a modest communal man.

Writers often juxtapose the optimistic confidence of men and the reluctance of women, as Rølvaag does in *Giants in the Earth*. In his stories of grim existence on the Canadian plains, Sinclair Ross depicts the man's stubborn refusal, despite storms and tragedy, to give up independence on the land and the wife's fear of isolation and failure. In Ross's classic Great Plains story, "The Lamp at Noon," Ellen fights against her rising panic, exacerbated by dust so thick she lights the lamps at midday. She pleads with her husband to abandon the struggle to farm and move to town, where he can work in her father's store. But Paul refuses: "Even as a desert it's better than sweeping out your father's store and running his errands" (*The Lamp at Noon and Other Stories*, 1968, 10). She longs for town and some of the amenities she enjoyed as a young schoolteacher. Closed in by two barren rooms, her solitude broken by her baby and a monthly trip to town, Ellen pleads for some relief. But Paul dismisses her pleas. "You're a farmer's wife now," he tells her (12). His concern is focused on the land. After the storm, when he sees the land "mounded smooth with dust," he returns to the house to find Ellen and the baby are gone. Searchers find her clutching the dead child and insane.

In "A Field of Wheat" Ross tells the story of John and Martha, whose lives are pitted against the wheat, the land itself. "Not an heroic struggle to give a man courage and resolve, but a frantic, unavailing one. . . . it was the wheat that was invincible" (68). When the inevitable hailstorm bears down on their perfect crop, which is not insured, destroying it, and invades even the house through broken windows, Martha rebels, until she witnesses John's sobbing in the barn with the animals. She takes strength from his unacknowledged weakness. The balance restored, they will persevere (76). In another story of invasion, "September Snow," part 2 of "Not by Rain Alone," Will leaves in a blizzard to search for his cattle, a concern that takes precedence over his wife's approaching childbirth. Stranded overnight by the storm, Will returns to find his kitchen door open, snow drifted into the room, and Eleanor in the cold bedroom in the throes of childbirth. When she dies, Will is left with the baby. The cattle have drifted home on their own.

The conflict over work and reward is not always within families. Robert Stead's novel *Grain* (1926) is a moralistic tale of the choices one must make between work and community. Gander Stake resists all efforts to make him leave his farm. He is fascinated by his neighbor Jo Burge, but he is fascinated even more by his other love, machines.[5] As Dick Harrison points out, the Stakes concentrate on "mindless production," on farming as industry (105). When his brother leaves home, Gander quits school to help his father, Jackson. When the war comes to Plainville, he resists the invitations to enlist, in part because he is repulsed by the undemocratic tone the drill sergeant uses on some town recruits (166). To Gander, the drill team represents the deadening effects of society's demands. The farm, on the other hand, in spite of the endless work it requires, means a selfish kind of freedom. "His life was on the farm, where he left other people alone, and asked only that they do the same to him" (188). Only when his relationship with the married Jo threatens to go beyond friendship does he flee to the city.

Frederick Manfred, in his novel *The Golden Bowl*, explores the conflicts that arise when a strong individual is faced with the challenge of subduing and surviving on the land. Set in South Dakota in the 1930s, when the Dust Bowl was at its worst, Manfred establishes an ironic contrast between the mythic ideal of the simple yeoman farmer recreating the garden of the world and the Thors and Maury slowly shriveling up on their barren acreage. The land's mythic promise of the garden, hidden beneath years of drought and neglect, is implicit in Iver (Pa) Thor's determination to work even if the land is dead and in the fertile promise of his daughter Kirsten. Pa Thor's effort to draw the drifter Maury Grant into his family represents the myth of the democratic utopia: anyone willing to work can become a part of the family community.

The story that Manfred layers upon these underlying myths is a realistic portrait of South Dakota in the depth of the Dust Bowl. The Thors are self-sufficient by necessity: everyone else has abandoned the land. Their farm is a parody of the bucolic ideal, not a neat white farmhouse with picket fence and protective shade trees but the ultimate desert setting, a paintless shack amid drifts of dust.

Pa and Maury personify the myths and realities of fertility and drought. Pa Thor's optimism – what we might call a "garden" point of view – springs from his faith in the land, his own knowledge of farming, and his family's obligation to the land (131–32). Maury's lack of faith in the dormant land – his "desert" mentality – originates in his parents' farming failure, their deaths, and his resulting lack of roots and family ties. Ironically, the potential for growth exists only if one is committed to place. The man who rejects that commitment faces a barren existence, something that Maury finally acknowledges.

Pa's faith is not easily passed on to Maury, for whom the empty land affirms that "only empty people kin live in an empty country, people empty in their soul" (131). He sees only the land itself, parched and unproductive. Not until he has withstood tests and failures can Maury see the mythic "golden bowl," the earth's promise.

Near the novel's center Manfred includes an incident that encapsulates

Maury's conflict with the land. In an effort to force some water from the land, Maury, Pa, and Ol' Gust dig Pa Thor a deeper well. After Gust drops a wrench, Maury descends through the narrow casings into a black pit created by cave-ins below the casing and finally into the water to retrieve the errant tool. Maury's experience is a form of baptism, total immersion into the farm and the land itself. His own cramped ascent in a fetal position is a symbolic rebirth and, at the same time, a realization of death: he experiences the suffering of the Thors' son Tollef, who perished in a dust storm (127).

To avoid a repetition of the past, Maury continues to deny the mythic promise of the garden. He abandons the Thor farm and drifts west soon after the incident in the well. He is as "free" as anyone can be: isolated, impoverished, and afoot. Maury's encounters with the land and with people begin to stir in him the unconscious commitment to the land that was prefigured by his descent into the well. Finally, admitting his need, he heads east, back to the Thors' farm.

Kirsten Thor is a very real woman who links Maury symbolically to the Thors and, what is more important, to the land. Manfred is careful to establish Kirsten as much more than a comely farm girl. Throughout the novel he balances descriptions of the dead land with images of the virginal Kirsten. The relationship increases in complexity as Maury's efforts to resist his attraction to the place itself intensify. Kirsten's own animal nature makes her clearly a fertility symbol, an earth mother, a fact that Maury instinctively recognizes as both a promise and a threat. At first his feeling toward Kirsten is pure lust for her physical body, but the connection between the girl and commitment soon becomes clear.

In a scene just before Maury's descent into the well, Kirsten and Maury swim in the moonlight. It is another form of baptism for Maury. At first they play, splashing each other like children. But their mood shifts when they notice the moon:

An enormous blood-gold saucer was slowly being shoved up over the rim of the earth by an invisible force. . . . The saucer expanded. It swelled. Raised. When the disc was almost free of the earth, the lower part clung to the dark horizon for a moment like a drop of water clinging to an object before it parts. Then the moon drew the reluctant part into itself and the blood-yellow orb rose slowly. (105)

The moon symbolizes their own condition. Like Kirsten, it is clearly a symbol of fertility, and like Maury, it reluctantly releases its hold on the land. At this point, however, Maury is too self-centered to realize the full force of his commitment to the girl and her symbolic and literal connection to place. He only feels trapped by his own desire. Soon after this, he leaves the farm and heads west.

Maury has been unfaithful to Kirsten and to the land. He ate at her parents' table, swam with her in the moonlight, descended into the depths of their land, and abandoned them all. However, as he journeys back to the farm (and before he knows that Kirsten is pregnant) he acknowledges his crimes against the land itself: "He had done something terribly wrong. He had, for four years, doubted the land. In the years to come, he would work doubly hard to make the earth, and his own heart, forget that he had been unfaithful" (196). On his return, Maury is confronted with conflicting myths, the garden in Kirsten's pregnancy and the desert in the worst dust blizzard they have encountered (210–24). But they are not defeated, because Maury has returned to stay. He deliberately takes up the work of the farm, the reward for those who believe in the mythic promise of the golden bowl.

Writers continue to explore the relationship between the mythic promises of land and society and the more prosaic reality. Douglas Unger's 1984 novel, *Leaving the Land*, focuses on three generations of Hogans from the 1930s to the present. The scene is the Hogans' South Dakota farm, marginal land settled in the last wave of homesteading. The patriarch, Ben Hogan, is a yeoman farmer who realizes his dream of owning a successful farm through ingenuity, good judgment, and physical strength. Like the earlier settlers, Ben must break the ground, work hard, and face the weather's un-certainties. World War II brings hard times. His sons are killed in the war. The monopolistic Nowell-Safebuy Company controls production, pro-cessing, and marketing in the same way that the railroads controlled the farmers' markets in the late nineteenth century. Ben Hogan loses ten thou-sand dollars when he tries to circumvent the company. Government poli-cies interfere with crops and shipping. He survives, but only the home-stead is left.

Ben's wife Vera is a stern, ailing woman worn down by farm work and isolation who embarrasses her daughter Marge on their trips to town (18–19). Like other farm wives in Great Plains fiction, Vera is simply a part of the farm. When Ben dies, she stays put; she moves to her car when she be-comes incontinent, and she dies after only three weeks in a nursing home, despite Marge's offerings of home water and her own canned goods.

Like Maury Grant, Ben's daughter Marge struggles against her con-scious desire to flee (83–84) and her unconscious attraction to the land. As her mother wears down, Marge reluctantly takes over the house. "She felt imprisoned by the kitchen as her men worked. She would much rather have been out there with them, working like a man, if she couldn't live in town" (20). Marge escapes to her "private place," a tangle of brambles and willows. It is a physical and psychological refuge that symbolizes her con-tact with the land: "She was alone, flat against the earth, able to distinguish each strand of grass from the next in a tiny clump, able to pursue the sudden leap of a frog in flight toward the creek and to capture it, give it a name, then set it free in the deepest pool of the creek, where she knew that, even in drought, its children would live" (83).

Despite her attraction to the land, Marge, like a host of other plains chil-dren, wants desperately to leave. Her marriage to Jim Vogel, the Nowell-Safebuy Company lawyer, a weak and ineffective man, is in keeping with her conscious rejection of her mother's vision of life: "There's a lot more to life than [romance]," Vera said. "There's having a home. There's having a life with both feet planted. . . . There's children and dogs and a garden to water. There's having a house and all the things that go with it, and all the work to keep that house a place where people want to come to your door, that's what there is" (81). But Marge rejects her mother's version of the "farm wife" myth. To her, the work is not worth this meager reward. She believes Jim is the antithesis of the things she tries to hate – the farm, the work, her rough father, her dull mother – but Jim also represents too many things that are opposed to her pioneer heritage, such as rootlessness, a corporate mentality, and a city man's attraction to things for show, including his house and his wife. Like Cather's Claude Wheeler, Marge finds marriage to someone divorced from the land itself an empty show. When Nowell-Safebuy closes its turkey-processing plant and Jim leaves town, Marge, like her mother, stays put in the big house her husband built in Nowell during the prosperous times.

Despite crop failures, war, the Depression, and corporate manipulation, the Hogans survive, verifying the persistent myth of the yeoman farmer. Unger explains the situation in sociological terms. The mythical evocation of the land and work as its own reward becomes not a dream from the past but a part of present reality:

[The Bates Corporation in northwest Colorado] discovered after intensive sociological research that family farmers are willing to work eighteen hours a day if need be and not just for money, but to hold on to the land. There is an immortality given to the earth, a sense of expansive dream passed from immigrant homesteader through generation after generation of his children in a self-perpetuating vision of freedom and wealth. Unit farm managers punched their time clocks after eight hours and drove home. Production dropped. It wasn't long before the Bates Land and Cattle Company began losing millions. (180)

The second part of the novel is narrated by Marge's son Kurt, who traces his mother's life without his father. Marge becomes the caretaker to both the land and the town, paying taxes on one, feeding the other at the Cove Cafe, where she works. The church, the traditional source of comfort and support, has become a seasonal warehouse for beets and potatoes (225). In its place, "[t]he town came to her for what they needed, to sit in her booths, eat the food she cooked for them, drink out of her cups" (212).

The town of Nowell is dying, but Marge and Kurt hold on. The yeoman farmer reappears in the form of Dan Gooch, an Indian rancher. He helps Marge and Kurt raise sheep on the homestead. Kurt's first experience with the sheep ends in his rejection of both the myth and the reality. Left alone, Kurt finds that tending sheep is harder than raising crops or tending turkeys: "I looked around. There were a lot more undoctored sheep than it seemed. My face and eyes burned from the Sioux's holy sun. I knew at that moment this was not my future – not this farm, this labor, not this whole sphere of human toil. I would do anything I had to do to get away" (249).

Kurt escapes to the Navy, where, presumably, he can be at sea on water rather than on grass. But his mother's letters draw him back reluctantly (134). Finally, on his return, when they are trapped together in the deserted farmhouse during a Christmas snowstorm, Marge passes the deed to the farm to her son, and Kurt accepts it, fully aware of its deeply rooted meaning:

I thought of my grandfather out in the first spring sun *gee-hawing* to his team, pushing his horses to their limits to drag a single plowshare a half acre a day through thick clay sod. Then I thought of the others like him still alive . . . still waiting out there for something, still holding on, counting the years by illnesses and deaths.

. . . I thought *there must be other secrets now and I don't know them.* (276–77)

For Marge, the reward for her lonely, unromantic life is this small act: to pass her parents' land on to her son. His initiation complete, his possession of the land assured, Kurt begins to understand what he has inherited: work, few material rewards, and fulfillment in the heritage – not in the ownership – of the land itself. It is the most persistent myth of the Great Plains.

Men and women learned the lessons of the Great Plains over and over. They discovered the land's fertility, and they struggled to establish the kinds of communities they wanted to live in. As regions were opened, more settlers came – from America and abroad. The myth of the safety valve was replaced by the myth of the melting pot, a less pejorative if not more accurate term. While the former focused on the less-than-honorable origins of the new arrivals, the latter incorporated much of the myths of the yeoman farmer and the democratic utopia: the promise of land and security and the vision of a free and equal society in exchange for work. To this vision were added some elements of the safety valve, such as escape from political and economic repression, and the added promise of religious freedom, with the naive hope for cultural acceptance in the new land. The myth's image is not one of a ragtag line of dispirited, impoverished slum dwellers squinting at the plains' unending horizon, but one of masses of solid, strong workers fanning out across the prairies and plains.

The myth of the melting pot was promoted by agents sent to Europe by immigrant companies, steamship lines, speculators, and railroads, which actively sought out settlers, especially from northern Europe. With glittering brochures and "gargantuan fruits and vegetables," their Lorelei call was verified by articles in guidebooks and emigrant newspapers and in the letters of successful immigrants (Billington 59–69). In the 1880s railroad agent Carl B. Schmidt brought the German-Russian Mennonites to the Great Plains. Schmidt and other promoters believed that "certain races and nationalities were especially suited to back breaking toil on farms and in factories." These people, they asserted, would "work harder, complain less and produce more than anyone else" (Hudson, "Towns of the Western Railroads," 46). Turner believed that the frontier transformed these immigrants into Americans: "This great American West took [European men, institutions, and ideas] to her bosom, taught them a new way of looking upon the destiny of the common man, trained them in adaptation to the conditions of the New World" (267). The idea of free land, rather than land as a source of revenue, made this amalgamation possible (244–45).

Of course, the myth was not fully realized. Conflicts in culture, custom, and religion fed the inevitable clash between generations when the initial dream of owning land had been realized.[6] A century after settlement many Great Plains communities retain their ethnic identity – Swedish, Czechoslovakian, Norwegian, Bohemian – and their dominant religious denomination, often Lutheran or Catholic. Annual festivals and celebrations commemorate these heritages. The crucible that Turner believed the frontier to be did not fuse these disparate people into one great melting pot; rather, it resulted in a stew of distinct parts.

Nevertheless, immigrants poured onto the Great Plains. In the nineteenth century nearly 20 million people entered the United States, and until the 1880s most of them headed for cheap lands in the West (Billington 60). They were confident that their lives, or the lives of their children, would be better. Evaliz, the narrator of Lindsay's *Shukar Balan*, describes the myth succinctly: "We are pilgrims of many nations, all fleeing Old World strife, looking for a new life of liberty and freedom" (121). Although Evaliz remains unassimilated into a culture that does not want to understand her Old World habits, she works ceaselessly so that her children "will be among the American people, to gain new knowledge that is so necessary, and to make something of their lives" (194).

Old Jules, Sandoz's account of her father's immigration from Switzerland to the Sandhills of western Nebraska in 1884, is the most provocative account of the immigrants' vision of the American melting-pot myth. Always planning and encouraging others, Jules believes his task is to create a community. "Jules saw his home and around him a community of his countrymen and other homesteaders, refugees from oppression and poverty, intermingled in peace and contentment. There would grow up a place of orderliness, with sturdy women and strong children to swing the hay fork and the hoe" (19).

Sandoz incorporates motifs of wilderness and community myths into her story. In the early years Jules adheres to the code of the lawless frontier, often taking the law into his own hands. As the community is established, he turns to the courts to battle the ranchers who run their cattle on the open range, indifferent to claim boundaries and the boundaries of government land. To realize his vision, Jules works tirelessly to build up the country. He encourages his family and friends in Switzerland to immigrate, writes letters to other prospective settlers, and works as a locator for homesteaders who come into the region.

Jules's approach toward the community he has struggled to create is a confusion of contradictory impulses. Because of his contentiousness, he is awarded and loses the post office, his symbol of community, time after time over the years. He encourages his neighbors to marry, believes women should bear children, takes in settlers for months at a time until they can establish claims, blames the wives when marriages fail, and comments only briefly when men and women are murdered or go mad.[7]

But Jules knows that without community his vision for the region will never be fully realized. He works especially hard to attract his own brothers, his fellow French Swiss, and Germans to these Nebraska claims because he knows they will be good workers. Over the years Jules sees settlers arrive in good years and old friends depart in years of drought, leaving their farms for the cattlemen's pastures and creating an empty place in his own immigrant community. With the inevitable rains, new waves of settlers appear to resettle the deserted homesteads. Not all of his recruits are fit for the task of establishing farms in the harsh, dry land. The last wave of settlers, the Kinkaiders, come after passage of the 1904 act that opened up the last of the available land. They settle the Sandhills, where Jules has established his second homestead, of orchards and vineyards. Isolated, dry in summer, cold in winter, barren of fuel, and far from the railroad, it is land that has been ignored until the last. These homesteaders are not the sturdy Germans, the witty and educated Swiss, or even the determined Americans of the 1880s, but rather "middle-aged, city-softened, dependent upon railroads and stores, too often set lone folk: bachelors, widowers, old maids, widows" (358). Nevertheless, Jules locates them and promotes marriage among them, importing wives if necessary.

Jules's vision of community is based upon his faith in the land. When others cannot sustain the faith or complete the work that the land demands, he is often disappointed but never deterred. He ignores the advice of those who tell him that the land is too harsh to grow crops and those who believe that the cattlemen are the rightful occupants of the land along the Niobrara River. Jules focuses his emotional effort on the establishment of a permanent community, but he puts all of his intellectual energy into new varieties of fruit trees and new crops. The proud Jules views the recognition he receives from the horticulture enthusiasts as justification for his faith in the "marginal land."

For the immigrants, the myth of the melting pot brings a mixture of hope and denial. While the promise of eventual ownership is an adequate substitute for material reward, the memory of home accentuates the loneliness of the first years on the plains. The sadness of all the immigrants is represented by Old Jules's memories of Rosalie, the sweetheart he left in Switzerland, who never has the courage to follow him to America.[8] All four of his wives must contend with this memory of his European past. Mary has her own memories. Most of the settlers do. "They all sang with strong young voices, led by Mary, who seemed always to know more and more songs of the homeland. Now and then a tear glistened in a wind-reddened eye as they sang of wandering lovers or sweethearts waiting and thought of those who did not wait or would not come to America" (212).[9]

Jules himself symbolizes both the promise and the danger of the myth of the melting pot. Although his success justifies his persistent faith in the land, the educated, refined Swiss has become rough and harsh. This is especially evident from the Surbers' point of view. They are Swiss immigrants who live in St. Louis and come to their Panhandle farm in the summers. Mrs. Surber is appalled at Jules's unkempt ways. Jules's friend Big Andrew invokes the wilderness myth when he explains to Mrs. Surber that Jules has himself become a symbol of the land he attempts to tame:

Jules is then only what he must be. . . . One can go into a wild country and make it tame, but, like a coat and cap and mittens that he can never take off, he must always carry the look of the land as it was. He can drive the plough through the nigger-wool, make fields and roads go every way, build him a fine house and wear the stiff collar, and yet he will always look like the grass where the buffalo have eaten and smell of the new ground his feet have walked on. (375)

On his early hunting expeditions, Jules sees the promise of the land in the clear streams, the white bluffs, the plum thickets that form a thick canopy, and the matted wild grape. Jules's wild orchard is not the quiet refuge of *O Pioneers!* but full of life. It symbolizes the land's fecund potential for the community:

Over them, and as far as they could see in the dim leaf haze, the thicket was roofed with a solid cluster of wild grapes, blue with bloom. The thorny brush that supported the vines was almost bare, but the ground underneath was purple-red with overripe plums, sweetish, decaying food for the swarms of wasps humming drowsily as they worked.

"Fruit enough for a whole village," Jules said grandly. "Plum jell, grape wine!" (80)

Years later, the community – a mixed pot of immigrants, Yankees, and Kinkaiders – comes to his cultivated orchard. Jules's steady faith in the fruit of the land has resulted in realization of the garden myth for the immigrants from Europe and across America who have gathered along the rivers and among the hills of the high Nebraska plains. They have created a new civilization.[10] The cold, the suffering, the feuds, and the isolation are not important to Jules. His own family, his house, his appearance matter even less. It is the orchards, the changes in the pale, weak people, and the prosperity that brings fine draft horses to the fields and the music of a record player to Mirage Flats that are important. For a while, the society Jules creates in the Nebraska Sand Hills is as close to equal as a society on the high plains can be:

But prosperity, unless too great, brings neighborliness. Where once each little shack curled pungent blue smoke from its stovepipe reaching crookedly into the sky, now wagons, buggies, saddle horses, and a few cars were grouped about certain homes on Sunday for big dinners. Three kinds of meat, perhaps, in big gray roasters or black kettles, beans, become a staple during the leaner years, corn, salads, choke- and sand-cherry jams and jellies, wild plum preserves, with cake, stacks of pie and cookies, until there was scarcely room for the plates. Pure democracy excluded only the fat old widows who were afraid of horses and could not "hoof it," as the Kinkaiders expressed it. People like the music teacher were always remembered by somebody who could just as well swing "round that way." . . . Every Sunday Mary cooked dinner for perhaps fifteen to thirty people. Often all Sunday afternoon the uninvited came. (388–89)

The new civilization is not realized without suffering. Jules limps from a fall down the well that crushed his foot. His second wife slowly goes insane. Jules's treatment of his wives and children is cruel. And yet, it is clear that Mari Sandoz – the quiet, shy Marie of the narrative, and the only one to leave the Panhandle – believes that her father embodies the myths of the garden in the desert and the immigrants' melting pot and that fulfillment of those myths is, in one sense, justification for the suffering the vision demanded.

The conflicts implicit in the myths persist in Great Plains fiction. The land may prove bountiful, but it demands undivided attention and unrelenting work. Hundreds of thousands of home-seekers, whose faith in the land fed the myth of the garden, believed also in the possibility of a democratic utopia and the melting pot on the prairie homesteads. Ironically, it is the children who melt into American society, leaving the first generation isolated on the farm, perhaps successful after years of work but strangers in a society that may include their own children. The immutability of the land, the willing sacrifice of those who fight to survive the harsh climate, the pressures to abandon their cultural heritage in exchange for the sameness of American culture and material success, and the promise of reward, whether it be survival or security, persist. The dream may be deferred, but it is not abandoned.

CHAPTER FIVE

The Enclosed Garden:
Coming to Terms with Place

As people settled in on the Great Plains the myth of the garden was revised in light of actual conditions. According to Henry Nash Smith, "By 1900, more than thirty-five percent of all American farmers had become tenants" (190), their bitter struggle to be told by Great Plains writers such as Garland, Lois Philips Hudson, Winther, Manfred, and Stegner. According to Smith, the garden myth was destroyed by the Industrial Revolution, which transformed nineteenth-century America from an agrarian to an industrial society; however, it is doubtful that the dream of the yeoman farmer could ever have been realized on the high plains. Those farmers who adapted and survived followed the pattern advocated by John Wesley Powell, increasing their holdings, raising cash crops on large acreages, and sometimes grazing cattle as well. For most settlers, the attempt to transfer the garden to the Great Plains ended with the realization that "Eden could not be recaptured by fervent prayers and incantations and that proper land utilization in the central Great Plains required more than a boomers' combination of naivete, wishful thinking and fraud" (Emmons 197).

Because of these realities, the garden in Great Plains fiction is not a retreat that prepares one to return to civilization as it is in classical pastoral literature: time and space intervene, so that settlers have no place and no people to return to. Instead, civilization must be established *in* the wilderness. Harold Simonson has suggested that the closed frontier is a metaphor for American tragedy, a reluctant recognition that possibilities are finite, progress limited. "The existentialism symbolized by a closed frontier replaces the idealism engendered on an open frontier. Instead of a limitless frontier, there is a wall. The tension comes from the illusory prospect of the one and the certitude of the other" (*The Closed Frontier* 6).

Great Plains writers are fascinated by space and its relation to human-sized enclosures.[1] The tension between eternal horizon-to-horizon space and the need to create some refuge to close off space and time is central in Great Plains fiction. The bowl of sky that symbolizes unlimited opportunity to one can threaten psychological erasure to another. A grove of trees or the prairie house becomes the symbol of finite space, a refuge to one, a trap to another. Perhaps these images of enclosure persist because even after almost one hundred years we are reluctant to admit that there is no place to go. Wright Morris has suggested that the plainsman is attracted to space travel because once the "fiction of the westward course of empire" proved an illusion, "[n]ext on the agenda loomed the sky" (*Fork River Space Project*, 1977, 54–55).

As early as 1891 Garland's realistic tales of rundown farms in the Wisconsin coulees, on the Iowa prairies, or on the Dakota plains set forth situations that illustrate the inescapable drudgery of farm life, the futility of hope. Cather and Rølvaag write in the 1910s and 1920s of the limitations men and women faced in the generation that inherited the wilderness. Greed, materialism devoid of taste, and foolish pride prevent Claude Wheeler and Peder Holm from achieving the heroic stature of Alexandra Bergson or Per Hansa.

The Enclosed Garden 97

This sense of helplessness persists, especially in stories of latecomers, who had to struggle not only with the land but also with landlords and townspeople who set up barriers for newcomers, particularly for immigrants. For Winther's Grimsens or Lindsay's Evaliz and David, the garden is a rented farm, and the society a Yankee mix suspicious of outsiders. In stories of drought and the Depression, natural forces dry up the garden.

In *The Beet Queen*, Louise Erdrich conveys this sense of uncertainty through images of pure space and cold. The land itself seems to have evaporated. The names Mary Adare and Argus are plays on words and on space itself. Mary's mother deserts her children and flies off with a stunt pilot. Erdrich repeatedly describes Argus from the air. Mary says, "[S]ometimes before sleep I looked down from my bed and saw Argus as in the postcard view I sent to my mother. It was small, a simple crosshatch of lines on the earth, nothing that an ice age or perhaps even another harsh flood could not erase" (60). The land, the town, the lives of those connected with Koza's Meats, where Mary finds a home of sorts, seem ephemeral. Her cousin Celestine reports that Mary "tells me about holes in space that suck everything into them. They even suck space into space. I cannot picture that. In my mind I see other things, though, drawn away at high speed into the blackness" (250). Ironically, when the air becomes substantial, it solidifies into ice: "The rain had gone solid as it fell. Frozen runnels paved the ground and thick cakes of ice formed beneath the eaves where the dripping water solidified midair" (34). Isolated, injured, abandoned, paralyzed, fanatical, even dead, the people in Argus and especially those who come and go at Koza's Meats continue to exist in their frozen world, feeling, as Mary's brother Karl says, "part of the senseless landscape. A pulse, a strip, of light" (285).

The novel closes with Celestine and Mary driving in the annual Argus beet parade with the body of Sita Koza, driven insane by the arid land and her empty life, killed by loneliness and pills, propped in the seat. The paralyzed Indian war hero, Russell, looking stuffed, rides on a float in the same parade. Russell, Dot the Beet Queen, Sita, and even the town itself have been used up and dried out: "We needed a kind rain, a blessing rain, one that lasted a whole week. We needed water. . . . Whole congregations prayed for the drought to cease. But the days were rainless, hot, and everywhere the earth dried and cracked" (276–77). Only Dot escapes. Like her grandmother, who took flight when her mother was a child, she flies off with the stunt pilot hired to write her name in the air (300–301). For Erdrich, as for Wright Morris, the sky's the limit when the land has become unbearable.

The enclosed garden is not always a physical or even a psychological enclosure. Declining expectations can lead characters to reevaluate their dreams. The myth of the bountiful garden is replaced with another Old Testament image, that of the suffering Job. The focus is not on the garden's promise but on the sufferings of the desert. Like Job, the farmers face multiple disasters for which they are blameless, and they feel that they have been set upon by Satan to test their faith. Job loses all his material possessions, his family, his friends, and yet he continues to work. Even in the face of physical debility Job refuses to give up. In Great Plains fiction, to surrender is to die; however, it is usually not faith but entrapment that makes the farmers keep waiting for some reward.

Many Great Plains stories reflect a deterministic philosophy that is diametrically opposed to Job's stubborn faith; yet they share with the biblical tale the refusal to submit to nihilism. Their persistence is especially evident in the six short stories in Garland's original edition of *Main-Travelled Roads*.[2] By the time Garland began to write, Americans were ready to accept a new Western figure and a new Western myth. As Smith explains, Garland's plowman "is neither the yeoman of agrarian tradition nor a picturesque rural swain, nor a half-barbarian like Ishmael Bush, not an amusingly unrefined backwoodsman, not even a victim of a perverted land system. His most direct relation is to nature, and even though this relation is one of conflict, it confers on him a certain dignity and tends to enlarge his stature by making him a representative of suffering humanity, or man in general" (241).

Garland's story "Up the Coolly" is an especially grim, Job-like portrait of the farmer as suffering victim.[3] Garland contrasts the lives of two brothers, the impoverished Grant McLane, who stayed on the marginal Wisconsin farm, and Howard, who drifted away and found success as an actor. On a return visit, Howard's bucolic memories contrast with the hopeless reality Grant endures. Howard reclines comfortably on the train, enjoying the "panorama of delight" that passes before him. "The farming has nothing apparently petty about it. All seems vigorous, youthful and prosperous" (54). But Grant has lost the family farm in part because Howard was too busy to care. He says to Howard, "You might have known we were as poor as Job's off-ox. Everybody is that earns a living" (66). The farm, with its "sordidness, dullness, triviality and its endless drudgery" (61), shocks Howard and has embittered Grant. Like Job, Grant has lost everything – his farm, his wife's respect, his health, and his zest for life. Only work is left – in mud, with the animals, a barely human existence.

A romantic, Howard wants the Western garden to persist. He escapes his brother's wrath by walking into the countryside, but his interlude does not eradicate thoughts of the inequity and injustice of his good fortune and his brother's misery. He is hurt and angered by his brother's bitter accusations. For his part, Grant does not accept his brother's efforts at reconciliation patiently: "Singular we fellers here are discontented and mulish, ain't it? . . . Singular we think the country's goin' to hell, we fellers, in a two-dollar suit, wadin' around in the mud or sweatin' around in the hayfield, while you fellers lay around New York and smoke and wear good clothes and toady to millionaires?" (71).

Grant's wife Laura is trapped too. She looks longingly back to her days as a teacher. "I was a fool for ever marrying. . . . I made a decent living teaching. I was free to come and go, my money was my own. Now I'm tied down to a churn or a dishpan, I never have a cent of my own" (90). The other women, whom Howard knew as lively girls, live even worse lives on barren homesteads further west, or, left behind, they have become old-maid teachers. "Marriage is a failure these days for most of us," declares his old friend Rose. "We can't live on the farm, and can't get a living in the city, and there we are" (82).

Howard realizes that his brother's bitter discontent is shared by most of his neighbors. The free land in Dakota is gone, and renters must agree to terms that would "skin a man alive." In the light of such despair, Grant rejects Howard's offer to buy back the family farm. Physically, he does not have the strength to maintain the old farm. Psychologically, he is worn down. His life is over: "I mean life ain't worth very much to me, I'm too old to take a new start. I'm a dead failure. I've come to the conclusion that life's a failure for ninety-nine per cent of us. You can't help me now. It's too late" (97). The garden that persisted in Howard's memories has become a scene of toil because of Howard's neglect and Grant's bitterness.

This pattern persists. In much Great Plains fiction the farmer is unable to leave and unable to create a home where he is. The root causes of failure are not always external. In Manfred's novel *This Is the Year* (1947), Pier Frixen, who understands neither his wife nor the land, loses both because of his stubborn refusal to commit himself to either with affection and understanding. Pier treats his wife and his land with equal indifference, taking satisfaction from both without reciprocating their affection or acknowledging their needs. The county agent, Pederson, whom Pier calls the "Old Dreamer," warns Pier on his wedding day to "get acquainted with your working mate," and he means the land. But Pier, full of pride and self-confidence, rejects not only Pederson's educated advice but the past as well: he takes over his father's farm on his wedding day and soon forces his parents to retire in town. To him, farming is a simple matter of imposing his will on the land. "If all the farmers here 'bouts would farm their land clean like me . . . if they'd cultivate on time, if they would plow neat and straight, the land would stay as sweet as it's always been" (26). Pier adheres to his philosophy, treating the land and his wife Nertha with straightforward self-satisfaction. He ignores Pederson's advice to contour his hillside plowing, and because his father farmed across the hillside, he plows down the slope, so that over the years the rains dig a gully that threatens the very foundation of the Frixen home. Similarly, Pier ignores the doctor's advice to take care that Nertha gets the same satisfaction from their sexual relations that he enjoys. Abandoned both physically and emotionally, Nertha slides into fanaticism and madness. After a self-induced abortion, she is as barren as the land Pier has abused. At the novel's end Pier is trapped into leaving the land, and Nertha is dead. The bank forecloses. Pier walks away from his own farm sale.

For Grant McLane and Pier Frixen, the garden has become a cage, trapping them in a loop of failure and hope that repeats endlessly. Their ability to see other options is clouded by their commitment to the land and their narrow exposure to the rest of the world. They express in their work the emotions that they cannot articulate to their wives and children. In Sinclair Ross's story "A Field of Wheat," John retreats to the barn and his animals grieve over the loss of his crop. His wife, who watches silently, realizes that "John was gone, love was gone; there was only wheat" (68). Forces beyond their control – depression, storms, foreclosures – lead them to reassess, but they will never of their own free will leave the land that causes so much suffering. Manfred's title reflects their futile optimism: this *may* be the year.

On the prairies and plains, where men and women have had to create the smaller spaces that define them, physical space becomes significant. The most persistent image of refuge is a physical place that symbolizes not only emotional and psychological escape but also physical contact with the land. On his visit to Ántonia's farm Jim Burden can slip back into a pastoral retreat in her triple-enclosed orchard, a place of "deepest peace" (341). In Cather's *The Song of the Lark*, Thea Kronborg finds refuge from the narrow confines of Moonstone in her attic room, in the Kohler's lush garden, and in the Sandhills with Ray Kennedy. The maturing Laura finds moments of childish freedom running across the prairie and envisioning "violets and fairy rings and moonlight over the wide, wide land" in Wilder's *By the Shores of Silver Lake* (270–71, 290). Judith slips into her retreat to hide from Caleb in Ostenso's *Wild Geese*.

For Claude Wheeler in Cather's *One of Ours*, the timber claim on his farm is a refuge from the perfect, cold house his wife Enid keeps for the newlyweds. The family of quail living in the deep grass, safe from hunters, make him feel equally safe from Enid's silent disapproval. "The timber claim was his refuge. In the open, grassy spots, shut in by the bushy walls of yellowing ash trees, he felt unmarried and free; free to smoke as much as he liked, and to read and dream . . . and let his imagination play with life – that was the best he could do" (183). The woods represent an unredeemable past for Claude: he knows his relief is only temporary.

Phyllis Young's "bower" shelters her from the family conflicts that arise when her husband Ralph and his two brothers and their families are forced back onto his parents' farm during the Depression in Dorothy Thomas's *The Home Place* (1934). The sullen anger of her sister-in-law especially irritates the pregnant Phyllis, and the drought has left them all depressed. Even nature reflects their desperate state:

Her bower hid her from the road and left the field and house in clear view. . . . Down near the dry creek-bed she saw something moving, and as they came nearer, she made out a pheasant cock and three hens going their slow rhythmic way. They were not shiny, superb, as pheasants ought to be. They were dull, bedraggled, and scrawny. The sight of them made her sadder than anything she had known during the winter. (118)

The sight of the pheasants releases emotions Phyllis has suppressed in the crowded household: "the ruined pheasants made her cry with sudden, hurting sobs" (118).

In his memoir, *Wolf Willow*, Stegner describes his boyhood refuge in the river bottom:

As the prairie taught me identity by exposing me, the river valley taught me about safety. In a jumpy and insecure childhood where all masculine elements are painful or dangerous, sanctuary matters. That sunken bottom sheltered from the total sky and the untrammeled wind was my hibernating ground, my place of snugness, and in a country often blistered and crisped, green became the color of safety. When I feel the need to return to the womb, this is still the place toward which my well-conditioned unconscious turns like an old horse heading for the barn. (22)

In Unger's *Leaving the Land*, Marge Hogan's small clearing where she hides from her brothers and her conflict with her father is a tangle of brambles in autumn, but in summer "the purple flowers of foxglove and thistles, the white trumpets of the creeping jenny tried to overrun the dark green grass" and "there was a tiny border of wild roses" (82–83). In her retreat Marge feels secure, but the tiny gray insects that climb into the center of the rosebuds and tumble "into the dark center of the rose's fruit" (83) signify what Marge knows subconsciously, namely, that even her retreat is not inviolable: there is no Eden in South Dakota.

Some characters create mental refuges. Amalia Stoltz is married to Herman Holmsdorfer in Aldrich's *Spring Came On Forever*. She silently acquiesces to his demands – she cooks, sews, tends his chickens, and helps him plant – but she lives in two worlds, "the practical one in which all others moved . . . and another world in which she existed apart from them, entirely aloof in her thoughts and with nothing in common in her emotions" (68). She imagines her escape as a room "from whose windows one looked into a dim cool clearing in the woods, and in whose shadowy confines there was love and understanding" (89). Amalia equates emotional comfort with trees and enclosures. On the open prairie she is exposed to a husband who intimidates her. She is freed when a blizzard kills her husband and her father (136), and her room becomes less important, for she can live as she pleases in her house and on her homestead.

In Sandoz's *Slogum House*, Ruedy's carefully tended garden is a symbol of renewal, fertility, and protection. Here Gulla's victims find a refuge. Ruedy's stream flows naturally, but his garden is not a gift. He has labored to create his home: "Where the bogs had been lay the gardens of vegetables for Slogum House and the market at Dumur, the rich earth soaked black by the spreading laterals that fed back into Spring Branch" (103).

Larry Woiwode unifies the land and refuge in the controlling image implicit in the title of his novel *Beyond the Bedroom Wall* (1975). Preparing for the burial of his father, the patriarch of the Neumiller family, Charles revisits the family's North Dakota homestead and remembers that as a child he would sit in the cedar-lined closet of his bedroom imagining a forest he had never seen: "[H]e visualized the walls of his bedroom around him, and around his bedroom the house, and around that the farmyard, the shape of the creek around the fields, the shape of the county around the creek, and around that the rectangle of North Dakota, at the center of North America, and felt enclosed in layers of protection, invulnerable" (44). Years later, when another Charles, the grandson now living far from the homestead, learns of the death of this Neumiller, he can draw on only vague memories of the closet in the parents' bedroom and his grandfather's reassuring presence (437–38). It is clear that the elder Charles's vision is possible because the house is solidly connected to the land and a part of his own experience.

In Martha Berglund's *A Farm under a Lake* (1989), Janet Hawn has an epiphany similar to Charles's on the Illinois prairie. The frontier void between settlement and the unknown becomes vertical, and connection to the past is once again rooted in the land. Berglund inverts the ubiquitous ocean metaphor: "I realized that we live between land and sky, on the frontier between two great countries. I had forgotten how sky is as much a country to live in as land. I had forgotten that we live in the sky and under it; we live on the land" (86–87). Both Woiwode and Berglund regard the individual's connection to the land as rooted in a vision that encompasses space and time.

The house as refuge can be a more problematic symbol. Margaret Laurence, for example, considers "the prairie as personal identification," as Thacker and other critics have pointed out (Thacker 219). The refuge symbolizes the private self, or the attempt to put the self in a specific, protected place. The girls who grow up in Manawaka, full of self-doubt and insecurity, may find stability or threatening reality in the houses they inhabit.

In Laurence's *The Stone Angel* (1964), Hagar Shipley, ninety years old and dying, refuses to leave the house she shares with her son and his wife. Her room, full of photos that link her to the past she wants to remember, is her reality, a solid point of reference in a world that is rapidly fading (16). Hagar dimly realizes that she has trapped her daughter-in-law Doris, who must care for her, in her own home, but her room is the only safe refuge she has known. Her storekeeper father's huge brick house, the rundown farm she endured when she was married to a common dirt farmer, Bram Shipley, the rooms she lived in when she kept house for Mr. Oatley after she fled Bram, the deserted cannery she shares with a drunk insurance agent in her last effort to assert her independence, and her bed in the hospital ward are all vulnerable, easily invaded.[4]

In *A Bird in the House*, the child Vanessa seeks hiding places in her grandfather's huge house. It is not a simple prairie home but elaborately overbuilt, full of doors, the living room alien territory (36). In it lurks her family's intimidating past and her grandmother's insistence on order (38). Vanessa's refuge is a wheat field, a place that follows the natural order of chance:

It was late summer, and the wheat had changed colour, but instead of being high and bronzed in the fields, it was stunted and desiccated, for there had been no rain again this year. . . . I put my head down very close to the earth and looked at what was going on there. Grasshoppers with enormous eyes ticked and twitched around me, as though the dry air were perfect for their purposes. A ladybird laboured mightily to climb a blade of grass, fell off, and started all over again, seeming to be unaware that she possessed wings and could have flown up. (49)

Like the ladybug, Vanessa does not know that she could enjoy limitless possibilities away from the house and Manawaka.

In *The Diviners* (1974) Laurence creates a refuge for Morag Gunn. Her farm at McConnell's landing, even though it is in Ontario, is a point from which Morag can review her uncertain present, her past in Manawaka, and the deeper pioneer past. In Manawaka the child Morag never feels secure – not at home with her foster parents, who love her and shame her, not at church or at school or at work in the store selling clothes she cannot afford. She tries every means to escape: she excels at school so that she can go away to college. She escapes middle-class mores in a brief encounter with Jules Tonnere, whose physical strength makes her feel momentary security (138–39). She flees into marriage with Brooke Skelton, who gives her a home in a city apartment and an upper-middle-class social circle and treats her as a child, condescendingly criticizing her first efforts as a writer. Her Toronto apartment becomes "a desert island, . . . a cave, a well-lighted and beautifully appointed cave, but a cave just the same" (254). Her flight from Brooke to Vancouver is not successful either, and her search for ancestral roots in Britain leads her back to Manawaka.

McConnell's landing is an island that Morag realizes may be as tenuous as all her other refuges, and no protection for her daughter, Pique:

Maybe I should've brought Pique up entirely in cities, where she'd have known how bad things are all over, where she'd have learned young about survival, about the survival tactics in a world now largely dedicated to Death, Slavery and the Pursuit of Unhappiness. Instead, I've made an island. Are islands real? . . . Islands are unreal. No place is far enough away. Islands exist only in the head. And yet I stay. . . . I can bear to live here until I die, and I couldn't else-where. (356–57)

Morag's link to the past is the house itself, a one-hundred-year-old log structure. Here she confronts her spiritual foremother, Catharine Parr Traill, a pioneer woman who intimidates and inspires the modern-day Morag. The house is a halfway point between past and present, wilderness and civilization. It is made of logs, and the door frames and window sills are of hand-hewn timber, but the floorboards and doors are from a saw-mill. Morag's secondhand furniture reflects her own ambivalent present (93).

For the pioneers, survival was a question of physical possibility, "the sheer unthinkable heart-breaking slog" (94). Morag feels sorry for the women, for the loneliness, isolation, strain, despair, overwork, and fear that drove them mad, but she feels impelled to challenge the evidently boundless energy of Catharine, "drawing and naming wildflowers, writing a guide for settlers with one hand whilst rearing a brace of young and working like a galley slave with the other" (95), while she, Morag, runs that same house with "a little help from the electric fridge, kettle, toaster, stove, iron, baseboard heaters, furnace, lights, not to mention the local supermarket" (96). Morag feels caught between "Catharine P. T.'s" past, full of the physical challenges of homesteading, and her own psychologically complex present. In her attempt to rid herself of her own confusion Morag must bury the pioneer woman in the past; her refuge must be free of memories that would overwhelm progress toward the future:

I'm not built like you, Saint C., or these kids, either. I stand somewhere in between. And yet, in my way I've worked damn hard, and I haven't done all I would've liked to do, but I haven't folded up like a paper fan, either. I'll never till those blasted fields, but this place is some kind of a garden, nonetheless, even though it may be only a wildflower garden. It's needed, and not only by me. I'm about to quit worrying about not being either an old or a new pioneer. So farewell, sweet saint – henceforth, I summon you not. (406)

In *The Fire-Dwellers* (1969), Manawaka refugee Stacey Cameron MacAindra expresses almost the same sentiments. Isolated in Vancouver, she is trapped between her fierce loyalty to her husband and four children and her intense guilt over her desire to escape the oppressive sense of responsibility. Her cluttered home is her refuge, but it is also a trap. She refuses to leave when her husband's job gives them financial security. She does not enjoy Morag's isolation or her links to the past. Ultimately, Stacey draws on her own inner resources to regain her equilibrium. In Laurence's works, then, the house can be an enclosure, a trap, a refuge, or a link to another time and place.

The house as refuge is a familiar motif in other Great Plains works. In

Wilder's Little House books, Ma carries her shepherdess, her symbol of home, from log cabin to dugout to surveyor's shack. The dugout on Plum Creek in Minnesota is perhaps their most secure refuge. The home is a veritable fortress, the wall so thick the sun "stayed near the window." But the entry is covered with morning glories, and the interior is clean and whitewashed (9–11). It is not a cave but a snug retreat. In *The Long Winter*, the weather forces the family to move to ever more constricted spaces. First they move from their Dakota homestead into the store in town. When the blizzards continue and the cold hangs on, they are reduced to the area around the stove. When they run out of wheat, Pa goes to Almanzo and untaps the seed wheat the young farmer has hidden in his false wall. Almanzo's house literally saves the Ingalls family from starvation (chap. 23).

For Elof Lofblum in Manfred's *The Chokecherry Tree*, his father's house at Chokecherry Corner is a refuge from his failure at school and as a salesman. The town is so unimportant that on his return he must jump off a truck because the driver refuses to slow down. The small, misshapen chokecherry tree, surrounded by towering cottonwoods, represents Elof, an insignificant resident. His mother has died, and the combination grocery store and home is rundown and lonely, inhabited only by his demanding and unaffectionate father. Nevertheless, Chokecherry Corner is full of smells that call up memories of family rituals (12). When Elof contemplates himself and his place in this small world, he decides that "hate with room and board was better than hate with no board and room at all" (21). Ironically, in this refuge Elof undergoes his ritual initiation into the worlds of work and love. He endures the ignominy of wearing shoes several sizes too large and the pain of blood poisoning in his foot, gradually adjusting his limits and expectations. He learns to tolerate his father and to find a place in the community. And after one more foray into the outside world as a salesman, he marries the farmer's daughter, Gert, and takes over his father-in-law's gas station across the road from his father's store.

Often, the home is not a given but must be found. Ma's quest is implicit as the Ingalls family moves from Wisconsin to Minnesota to Dakota Territory. The search is explicit in Wright Morris's *The Home Place* and *The World in the Attic* (1949). In the first novel, Clyde Muncy arrives from New York at the farm of his Aunt Clara and Uncle Harry. He waits for his Uncle Ed to die, his eye on the old man's place across the road as a home for his family, refugees from their uncertain life in the city. But when Ed dies and the house can be his, Clyde realizes that he cannot assume someone else's house any more than he can graft his own childhood onto his city-bred children: "But with the people gone, you know the place is inhabited. . . . There's a path worn into the carpet, between the bed and the door. . . . The pattern doesn't come with the house, nor the blueprints with the rug. The figure in the carpet is what you have when the people have lived there, died there, and when evicted, refused to leave the house" (*The Home Place* 132). Clyde feels "like some sly peeping Tom" (138). When he and his wife decline the house, Clyde feels a sense of satisfaction that living in the house would never bring. "I felt like a man whose job it was to close up a church" (145).

In *The World in the Attic*, Clyde and his family, moving on, stop to visit Bud Hibbard, Clyde's boyhood friend, who is also waiting for his house. The Hibbard house was built by Bud's uncle, Clinton Hibbard, for Caddy, his imported "city, Southern" wife (from Indiana) (84, 105). Caddy, a "Hibbard by law but not by anything else" (81), lives a petrified existence shut in the front of the house, while Bud's grandparents, Aunt Angie and Uncle Bill, like caretakers, live in the back room (83). Bud's own house is a square box, a house that has failed (60–61), but he waits patiently.

Caddie Hibbard's house is out of place, "a wooden house, with windows that rose from the floor to nearly the ceiling, the shutters were all on the inside, rather than out. . . . the house, like Caddy, had been imported – it was not grown here" (90). It reflects a dream of gracious living, a refuge from the dust and space of the plains. Like Laurence, Morris regards the house as a link to the human past. It is a man-made symbol, a place created from the empty space of the sea of grass. It contains the inhabitant's personality, an indelible print that cannot be erased or replicated. Clyde

Muncy, who tries to return with his non-native family, finds that the home place cannot be his home, but Bud, a part of the Hibbard clan, moves into Caddy Hibbard's house: her attic is a part of his past too.

Many Great Plains writers depict the house not as a refuge but as a trap or even a tomb. In Haruf's *The Tie That Binds*, first Ada and then her daughter Edith is trapped on the open plains. Ada, caught in a loveless marriage in an indifferent country, regards the threat as personal:

It was a hell of a big piece of sandy country, with a horizon that in every direction must have seemed then . . . to reach forever away under a sky in summer that didn't give much of a good goddamn whether or not the bags of corn seed Roy was going to plant in some of that sand ever amounted to a piddling thing, and a sky in winter that, even if it was as blue as picture books said it should be and as high and bright as anybody could hope for, still didn't care whether or not the frame house Roy was going to build ever managed to keep the snow from blowing in on Ada's sewing machine. . . .

No, Ada never got over the shock of this country. There was too much of it, and none of it looked like Iowa.(18)

As her children grow, Ada shrinks. She dies at the age of forty-two of more than a virus. It was "all those years of looking east; it was two decades of being married to Roy" (28). Her husband ignores her dying wish to return to Iowa and buries her on the plains (32).

Edith is entrapped first by her father's impotent rage and then by her brother Lyman's insanity. Lyman travels all over the United States for twenty years, but after a car wreck, he retraces his travels within the house that becomes his safe haven from a world he can no longer cope with. As he becomes more violent and unmanageable, his refuge becomes Edith's prison. To her, the house symbolizes psychological suppression, "a lifetime of staying home" (111). As they confine themselves more and more to the house, and then to only the first floor, the relationship between brother and sister becomes incestuous. Their lives are so constricted that they are literally inseparable. The house is like a mental box. Edith's only escape is to set fire to the house and destroy them both in their home, their prison (239).

These places of refuge and confinement reflect a central theme that runs through Great Plains fiction. On the plains the sky is the limit, but for some the open space threatens erasure: they need the close reference points of ground or trees or walls to reassure them of their existence. Others find the walls themselves threatening or confining. The attention to enclosed space reflects the ambivalence that Great Plains writers feel about the ultimate enclosure, the end of the frontier.

One of the most devastating portraits of the closed frontier is Rølvaag's study of Beret Holm in *Peder Victorious*, the second volume of his trilogy.[5] Beret is closed in as almost no other Great Plains character is.[6] Her children are drawn into American culture, speaking English with more ease than Beret's beloved Norwegian and finding friends outside the close community of Norwegian pioneers. At first Beret feels trapped and physically isolated on the great barren plain. In the weeks following Per Hansa's burial Beret dreams of returning to Norway, but that path is blocked. Her husband lies in the nearby churchyard: "[O]ught she to leave him to lie here alone in an alien land?" (17). Her children, her friend Sorine points out, would be strangers in Norway. The present tasks push her homeland further and further away (171). With effort, she assumes the role as head of the household, doing chores and making the decisions that bring her remaining family through many difficulties. Ironically, Beret's instinctive feel for the animals and the farm results in prosperity, but even as she sets an example for the community in her farming practices, her reluctance to embrace American culture isolates her. Beret's refusal to speak English is a deeply personal matter. To acquiesce to the English around her is to surrender her soul. When the Reverend Gabrielsen, the well-meaning but meddling pastor of her Norwegian church, points out that a new language does not change one's human status, Beret expresses her belief that it is a sin for the Norwegian pastor to preach in English (206).[7] Neither the minister nor her own children can understand Beret's fear. Peder sides with Gabrielsen and embraces English at school and at church.

To the puzzlement of her children, Beret's solace is only in animals and things that cannot change: Rosie, the cow that came west behind their wagon; the table Per Hansa made out of their homemade wagon; the immigrant chest and the old box given to her by her father on her confirmation, which she uses as a money box (196). As her children become more comfortable with English and with Americans, Beret is cut off from their society, feeling uncomfortable in her children's school and even at Norwegian social gatherings in her own church.

The most tragic consequence of Beret's isolation is the growing distance between her and her youngest son, Peder Victorious, the baby born in the first terrifying years on the prairie. When Beret accompanies Peder to a school meeting where he is to recite the Gettysburg Address, Peder senses the incongruity. "Mother in this place! The incredible had actually happened – she had stepped out of her own world and had accompanied him into his. There she was sitting beside Pat Murphy, just as though she, too, belonged here" (110). Beret's isolation threatens to cut Peder off from both the Norwegian and English-speaking communities. She removes Peder from the country schoolhouse because she does not like Irish and Norwegian children attending the same school. "The authorities made a terrible mistake when they threw us in with those people. And it is no better for them than it is for us. We should never have had the school together – you can't mix wheat and potatoes in the same bin" (104). Ironically, in the all-Norwegian school, Norway is depicted in the textbook only by a picture of "a combat between a man and an infuriated bear" and a paragraph entitled "Norway" (142). Peder finds no close alliance with his mother's homeland here. Unless he makes a choice, Peder will be shut off as she is from both Norway and America. He chooses America, and within a few weeks Peder speaks only English, even at home.

Peder's friendship with his Irish neighbor Charlie Doheny and his growing love for Charlie's sister Susie results in Beret's further alienation. On the eve of Peder's confirmation, Beret and her son walk across their farm to the sacred Indian mound. Beret confronts Peder with her knowledge of their liaison. Confused by her threats and unvoiced fears and the minister's insistent praise, Peder cannot voice his vows of confirmation. In the following months he seldom talks to his mother. He dreams not of farming or the ministry but of America and politics. Simonson sees in Beret's resistance to things American Rølvaag's own disenchantment with the American dream (*Prairies Within* 55). Seen in this light, Beret's conflict represents not only the immigrant's inability to adapt but also the cultural and psychological wasteland of American values. Peder, in embracing this America, becomes a symbol of the immigrants' capitulation to a corrupt America (see also Blegen 103–4).

Finally, Beret reverts to the depression that plagued her in her early days on the open prairie. While Peder, Susie, and the other young people are rehearsing a school play, she hears a voice telling her, "Now goe, and smite Amalek, and utterly destroy all that they have, and spare them not" (309).[8] She tries to ignite the schoolhouse, but a downpour douses her effort. Beret is confused. "The Lord Himself had commanded her to destroy this place of wickedness – it must burn!" (310). Beret's act is a final, futile gesture, but it is also a form of release. When she is safely back home, the baptismal effect of this experience becomes apparent. She tears the crepe of mourning from Per Hansa's portrait, throws off her water-soaked clothes, and builds a fire. In a benevolent trance that is a sharp contrast to her earlier confusion, she hears the voice of Per Hansa tell her to let Peder have his way.

Beret's acquiescence is an affirmation of Peder's place in the new world and her own surrender: Peder's marriage leaves her entirely alone. All of Beret's frontiers are closed. Psychologically, she is cut off from her church and therefore from her Christian mind and conscience. Socially, her language isolates her from her children, their families, and the increasingly Americanized Norwegian community. Nevertheless, she has an inner strength: her faith, her Old World things, her animals, and her land are connections between past and present. She possesses just what Per Hansa dreamed of; however, it has brought physical and psychological isolation, not freedom and happiness.

The psychological entrapment that Rølvaag depicts is evident in other Great Plains works. Alpha Neumiller in Woiwode's *Beyond the Bedroom Wall* actively seeks relief within her husband Martin's Catholic faith because it ties her to an ordered past (256). Alpha weakens as the family moves from the Dakota homestead to Illinois, "the turning point in their closed world" (538), and she dies in childbirth at thirty-four. Others share this suffocating isolation: Mrs. Bentley, trapped in a dusty town and a dry marriage in Ross's *As for Me and My House* (1941); Laurence's Morag, Vanessa, and Hagar; Harauf's Ada and Edith; Erdrich's Mary Adare and Sita Koza in *The Beet Queen*, Marie Lazarre Kashpaw in *Love Medicine*, and Fleur Pillager in *Tracks* (1988). In these stories, loneliness arises not only from physical isolation and the enervating effects of work but also from sexual alienation and an acute sense of displacement. The culture around these women is unfamiliar because of marriage, a different language, a new religion, or a white instead of an Indian community. For some, the open landscape exacerbates the psychic isolation that they experience. They become passive, withdrawing from normal human intercourse. They are enclosed not in a place but within themselves.

Some try to find the means to escape the enclosed garden. Garland often introduces a savior in his stories, but when he is being realistic rather than romantic the generous intentions of the rescuer fall far short. In "Under the Lion's Paw," Council's well-meaning help ironically restricts Haskins even more. Butler appears at first to be a benevolent redeemer, but in reality he is a parasite who profits from the desperation and hard work of others. In "Up the Coolly," the letter that would have alerted Howard to his family's distress is lost, and Howard loses his opportunity to help. In Garland's more romantic stories the savior sometimes succeeds in his rescue. In "A Branch Road," Agnes escapes the drudgery of the farm and the cruel indifference of her husband, Ed Kinney, with Will Hannan. Garland repeats this escape motif in two prairie novels, *Jason Edwards* and *The Moccasin*

The Enclosed Garden 115

Ranch. In both novels the savior functions similarly as a deus ex machina. Jason Edwards, like Haskins, is a man defeated by economic and natural disasters, first in Boston and then in Boomtown. He is rescued and returned to the East when his daughter consents to marry an Easterner she earlier refused. *The Moccasin Ranch* focuses on the defeated wife who, like Agnes, flees from the isolation of her husband's prairie claim with another man.

For some, religion or art or physical escape results in release. Beret Holm, Alpha Neumiller, and Marie Lazarre Kashpaw turn to religion with varying degrees of success. Morris's Sharon Rose and Cather's Thea Kronborg find an outlet for their submerged emotions in music. Claude Wheeler flees the burden of his father's farm and his empty marriage by going off to World War I. But these are exceptions: most characters in Great Plains fiction must come to terms with the place where they are.

In the final volume of his trilogy, *Their Fathers' God*, Rølvaag traces the efforts of Peder Holm to create a place for himself in the new world that destroyed his father and isolated his mother. His search reflects the struggle of the first and second generations to define their own vision of the democratic utopia, to melt into American society. Peder has cut himself off from the Norwegian community, his family, and the land. His most isolating act is his rejection of his son's baptism. Both Beret and Susie secretly baptize "Petie" in their respective religions because Peder makes it clear that he regards such acts as foolish superstition. When Susie's priest cautions Peder to be considerate of Susie and "give her the same freedom that you reserve for yourself" in matters of religion, Peder dismisses his admonition as "Poppycock!"

Peder's reliance on his own intelligence and common sense is as dangerous as Beret's isolation: "[T]here were times when he built and built until the whole structure toppled over in a hopeless ruin, and existence lost all meaning. [. . .] At such times the despair over his own impotence might grow so heavy that it threatened to strangle him" (96). Systematically, Peder rejects every aspect of his past, even his obligation to the land itself.

He relegates his mother to the roles of housekeeper and nursemaid, roles that she values but Peder regards with indifference. Unlike his father, Peder does not regard work as a reward. He abandons growing crops on the land to raise cattle because "the joy he used to get from his work was gone" (148). Unlike Beret, he regards cattle as profit, not as objects of affection. He takes the advice of experts rather than from following his own instinctive feel for the land that as Per Hansa and Beret did.

Peder is even tempted to abandon his wife. In the section ironically entitled "And They Shall Be One Flesh," Peder is drawn to Nikoline Johansen, an intelligent, socially aware Norwegian who is the antithesis of the simple, naive Susie. Unlike Peder, Nikoline is anchored in her awareness of Norwegian heritage. In one of their discussions Peder asks her about *hilder*, the Norwegian word inadequately translated as "mirage." Nikoline's explanation reflects her awareness of the physical and psychological implications of illusion: "[A]ll the islands stand on their heads in the air – they just float there. The ships sail with their masts pointing down; up in the sky, you understand. [. . .] All space is a magic mirror . . . you see only phantasms floating in a great stillness . . . you don't dare breathe for fear they'll pass away" (234). It is clear that *hilder* is the Norwegian answer to Peder's fruitless search for answers inside his own mind. The magic mirror reflects the inner life, the truths that can be revealed to one who can see. But Nikoline tells him that because he is an American he cannot attain it: "[Norwegians] know when we see hilder; we can tell it and make allowance. You Americans believe all you see until you run your heads against a stone wall; then you don't believe anything anymore" (235). Simonson points out that Nikoline's judgment is not on Peder alone but on the "American mandate to turn one's back on the country of family origins" (*Prairies Within* 79). In this she echoes the warning of Reverend Kaldahl, who speaks for Rølvaag, that immigrants must preserve their traditions or America will be a "perfect democracy of barrenness" (*Their Fathers' God* 210).

When Nikoline decides to return to Norway, their leave-taking occurs in her Aunt Sorine's orchard, clearly a symbol of many things. It was planted by the pioneers. The fruit has been picked, but there are overripe plums still to be gathered. In this fecund setting, Nikoline tells Peder that she is returning to Norway because she has taken the wrong road. "I've tried [America] and know. I'm not so stupid as I look" (312). Involved in the political battle for county commissioner, Peder is feeling confident of his success, but Nikoline cautions him, "You should know by this time that Success and Happiness don't live on the same road! [. . .] If you want one, give up seeking the other" (313). Rølvaag drew this concept, that satisfaction is *either* success *or* happiness, from Ibsen's *Brand*. The attempt to achieve both, Rølvaag clearly implies, is an American aberration from Ibsen's concept of the ideal.[9] Nikoline tells Peder, "It's queer with the Americans, you want heaven, and aren't willing to pay the price." Peder declares that it can be done. Nikoline counters, "Yes, in the fairy tales. There the hero slays the monster and gets the princess. The only trouble is that just at that point the tale ends" (314). This is precisely Rølvaag's point: his fairy tale about the dragon-slayer, *Giants in the Earth*, ended with the founding of the kingdom at a great price: the death of the hero, Per Hansa. But this is not a fairy tale. Nikoline warns Peder that Paradise is "Beautiful . . . and terrible, too" (315). Peder, who believes he is safely inside the enclosed garden, does not understand her warning. "I too have stood at the gate and looked into Paradise. What I saw was not hilder. The flaming sword does not frighten me. What I've been hunting for all my life I've seen with my own eyes, I know it exists. And now I think that I can make the journey alone" (317–18).

Peder's confidence in himself is, of course, misplaced. He will not be the one to fulfill the promise of the West. For Rølvaag, Peder clearly is the American Adam, cast out of Paradise. The garden is denied to those who have chosen to ignore their past and the community's allegiance to the collective present. Peder's isolation is brought home to him in a scathing personal attack by a political opponent who recounts all the community knows of Peder: his mother's apparent insanity, his hasty marriage, his freethinking, and, finally, the baptism Susie has hidden from him but not from the community (331–32). After the speech, Peder returns home and smashes Susie's religious objects; he awakens the next morning to find his wife and baby gone from his home (336–38). At the close of the novel, Peder, like Beret, is wholly alone.

In her novel of withdrawal, *The Professor's House* (1925), Cather explores the interrelations of past and present. Surrounded by family obligations, his great scholarly work completed, the aging Professor Godfrey St. Peter feels trapped. He must come to terms with the myths of the past as they relate to his own history. St. Peter has confined himself to his empty house in a small town on the shores of Lake Michigan, the eastern rim of the plains and prairies. The walled garden of the old, cramped house is as unlike a Midwestern garden as it could be. "The professor had succeeded in making a French garden in Hamilton. . . . In the spring, when home-sickness for other lands and the fret of things unaccomplished awoke, he worked off his discontent there" (14–15). Cut off from the mundane town, St. Peter creates his own physical and intellectual world. What the garden walls in or walls out is debatable (see Maxfield; Rosowski, *The Voyage Perilous* and "The Pattern of Willa Cather's Novels"; and Yongue).

Even more isolated than the garden is St. Peter's study, an attic retreat that he shares only with the family's seamstress, Augusta, and with the empty female forms she uses in her craft. When St. Peter asks to continue to rent the old house from her uncle, Augusta is puzzled, and she is even more bemused when St. Peter refuses to let her take away her forms. "I can't have this room changed if I'm going to work here," he declares (21). For St. Peter, houses and things are anchors in a changing world.[10]

St. Peter seems powerless to break free and move into the present. He is attempting to sort out the significance of the past so that he can face the end of his own life. In this sense, St. Peter represents the fading pioneer spirit. Reluctantly brought west by his pioneering parents, he has not participated in the mythic visions that lured his father onto the open frontier. He looks back to the memory of blue water, to the Indian past, and to the Old World myths of El Dorado and exploration rather than to the New World democratic myths of Manifest Destiny and the yeoman farmer in the garden.

St. Peter's vision of the past is personified in Tom Outland, a young man who breaks in upon the professor's present when he appears at the professor's door bearing gifts of ancient Indian pottery. He settles in Hamilton, courts the professor's daughter, Rosamond, proves to be a brilliant student of physics, and leaves to fight and die in World War I. The patents for his inventions he wills to Rosamond, whose husband, Louie Marsellus, creates a fortune from Tom's legacy. To the professor, this crass materialistic treatment of a past reality signifies all that is wrong with the present.

St. Peter does not want to preserve this Tom Outland. Rather, Outland is the professor's link with the heroic past of the Southwest and the romance of prehistoric Indians. St. Peter wants to bring that past into the present. To this end, the professor is transcribing his friend's diary. Tom's story of his Indian discoveries is the middle third of the novel. In a sense, the ruins Tom discovers are the ultimate walled-in garden. Protected for centuries in the narrow canyons of the mesa, they, like the professor's garden and attic, are isolated by time and space. Tom comes to realize not only that the ruins are physically inaccessible but that "as a culture, these people were isolated, cut off from other tribes working out their destinies" (220). The parallels between Tom's own studies of theoretical physics and St. Peter's dedication to historical scholarship, both isolating activities, are clear.

Left alone when his family takes a European vacation, St. Peter attempts to establish his own link to the past through Tom's diaries. He envies the escape into death that enabled Tom to avoid the jealousies, envy, and bitterness that have spread among the St. Peter family and his colleagues at Hamilton as a result of the wealth Tom's patents nourished. He remains suspended between his memory of Tom's past and his own family's move into a new home. In this state, the professor discovers another boy: the original, unmodified Godfrey St. Peter, left behind in Kansas (265). He feels himself that boy again, his original self: "He did not regret his life, but he was indifferent to it" (261). St. Peter begins to long for death, "eternal solitude . . . a release from every obligation, from every form of effort" (272). When his family sends word that they will soon be home, St. Peter tries desperately to think of a way to avoid meeting them (275). When the window of his study blows shut and the gas from the stove threatens to overwhelm him, St. Peter suddenly faces his own passivity: "[S]uppose he did not get up – ? How far was a man required to exert himself against accident?" (276). The faithful Augusta hears him fall and opens the window to revive him.

His brush with death reduces the professor's expectations and, sadly perhaps, releases him from his familiar, private past (282). "Theoretically he knew that life is possible, may be even pleasant, without joy, without passionate griefs. But it had never occurred to him that he might have to live like that" (282). St. Peter can face the future with a modicum of confidence, if not with enthusiasm. "At least, he felt the ground under his feet. He thought he knew where he was" (283). He is not entirely walled in.

In his novel *The Big Rock Candy Mountain* (1943) and in *Wolf Willow*, a blend of memory, history, and fiction, Wallace Stegner explores other aspects of enclosure that explain the sense of alienation pervading so many Great Plains works. Stegner's Whitemud stories are an attempt to set the points on the compass, to come to terms with a time and place that, as Wright Morris points out, Stegner could point to as home even if the world or his own poles shifted: Whitemud is East End, Saskatchewan, Stegner's boyhood home.

It is not place but time that encloses the Mason family in *The Big Rock Candy Mountain*. As Stegner commented, "I obviously had Turner in my mind . . . and the ending of the frontier and what it does psychologically to whole bodies of people" (Stegner and Etulain 61).[11] The father, Bo Mason, is a frontiersman, as uncomfortable with society's laws as Ishmael Bush, looking for the romantic West of perfect freedom and instant riches: "[H]e would never quite grant that all the good places were filled up. There was somewhere, . . . some Big Rock Candy Mountain where life was effortless and rich and unrestricted and full of adventure and action, where something could be had for nothing" (92). Bo imagines himself a dragon-slayer, a man who takes risks and expects unlimited opportunity and rewards in return. But he is not a worker like Per Hansa or Alexandra Bergson: he is a dreamer, drawn to the West's promise: "Here in Dakota there was something else. Here everybody was his own boss, here was a wide open and unskimmed country where a man could hew his own line and not suffer for his independence" (47). But it is 1905. The frontier is closed. In his quest Bo finds, not riches, but the "lost and derelict." His wife Elsa wonders, "Were they all over, . . . or was it just that Bo took them always to the fringes of civilization where the misfits and the drifters all congregated?" (268). When he fails at legitimate occupations, Bo turns to the underworld – illegal bars, whiskey-running, and gambling – the only place where frontier values are still useful. Ultimately, all of his dreams fade to nothing. A son dies, then his wife dies, and his other son leaves for school. Bo's world constricts until he ends it in murder and suicide.

It is not only the disappearing historical past that limits Bo. Elsa and his younger son, Bruce, pull him away from the fringes of society into the respectable present, but at the same time he pulls Elsa into the underworld, into "psyche-isolation." The restless Bo keeps his family on the move, so that his wife has no time and no legitimate avenues into society (397). Elsa is isolated in an increasingly restricted world by moves, illness, and finally death. "All you could do was shut your mouth and make the best of it," she thinks (399). In Whitemud, Bo attempts to conform to this new order, but years of drought and the failure of his wheat crops trap him into pursuing profits from illegal whiskey runs across the border.

To point up the hopelessly limited lives of Bo and Elsa, Stegner relates the summer idyll on the homestead (an important part of *Wolf Willow* as well) from Bruce's point of view. The boy is too young to fully understand his father's entrapment. The town and the farm that represent stifling responsibilities and failure to Bo mean home to Bruce. On the farm in the summers, the boy attains the kind of freedom his father can only dream about: "[I]t was that summer that he somehow lost his identity as a name. There was no other boy to confuse him with; he wasn't Bruce, but 'the boy,' and because he was the only thing of his kind in all that summer world he needed no name, but only his own sense of triumphant identity" (180). As critics have pointed out, Bo is a tragic anachronism, the waste of human and natural resources that hollow myths and unchecked individualism have meant to the West (Robinson and Robinson 114–15). Like Natty Bumppo, Bo straddles the time line between the primitive past and the technological present. As Stegner explains:

It's perfectly clear that [Bo] doesn't have the qualities for the changed world. He's made for a world that's just passed, just barely passed, and so he goes looking for a place where that world is still possible. . . . One of the nicest things about American independence, which was born of free land, as far as I can determine . . . is that you can tell the world to kiss your behind and go off. That is freedom; it is also irresponsibility, social irresponsibility. When the world tightens in around you, you can't do that anymore, and it probably means a lot more unhappiness for people of that stamp. (Stegner and Etulain 49)

The home that entraps and limits Bo, Elsa and Bruce long for as security. Ironically, at the novel's close Bruce heads for Salt Lake City, where his parents and his brother are buried. The family plot, provided with "perpetual care" by the restless Bo, is the only "home" the family ever has.

In *Wolf Willow*, Stegner focuses on the land itself. In this work, speaking in his own voice and invoking once again his own boyhood, Stegner examines his tenuous link to a historical past in a place that proves as elusive as the myths Bo pursues. Here the family's homestead represents the psychological separation between frontier and community, between farmland and cattle ranches, between a child's sense of adventure and, in retrospect, an adult's sense of tragic loss. To Stegner, it is "the place where the Plains, as an ecology, as a native Indian culture, and as a process of white settlement came to their climax and their end" (4). As a child, Stegner felt no connection to the past in Whitemud; instead he adopted his Norwegian grandfather as his "past" (112). Right before him was the Indian past – Cree, Assinboine, Blackfoot, and the interloping Sioux, Nez Pierce and Gros Ventre (112–15). "All of this was legitimately mine, I walked that earth, but none of it was known to me" (112). With a child's innocence, he entered a world that "had neither location nor time, geography nor history. But it had a wild freedom, . . . I was blessedly free of most conventional restrictions, and its very liberation from the perspectives of time and place released our minds for imaginative flights into wonder" (29). Here there were no monuments, museums, attics, old trunks, no books, no ghosts to acknowledge and locate the past (29). The town dump, "our poetry and history," hinted at the past (34); "it is all *we* had for the civilization we grew up in" (36).

In *Wolf Willow*, Stegner searches for the deep past of continuous history: one cannot anchor in a land with no past and no physical landmarks. As Stegner points out, the past that is forcefully grafted onto the child by "five thousand years of Mediterranean culture and two thousand years of Europe" seems ludicrously out of phase with the reality of the prairie town (24).[12]

Place is hard to preserve on the Great Plains. In Whitemud the farms returned to rangeland. In Morris's novels this tenuous past is embodied in places – the worn-out farmhouse that Clyde Muncy covets, the boarded-up rooms where Miss Caddy Hibbard wastes away. These are visual, memory-laden anchors. For other Great Plains writers, the graveyard, the ordered fields, the timber claim, the title deed, the family's beet fields, the hidden patch of cool grass, even the dried-up fields can be the points on the compass, the connection with the past and with the land.

Beret, Bo Mason, Godfrey St. Peter, and other isolated characters in Great Plains fiction come to realize that the mythic West is in the past, a romantic memory sold off and turned into profit by those insensitive to the holy reality of lives and civilizations that stretch back before time. We cannot preserve the past or prevent the incursions of the present into our lives. Finally, we must give up the past, abandon isolation, and embrace society, however diminished it may be. In the enclosed garden the myth of endless opportunity, of a past stretching unbroken behind, creating a path for the future, is an idea conserved in a Norwegian Bible, a meticulous diary, objects that mean little to the uninitiated.

CHAPTER SIX

Afloat on the Sea of Grass:
Transforming the Myths

In the twentieth century we persist in dragging our notions of the mythic past into the present, re-forming them in advertising slogans, films, televisions shows, museums, and theme parks. As David Lowenthal points out, we never have gotten it quite right: the traits we idealize "only partly conform with the goals of the pioneers themselves" (14), and they are far removed from historical fact. The expectant myths have been transformed into unheroic, ironic, sometimes antipastoral, sometimes comic motifs. With almost predictable regularity, twentieth-century scholars have reexamined the transformation of the earlier myths, explaining the recurring patterns in a variety of ways. Lucy Lockwood Hazard, writing in 1927, attempted to do for literature what Turner had done for history: to explain the significance of the concept of the frontier in both the conscious and the unconscious development of American literature.[1]

Vernon Louis Parrington was the first critic to trace the region's cultural and intellectual history (Etulain 418). The unfinished third volume of Parrington's study, *Main Currents in American Thought: The Beginnings of Critical Realism in America, 1860–1920* (1930), deals with Middle Border literature as part of a much broader conflict between a fading agrarian economy and a rising industrial complex. Parrington's study reflects the political and literary biases of the 1920s; nevertheless, it traces developments in the myth that are familiar and predictable. As settlers learned what sort of living the prairies might provide, the myth of Manifest Destiny was replaced by the myth of the garden (259). By the 1880s, Parrington points out, the conflict was not one of man against nature but an economic conflict. The myth of the democratic utopia faded not only because of the closed frontier but also because production for consumption had been superseded by production for profit (277).[2] The failure of Populism was the culmination in reality of the failure of the myths of the garden and the democratic utopia.

In his analysis of the profit motive of the settlers on the Great Plains, Parrington attempts to refute the myth of work and its attending reward. The forces that drove men and women westward seem to have been less an extension of the visions of early explorers than a greedy, self-seeking kind of opportunism. If Parrington's assessment is accurate, then it is not hard to understand the disillusion that deepened into gloom as falling prices and market values, mounting debt, and increasing economic centralization encroached on the farmers' narrow margin of credit (Parrington 260). Clearly, the promise of "preemption, exploitation and progress" was as much a chimera as the myth of endless open frontier had been.

Writing three decades after Parrington, Leo Marx analyzes the relationship between technology and the older pastoral vision in *The Machine in the Garden* (1964). Marx sees the conflict not as an economic struggle between agrarians and industrialists but as a philosophical contrast between the pastoral and the technological. The conflict arises not from a division of the populace into one camp or the other but from their necessary coexistence. "It is difficult to think of a major American writer upon whom the image of the machine's sudden appearance in the landscape has not exercised fascination" (16). Marx's complex pastoralism, the tension between the wild landscape and the transformation symbolized by the encroaching machine that sometimes runs amuck, permeates Great Plains fiction. As we have seen, the refusal to relinquish the vision of the pastoral world leads to the closed garden, to defeat or isolation, and abandonment of the land can as easily lead to destruction. The balance is difficult to achieve.

Transforming the westering myths into a usable past is a formidable task. As Wright Morris explains in *The Territory Ahead* (1957), "With the passing of the last natural frontier – the series of horizons dissolving westward – the raw-material myth, based, as it is, on the myth of inexhaustible resources, no longer supplies the artisan with lumps of raw life" (9). Of course, we constantly redefine the prairies and plains: unending space has become a network of identifiable places; the "northwest passage" led to Oregon and California, not to China; the formidable desert is now a cultivated field susceptible to crop failure; the democratic utopia, a typical pastiche of American communities; the safety valve, an economic trap; the melting pot, indistinguishable American culture.

The transformation Morris has in mind is not merely a change in attitude but a transformation of the material of the myth itself.[3] The raw material that is experienced by the senses is transformed by the imagination into more raw material. The frontier becomes not a place but an idea. As Morris demonstrates in his own fiction, the combinations are infinite. The task is not easy, but it is necessary. Only by rearranging the puzzle pieces (an image Morris uses), reevaluating and transforming the past, can we render it useful in the territory ahead. Otherwise we merely report on the nostalgic and useless past.

On the Great Plains the past would seem to be a simple matter of a century or so of history, but as we have seen, surfaces – the empty land, the stolid inhabitants, the myths of promise – are deceptive. Some Great Plains writers find their raw material in the deep past, which can symbolize the psychological aversion to the isolating open spaces. In *The Bones of Plenty*,

Lois Philips Hudson combines images of prehistoric dust, ice, and wind as symbols of insecure lives. The child Lucy Custer imagines that the snow is a glacier, miles deep, "that once surmounted this land to press the dinosaur bones down into the ground and swallow up the long-haired mammoths. She was the solitary creature on it – misplaced there so many ages before it was her turn to live" (337–38).

In Morris's "The Origins of Sadness" (*Collected Stories*, 1986), the scientist Schuler searches, ironically, for the origins of human feelings in fossil fragments, ignoring human remains. Scouring the gully crevices of the Solomon River, he believes that perhaps through these silent plant and animal forms "nature herself spoke" (260). His only other contacts are with his silent Indian wife, the parrot she "talks" to, and a caged ape. At the close of the story Schuler falls into a rocky crevice. "Had he come here to slip time's noose?" (273).

The most complete treatment of this very bottom layer of the Great Plains mythic past is in *Badlands* (1975), Robert Kroetsch's story of paleontologist William Dawe, who, in the words of his daughter Anna, "went out and looked for that past. Appropriately enough with a pick and a shovel and an awl and a chisel and a hammer" (4). Kroetsch's narrative is itself a conscious artifact, broken by Anna's ironic commentary. Kroetsch mirrors Dawe's 1916 search along the river's eroding shore in Anna's 1972 search along that same river for the truth about a father she knows only from his field notes (2).

Kroetsch explicitly questions the function of the past in an exchange between Dawe and the photographer Michael Sinnott: "Everything is vanishing here," Sinnott says, "Every form of life. The Indians. . . . The homesteaders who replaced them." Dawe challenges Sinnott's historical sense: "Look at the dinosaurs. Seventy million years later. The bones are still here. Right here in the rock and the earth." Sinnott points out that bones he photographed on their removal were torpedoed and sunk on their way to England. "We pass along this little conundrum of the soul's pathway, only my photographs remaining" (117–18). In this passage, Kroetsch poses an interesting conundrum of his own. What is the raw material – the bones, the photos, the field notes, or the novel? And who preserves the record – Dawe, Sinnott, Anna, or Kroetsch?

Dawe's search takes him literally beneath the present, the land's surface. The men must climb from the river up the cliffs to see the shortgrass prairie and present reality, "a ranch, a trail, a road to town . . . and men not talking compulsively about bones, men chatting about their horses, their hay crops . . . work and friends and family" (165–66). But this surface does not interest Dawe: he focuses on what lies under that surface. He finds his Indian shadow-guide, Anna Yellowhair, curled up in a grave (6). He descends into a mine in an unsuccessful search for a blasting expert (78–83). The party is caught up in a twister (201–7), a confusion of surface and air. Dawe is injured in a fall ("down past, down into Cretaceous times") and must direct the work of others at their major find (173–209). Finally, as they struggle to free their prized specimen from the layers of time, their blasting expert, the boy Tune, is buried while trying to repair faulty wiring, a newly covered specimen in exchange for the *Dawesaurus* (215–24).

Badlands closes very much in the present. Anna Dawe and Anna Yellowhair free themselves from the male's frontier past at the river's source, on the surface, in the present. As a renegade grizzly is deposited almost on top of them by a helicopter, Anna Yellowhair flings Sinnott's photographs of the vanished past at the approaching animal and Anna Dawe throws her father's field notes into the lake, the source of the burrowing river itself (266–70). In Kroetsch's novel, the past, buried under tons of prairie soil, encased in plaster, or recorded in meticulous notes, ultimately must be discarded if the next generation is to survive its own past.

Most Great Plains writers focus not on this complex interplay of the deep past and present surfaces but on the transformation of the historical past, the experienced raw material, into a usable present, stripped of clichés.

In *A Lost Lady*, Cather examines the loss of the more immediate pioneering past.[4] The problem is how to let go of the past without diminishing it. The past is embodied in two people, Captain Forrester and his wife Marian, and it is valued by their young friend Niel Herbert, who witnesses the changes in their lives. Cather focuses on their various efforts to preserve the past in a time and place that is not merely indifferent but actively opposed to it. On the surface Captain Forrester appears to be a force for change. He has been a railroad builder whose efforts tied the West to the rest of the country, bringing an end to the isolation of the farms, prosperity to the towns, and, some might say, outside control and ultimate ruin to those towns that depended upon the railroad for their existence. However, Cather means Forrester to represent not a despoiler but a captain of industry in the heroic mode, one who by strength of will has changed the face of the country.

The captain built his Sweet Water home on the site of an ancient Indian encampment, a fact that connects him literally and symbolically with the plains' first residents. The approach from town loops and curves through broad meadows that are "half pasture, half marsh. Any one but Captain Forrester would have drained the bottom land and made it into highly productive fields" (11). By leaving the marsh untouched, he acknowledges his debt to the past.

The marsh symbolizes the untouched wilderness and reflects the innocence of Niel Herbert, who is just twenty, on the verge of adulthood. An experience in the Forresters' marsh initiates his awareness of Marian Forrester's gradual separation from the land and from the past. When he approaches the house to leave a bouquet of marsh flowers outside Marian's bedroom, Niel hears her laughter mingled with that of a man who is not her husband. Niel is startled to realize that, like the marsh itself, unsullied in the fresh morning air "before men and their activities had spoiled it," Marian Forrester cannot remain an ideal but is also a part of the prosaic present.

A few years later the marsh is drained by Ivy Peters, a hard, practical, modern man who insinuates himself into Marian Forrester's life. To Peters, the marsh signifies, not the purity of the wilderness, but an admission by persons he resents that not all things must be put to practical use. To Peters, preservation of the marsh is a waste of good land, but Niel recognizes a deeper motivation: "By draining the marsh Ivy had obliterated a few acres of something he hated, though he could not name it, and had asserted his power over the people who had loved those unproductive meadows for their idleness and silvery beauty" (106).

Niel recognizes that this act not only reveals Ivy's cruel hatred of the Forresters but also reflects the loss of the mythic West: "The Old West had been settled by dreamers, . . . Now all the vast territory they had won was to be at the mercy of men like Ivy Peters, who had never dared anything" (107).

The transformation of the myth of the garden into a corruption of the myth of the democratic utopia is embodied in the captain and Ivy, representatives of the heroic past and the blindly practical present. Each for a while possesses Marian, who feels allegiance to both the past and her own future. As the novel opens, Captain Forrester's days of influence have already passed, but he is still a commanding presence. He knows that to the coming generations the railroad he dreamed across the continent will signify, not hope or possibility, but only accomplished reality. Even though he acknowledges the futility of conserving his dreams, he continues to adhere to his sense of propriety, which increasingly seems out of place. When his Denver bank fails, he stands firm against the other directors, young businessmen who have refused to make up the losses. In front of them, he opens his bank box and signs over his fortune. Judge Pomeroy, of the captain's generation, exclaims to Mrs. Forrester, "By God, Madam, I think I've lived too long!" (92).

The captain's time is passing. Debilitated by strokes, his fortune gone, he keeps time with a sundial so that he can literally see nature move time (109). When he is wholly incapacitated, the townspeople, who have kept their distance physically and socially from the Forresters, descend upon the household. His wife cannot hold them off. "They went over the house like ants, the house where they had never before got past the parlour; and they found they had been fooled all these years. There was nothing remarkable about the place at all!" (138). As the captain lies helpless and his wife retreats into apparent indifference, they belittle the Forresters, who have lived well without the things that signify success to these acquisitive offspring of the pioneer dreamers.

The antithesis of the captain and the heroic past is Ivy Peters, in his own words a "shyster," who encroaches upon the Forresters when they need income. He rents their land, drains the marsh, invests the captain's money for Marian, and finally possesses Marian Forrester herself. Ivy Peters is a corruption of the democratic myth: if all men and women are created equal, then there must be no one better than he is. Rude, arrogant, and defiant of anyone who represents authority or a finer way of life, he is not content merely to pry and poke about in the Forresters' house and their lives but must force the Forresters to meet him on his own level. He wants to destroy not only the marsh but their proud pioneering spirit as well. "There warn't any harm in the old Captain, but he had the delusion of grandeur. He's happier now that he's like the rest of us and don't have to change his shirt every day" (105). To Ivy Peters, Marian Forrester and her husband both symbolize the hated heroic past. He assaults her – putting his hands casually on her breasts, just as casually taking her money to invest it – for the same reasons that he drains the marsh: to destroy the last vestiges of beauty and independence in those who occupy the land.

Marian Forrester is a puzzling enigma, because she embodies the struggle to transform the myths of the past into the utilitarian present.[5] As long as the captain can support and sustain her, she remains loyal to his ideals, but alone she cannot survive on past heroics. Like the captain's hothouse narcissus and Roman hyacinths, which fill the winter air with a "heavy, spring-like odour" (70), Marian Forrester is a sensual being in a cold setting. She needs people to reflect her wit and personal charm and to provide money so that she can sustain a certain way of life, as essential to her as Sweet Water is to Captain Forrester. When the captain's health begins to deteriorate, he stays longer at Sweet Water, forgoing winter trips to Colorado Springs, and fewer old friends stop in on trips through the country.

Marian feels trapped. Still, her loyalty to the captain sets Marian Forrester apart for Niel (78–79).

Like the captain, Marian is a woman of adventure and courage who willingly followed her husband west. Yet, unlike her husband, she is not willing to let go of the fortune that has enabled them to live so well. Her sacrifices are diametrically opposed to his: she offers herself to Ivy Peters in return for money that will allow them to keep Sweet Water and all it symbolizes. Marian has succumbed to "rascality," as Niel puts it, because "it succeeds faster than anything else" (124). "I feel such a power to live in me, Niel," she explains. She refuses to succumb to the inevitable diminishment of the past and determines to use any means possible to preserve herself.

Marian Forrester symbolizes the transformation of the heroic myths of the pioneering era. She transfers her allegiance from the Captain's Sweet Water to modern society. Years after she leaves Nebraska, when Niel assumes she is dead, he hears stories of Marian, married to an Englishman, living in South America, surviving according to her own code.

A Lost Lady illustrates the ways we alter the old myths to fit our more prosaic world. The past is not dead but is preserved by those who, like Niel Herbert, acknowledge the connections between the past and the present, however tenuous those may be, and by those who, like Marian Forrester, alter the old codes so that they can survive in the present.

Not many readers would identify F. Scott Fitzgerald's *The Great Gatsby* (1925) as a Great Plains novel; yet the link to the optimistic westering myth of Manifest Destiny and the garden is obvious.[6] As Leo Marx points out, Gatsby and Nick, both Westerners, recognize the pastoral ideal. Gatsby tries to redeem it, and Nick understands the significance of his gesture (361). Nick recognizes the tension between the myth of the ideal garden – Daisy – and the threat of encroaching reality – the Valley of Ashes.

The pioneering myth is an integral part of *The Great Gatsby*. The story of Tom, Daisy, Nick, and Gatsby reflects the persistent theme of the search for place. All four have immigrated to the East, and to West Egg, just as their forebears headed west to conquer new territory, and Nick Carraway observes the summer's series of events from a decidedly Western point of view. Like Niel Herbert, Nick does not judge overtly, and yet both find the means others use to realize their ambitions repugnant. What they see about them tempts them, as it does Huck Finn, to light out for the territory, as if the territory were still there, fleeing from friends who have apparently betrayed the myths.

Fitzgerald frames his tale of Gatsby's attempt to realize his romantic dream with Nick's plains sensibilities regarding people and their place in the New World. Nick's innate sense of decency and his family's tradition of hard work and modesty provide a counterpoint to Gatsby's disintegration. Gatsby shares Nick's Western heritage, but in Gatsby it is manifested in a perverse way. Like Godfrey St. Peter and Marian and Captain Forrester, Gatsby wants to preserve something that is gone, but his dream is of a decidedly different nature. Where Cather's characters struggle to maintain the memory of an era through gestures and objects, Fitzgerald's Gatsby attempts to resurrect the past quite literally and, as a result of this act, to erase time. The sensible ones – Nick, Tom, and even Daisy – realize the futility of his effort, but only Nick acknowledges the significance of his gesture and recognizes its origins in Gatsby's acceptance of the myths. Born James Gatz, Gatsby was one of the farmers that Parrington, Smith, and others dismiss as unfit for heroic treatment until he jumped aboard Cody's yacht. When Gatsby's father appears for his funeral, Nick recognizes him as one of those typical farmers, a dull man who maintains his own dream about his son: "If he'd of lived, he'd of been a great man. A man like James J. Hill. He'd of helped build up the country" (169). He shows Nick his son's "schedule," written on the flyleaf of a ragged copy of *Hopalong Cassidy*, evidence that James Gatz naively believed in the myth of work and reward long before he discovered another ideal embodied in Daisy. His existential leap onto the yacht transforms James Gatz into Jay Gatsby. Meyer Wolfsheim shows him the crooked path to instant wealth. His own confidence, bred in Minnesota, a region where the myth of equality of people and opportunity persists, enables him nearly to realize his presumptive dream and regain Daisy.

Such a grand illusion could be acted upon only by someone for whom the myths of the garden and utopia are still very real. That Gatsby fails is not as important as the attempt itself. Nick realizes that he shares Gatsby's mythic sensibilities and that his own sense of complacency and stability make him different from the people around him. "I see now that this has been a story of the West, after all – Tom and Gatsby, Daisy and Jordan and I, were all Westerners, and perhaps we possessed some deficiency in common which made us subtly unadaptable to Eastern life" (177).

Nick leaves the East with a vision of the New World – the past – before him:

I became aware of the old island here that flowered once for Dutch sailors' eyes – a fresh, green breast of the new world. Its vanished trees, the trees that had made way for Gatsby's house, had once pandered in whispers to the last and greatest of all human dreams: for a transitory enchanted moment man must have held his breath in the presence of this continent, compelled into an aesthetic contemplation he neither understood nor desired, face to face for the last time in history with something commensurate to his capacity for wonder. (182)

As Marx points out, this is the vision, once a dominant image in American culture, of "the undefined, green republic . . . dedicated to the pursuit of happiness" (6). It is this promise that pioneers followed west, a "fresh green breast" that becomes a cliché the moment it is acknowledged. In Gatsby's West, if not in Nick's, the vision was still a reality, and Gatsby could leap at it by climbing aboard Cody's yacht and sailing away from his past. As Nick points out, the green light at the end of Daisy's dock was the focus of Gatsby's faith that he could again find the virgin world in Daisy. Nick's final comment poignantly points up this paradox of the future as past: "Gatsby believed in the green light, the orgiastic future that year by year recedes before us" (182).

The Great Plains have been transformed. There is no fresh, green breast, no green light. Limitless space has been divided into identifiable places. But the Great Plains as a concept can be carried away as memory or vision. Since Garland began writing in the 1890s, refugees from the cultural and social aridity of the plains and prairies have found that even though the region seems to be shapeless space, it cannot be lightly put aside. As Morag Gunn says in *The Diviners*, "I found out the whole town is inside my head, for as long as I live" (353). The land and the society that arises on it are the raw material that must be transformed if the inhabitants and the exiles are to avoid the losses that Marian and Gatsby suffer, if they are to overcome the paralysis of raw, unprocessed memory.

The necessity and danger the past represents are implicit as increasing distance in space and time from the family homestead that saps the strength of Charles and Alpha Neumiller in Woiwode's *Beyond the Bedroom Wall*. Their son Charles, an actor, tries to recreate his family on paper, even though he is isolated from the family's North Dakota roots. He feels this alienation acutely. He envisions a book like a journal, a geographical tracing of his mother's life. The incidents of her life would be "like large rocks in a stratum . . . each piece complete in itself, . . . bearing no outward relationship to any other piece, . . . so that an incident from childhood might have more temporal value than ten years of adulthood" (548).

Woiwode clearly outlines the difference between the sense of geographical locale that Charles intuits in his mother's early life, the "rocks" of her time and place, and the lack of terra firma in his own life: "The desolation, the bleakness and the anonymity of the city are identical to that of the plains, but more pernicious: man's constructed the city and chosen to live in it; the plain is a natural phenomenon he can always leave; swarms of people shoulder past more swarms in the city without touching another life; people move over the unpopulated space of the plain to have a specific effect on a particular person – so the city makes him more conscious than ever of the plain" (549). The act of writing, he imagines, would draw out parallels between his acted-out life and his mother's very real North Dakota existence. At the close of the novel Charles, like Morris's Clyde

Muncy, dreams of going home, of recreating a place that is firmly fixed in memory: "He could see a big, white, many-porched farmhouse, with a gambrel roof, perhaps, plus plenty of dormers" (598).[7]

Charles's brother Jerome has more haunting memories of their past, conjured up by their mother's stories of her own homesteader grandfather and her brothers Conrad and Elling. In the sleeping room of the Chicago hospital where he is an intern, Jerome remembers a childhood visit from his uncles, who declared the importance of the past (571). That same day his uncles were killed, and five years later his mother died in childbirth. Jerome, like Charles, has kept his past "locked into place, making it seem he was staring at a photograph that had been snapped of them at that moment, and begun receding into the depths of his mind, growing smaller and more faint and retreating as though they were spirits he'd taken by surprise" (573). The raw material of the past, untransformed by experience or ceremony, leaves Jerome and Charles paralyzed in the present.

A person without a connection to the land and to the past of those who first settled it can be threatened by loss of identity. In *Harvesting Ballads* (1984), Philip Kimball tells the story of rootless drifters searching for each other, for the past, and for stability across the central plains from Oklahoma north along the routes of harvest crews. The focus of this search for identity is Sorry, the son of Blanchfleur, who fled her family's farm with rodeo rider Roger Lyons. An orphan, Sorry is raised by the ranch hand Keeper. As a young adult Sorry learns who his parents were and finds his Uncle Marcus, but his ties to the family's Oklahoma ranch are not rooted deeply enough in his own past to provide him with any sense of continuity. The new knowledge of his identity only cuts him off from his familiar childhood with Keeper. Although Marcus can give Sorry the remnant of a family, he cannot pass on to Sorry his love for the land and his commitment to work, which would provide Sorry the connection he needs to be a part of Marcus's time and place.

The metaphor for this conflict is the rivalry of Marcus and Sorry for Isadora Faire. When Isadora chooses to stay with Marcus, Sorry knows he has lost his tenuous place on the land (337–38). When he returns to Keeper, he finds that Keeper has sold that place too: "Looked out across the road and pasture, the windmill a mile shimmering autumn heat. Born here. Grew up. Home. The rhythmic cant of the auctioneer from the barn. Going once. Part of me. Going twice. My own sweat and body. Going three times and. Gone" (343). Sorry, homeless, becomes the eternal pioneer.

This motif of the need for physical and emotional contact with the land pervades Great Plains fiction, especially as writers focus on the third and fourth generations, who are as mobile as their pioneering ancestors but lack a clear sense of their destination. "Crossing the Water," the closing story in Erdrich's *Love Medicine*, is the story of Lipsha Morrissey's search for his father and his place in the maze of complex interrelationships in North Dakota's Chippewa society. Lipsha has been raised by his grandparents without knowing which of their brood of blood and foster children are his parents. In the end, Lipsha knows his blood family and his true heritage. He is a symbol of the reconciliation of the forces of history, family rivalries, and political divisions. He is acknowledged by his father, Gerry Nanapush, as he drives him across the border into freedom in Canada. On his return home he pauses on a bridge that crosses the water, the Indian's symbol of the ancient source of life and death. He sees the water as the link between time and space, between the mythic past and the mundane present.

The transformation of myth as promised reality to myth as memory is an important motif in Morris's 1959 novel, *Ceremony in Lone Tree*.[8] The novel catalogs events surrounding the ninetieth birthday of Tom Scanlon. The opening passage demonstrates Morris's ability to transform memory into concrete reality:

Come to the window. The one at the rear of the Lone Tree Hotel. The view is to the west. There is no obstruction but the sky. Although there is no one outside to look in, the yellow blind is drawn low at the window, and between it and the pane a fly is trapped. He has stopped buzzing. Only the crawling shadow can be seen. . . .

At a child's level in the pane there is a flaw that is round, like an eye in the glass. An eye to that eye, a scud seems to blow on a sea of grass. Waves of plain seem to roll up, then break like a surf. Is it a flaw in the eye, or in the window, that transforms a dry place into a wet one? (3)

The fly is trapped behind the blind just as the old man is trapped inside the room, held there by the "obstruction" of the sky, exposed on the dry sea of grass. Tom Scanlon's three daughters, who live in the present, see nothing in Lone Tree. Tom Scanlon, who lives in the past, sees plenty through the flaw in the glass. "The fact that there is little to see seems to be what he likes about it. He can see what he pleases" (7). The children and grandchildren who have left Lone Tree are still a part of the landscape. Who they are has been shaped by brief encounters in their Lone Tree pasts. From time to time, they return, drawn to the place and the old man.

A generation and more removed from the pioneer period, the characters in Morris's novel exemplify the nostalgia, the withdrawal, and the wish fulfillment that accompanies the fading of one era into another. Here the focus is on the Wild West as well as the more prosaic Great Plains myths of settlers and town builders. Morris combines ceremonial and mythic elements in his quirky way to present an intricate set of rites that signal a powerful force for change in the West. The Wild West, with its emphasis on male domination, is fading.[9] The ceremonies in the novel simultaneously memorialize and encourage its demise. The opening command, "Come to the window," invites the reader to participate in a series of events that occur against a landscape that is hardly visible, in a town so dwarfed by sky that "it is hard to be sure if the town is still there" (6).

The first section of the novel, "The Scene," establishes the situation that culminates in the novel's third section, "The Ceremony." At first the reader assumes that the ceremony is the stated one: the family gathering in Lone Tree to celebrate Tom Scanlon's ninetieth birthday. Scanlon is the central

Afloat on the Sea of Grass 139

icon in Morris's Western funereal ritual. The old man was born in a covered wagon, now "inhabited by bats" but still parked outside his residence, the Lone Tree Hotel (16). Although Lone Tree is almost deserted, Scanlon stays in the hotel because "he has passed his life, if it can be said he has lived one, in the rooms of the Lone Tree Hotel" (96). Looking at the uninterrupted landscape, Scanlon can see "the scenic props of his own mind" (6). What he "sees" is the past – much of it events that occurred before he was born (17). As his children and grandchildren descend upon him, preparing his birthday celebration, the old man sleeps behind the lobby stove, the embodiment of the static, mythic West.

Other ceremonies, some of them dangerous and unsettling, appear unpredictably in the present. Charlie Munger, a random killer patterned after Nebraska's Charles Starkweather, has killed twelve people in ten days.[10] Bud Momeyer's nephew Lee Roy runs down and kills two mocking boys at school because he is "tired of being pushed around" (21). When he is apprehended, Charlie Munger says that he murdered all those people because he wanted to "be somebody" (21), an echo of the hero worship society awarded to gunmen in the Wild West. Lee Roy and Charles are twisted variations of the old rituals, killing not to avenge a wrong nor as part of an elaborate duel between good and evil but to appease feelings of inferiority in a faceless society. In the present there are no clear lines between chaos and civilization, between good and evil, but only random destruction, which can invade any place at any time. It is this, rather than the certainty of evil, that terrifies Lois and Walter McKee.

With these contrasting ceremonies established as the scene, Morris proceeds to the second section of the novel, "The Roundup." Family and friends gather in Lone Tree. Each has a role in the unfolding ceremonies. Scanlon's three daughters and their husbands, Lois and Walter McKee, their daughter-in-law Eileen and their grandsons, teenager Calvin and toddler Gordon, Maxine and Bud Momeyer and their daughter Etoile, and Edna and Clyde Ewing arrive, the McKees and Momeyers from Lincoln and the Ewings from the open road in the modern covered wagon, a motor home. McKee's boyhood chum Gordon Boyd shows up with a young divorcee he picks up in Nevada. Jennings, a writer of Westerns who searches for the West in drugstore novels and cowboy movies, is on the trail of the mass murderers and stumbles instead upon the scene. A rather gentle man, he functions as the ceremonial witness to the complex series of ceremonies that begins to unfold.[11]

Calvin, the present-day replacement for the long-dead heroic image of Scanlon, looks like Gary Cooper, but with his stutter he is a mute mirror of past heroes. Calvin's cousin Etoile is the ghostly echo of Samantha, a mythic image from the past of Scanlon's father (105). In a parody of the true West, Calvin courts Etoile by sending her leather-scented toilet water and a picture of his horse (87). Ironically, Etoile must physically arouse Calvin to awaken his latent sexuality.

Bud Momeyer and Clyde Ewing provide a satiric counterpoint to the more serious threat of random killers and the petrification of old Scanlon. Dressed in a red hunting cap, Bud stalks neighborhood cats with a salvaged bow and arrow to protect his neighbor's hamster farm. His forays are as ludicrous as Charlie Munger's are disturbing. Clyde, a costumed caricature of a Western hero, claims Cherokee blood and friendship with Will Rogers, a humorous version of the self-made Western man. This modern Westerner rarely steps out of the air-conditioned comfort of his mobile home. The Ewings have replaced children and the establishment of a family empire with Shiloh, a pedigree bulldog that they usually keep confined in their trailer home. In Lone Tree, Clyde allows the dog "to run a little" (195).

Poised between past heroics and present uncertainties is Gordon Boyd. On his way to the roundup and ceremony, Boyd considers his choices – to remain asleep in the past, dwelling on his boyhood antics and his infatuation with the young Lois Scanlon, who responded to his kiss and then married his best fried, Walter McKee, or to wake up and risk losing the past. Despite his feelings of awe and (not incidentally) inferiority before his friend Gordon Boyd, McKee won the hand of Lois, and he has made a success of his life. Among the men in attendance at the ceremonies, only McKee seems willing to face their full import. Forty years before, he witnessed Boyd's heroic attempts, and in the present, in Lincoln, he has witnessed senseless attacks by hoodlums and murderers. Against the forces of evil he feels helpless. "If McKee represented Good, . . . then the forces of Evil would carry the day" (51), he thinks. McKee is Modern Man, acutely aware of his limitations.

The possibility of a male-dominant future is embodied in young Gordon, a boy fascinated by his great-grandfather's guns and hostile to women because, as his grandmother Lois recognizes, he understands that women do not know all the answers (60–61). It is clear that unless a crisis occurs, the child symbolizes the future. He knows that by physical or psychological force he can be in control.

Juxtaposed against this myth of guns and force is the myth of the female pioneer, the nurturer and protector, who attempts to exist in the present and prepare for the future. If the men are asleep or ineffectual, the women are acutely awake. They exist along a continuum from the past into the present much as the men do. The female counterpart to the petrified Scanlon is Samantha, a romantic memory that Morris develops more fully in the companion novel, *Field of Vision* (142–51). Samantha is a part of the memory of Scanlon's father that parallels Boyd's only slightly more substantial memory of the young Lois. In the present, Etoile embodies Samantha, the woman who could shoot a buzzard from the sky (*Field of Vision* 149). One element of the ceremonies' climax is Calvin's gift to his great-grandfather – his new bride Etoile dressed as Samantha, riding behind a mule team (268, 276). Etoile is also a link to the future. Like Calvin's mother, Eileen, she speaks her mind and everyone else's. Physically beautiful and able to interpret Calvin's thoughts, she is the only possible mate for the present-day Western male, Calvin. The future is not especially promising for this pair, however. "The *worst* that could happen would be that [their babies] would have *her* [flat] feet and *his* stutter" (90). Like Scanlon's Samantha in the past and Maxine and Eileen in the present, Etoile will be a foil for the silenced Western man.

Lois and Maxine attempt to insert some stability and common sense into the lives of the men around them, but like their pioneer counterparts, they are isolated psychologically, if not physically. Remembering their mother's lonely and silent life in the old hotel, Lois acknowledges Maxine's silent endurance of the boyish Bud (69, 237–38, 264). Shapeless and faceless, Maxine is the family's drudge. Her only reward is the Amazonian Etoile. Lois McKee lives in fear of guns, especially ones wielded by mad killers unknown to her, or by her own precocious grandson Gordon, who has her where he wants her (57–62). Like her husband, Lois is keenly aware of the myths and realities that surround her: her petrified father, her grandson's disrespect, the random violence lurking outside her glass house. Like McKee, she feels powerless against these forces. Both Lois and Maxine attempt to influence the future. Maxine is tired of the silent courtship between her daughter Etoile and the McKees' grandson Calvin. "If something didn't happen to change the world, she would do it herself" (81). More important, Lois's act at the novel's climax reverberates against both the myths and the realities of the West.

The ceremonies that Morris presents to us, the observers, are interwoven in time and space. The pivotal figure in the conjunction of past and present is Gordon Boyd. His life is all ceremony – empty ritual or audacious presumption, depending on one's point of view.[12] When they were teenagers, McKee watched Boyd try to walk on water (*Field of Vision* 209), and he watched from the ditch when twelve boxcars passed over Boyd, who lay on the tracks. He witnessed the adult Gordon squirt pop at a raging Mexican bull (*Field of Vision* 59–60, 234). Boyd's foolish courage both appalls and fascinates McKee, who tells him, "[Y]ou have to make a fool of yourself since you've made such a mess of your life" (182), but as Boyd explains to his traveling companion, "[W]hat was America if it wasn't promises? And what were promises if a man couldn't live it up?" (259). This confused version of the myths has Boyd stymied.

On his way from his Mexican retreat to the ceremony in Lone Tree, Boyd passes through Nevada, where the clerk at the motel wants to know if she should wake him for the local ceremony, the atomic bomb test (29–32). The bomb becomes a central icon in the developing ceremonies, the melting of past into present, and the jolt into conscious awareness that Boyd has been trying to avoid. "What sort of bomb would wake him up?" Boyd wants to know (32). Is Boyd, like Scanlon, petrified in the past? His pilgrimage to the Lone Tree ceremonies is an attempt to find out if "it's there, or all in my mind" (42). The bomb that Boyd does not encounter in the Nevada desert symbolizes that instant of reality that we are constantly experiencing. It is this immediacy that Boyd wants to avoid: if the bomb goes off, and he proves to be awake, his past will be annihilated. His trip to Lone Tree, as his companion points out, is an attempt to recover the past, not confront the present.

The bomb is an inverted ceremony, an unpredictable spectacle that does not acknowledge orderly change but, rather, threatens unceremonious ruin. It is a logical extension of the six-shooter that defines Tom Scanlon and the boy Gordon. "How could you play at killing people without sooner or later killing them?" Lois asks, thinking not only of six-shooters but of larger guns as well (58). It is the nameless face of evil that dwarfs the random violence of Charlie Munger and the jealousy of Lee Roy Momeyer. It renders the antics of Bud and Clyde not only ludicrous but impotent. It is the jolt that forces us awake to face the present instant as it destroys the past, where we can sleep in memory indefinitely in Lone Tree, Nebraska, Nevada, or Mexico. Morris explicates this symbol in the clearest terms: "The past, whether one liked it or not, was all that one actually possessed. . . . the present was that moment of exchange – when all might be lost. Why risk it? . . . The meeting point, the melting point of the past confronting the present. Where no heat was thrown off, there was no light – where it failed to ignite the present, it was dead" (32).

The final ceremonial climax centers, ironically, not on Scanlon, but on the other members of the gathering. With a rented mule team and Etoile dressed in an old dress and sunbonnet to resemble Samantha (214–18), Calvin appears in the moonlight before the hotel just as Bud Momeyer mortally wounds the free-running bulldog Shiloh and Lois McKee, the only person who is truly awake, shoots off her father's antique pistol from one of the hotel's upstairs windows. Scanlon rises up from behind the stove, calls out, "That you, Samuels?" and falls over dead, "as if through a hole in the floor. Hardly a sound, no more noise than if a suit of clothes had slipped off a hanger, and the man who had worn them had vanished into thin air" (277). The birthday ceremony for the patriarch becomes a ritual of farewell to a way of life and a point of view.

The gun that explodes in Lois's hand is the bomb they all anticipated and feared. It brings Scanlon to life in the present and closes his past in death. McKee, the absent-minded hero "without a thought for himself," rushes to Lois (278). He and little Gordon see the pistol by her side and are duly impressed. The boy is jolted awake by the realization that the gun in his grandmother's hand is controlled by a woman. Lois, the woman who has been afraid of the past, is clearly in control of the future as the ceremonies come to a close. It is McKee who sums up the ceremonies' meaning: "Something he had taken for granted in the world was no more. Tomorrow would be different" (301). The past is dead and gone, but the present demands just as much courage and resolution.

On the Great Plains, raw material is a recyclable natural resource, repeated in endless variations, expanded into myth by Cather and Fitzgerald, its clichés transformed into metaphor by Morris. The movable image of the prairies and plains persists in the mind even when the place has been abandoned. The myths are embedded firmly enough in our national consciousness that writers can satirize and parody them with confidence: the myths are inverted, not transformed.

In *The Last Cattle Drive* (1977), Robert Day inverts the westering myths. Rancher Spangler Tukel heads his cattle *east*, across farmers' fields and through the banal small towns of Kansas. The narrator of this cowboy-farmer parody is Leo Murdock, a college graduate and teacher in small-town Kansas. To Leo's Kansas City friends, the towns of Gorham and Hays are "where the hicks" are. But Leo likes the West. According to Spangler, Leo's decision to trade his sports car for a jeep means that "it'll turn out you want to work on a ranch, be a cowboy. . . . You've been watching the Marlboro ads."

Spangler, who would be dead set against the Eastern dude Leo in a standard Western, accepts him out of confidence or desperation. When he becomes disgusted with trucking rates and schedules and decides to embark on an old-fashioned cattle drive from western Kansas to the Agriculture Hall of Fame in Bonner Springs, Kansas, he hires Leo as one of his hands. In fact, the drive is Leo's idea (61), the result of an off-the-cuff remark rather than a nostalgic romance for the fading days of the open road. Only old Jed, Spangler's other "hand," a relic of the past, has ever been on a cattle drive. The other cowboys – including Spangler – are a generation removed from the trail-driving days. Spangler acknowledges the irony implicit in his situation: "We're going to do this cattle drive just like we knew what we were doing. Just like the real thing. . . . I mean, I've never been on one of these deals before" (84). He looks back on "the good old days" without nostalgia: "They talk about the torch being passed from one generation to the other, and how the war broke all that up out here. Bullshit. This country doesn't have tradition. It's like instant coffee. . . . The west hasn't had four generations go through it. The twentieth century swamped us before we had a chance" (86).

Spangler's drive picks up more clichés when, on the first day, a movie company tries to "horn in." Uninterested in Spangler's project, they only want footage of a cattle drive (114). Like Spangler, they've cleared the way with the local officials, and so Spangler is forced to comply with their demands. They stampede the herd because "we need some film of these babies running" (116). Like marauding Indians, the interlopers beat a hasty retreat, leaving Spangler's crew to regroup the frightened herd. At the end of the day, Leo sums it up: "We had done it and we hadn't. It had been sunny, and the people had been friendly and curious. And we had been taken. The night was dark but not ominous. I realized just before I went to sleep how different our fears of failure were from those of the men who had done all this a hundred years before" (119–20).

Day parodies not only the cowboy-and-Indian popular romance but the region's governing myths as well. In this satirical reversal of mythic traditions, he uses a real place, the Garden of the World, frozen in concrete in Lucas, Kansas, as the second stop of Spangler's cattle drive. This garden is a network of cement caricatures, serpents, vines, and trees in the yard of a modest Lucas home. S. P. Dinsmoor, a self-taught folk artist, constructed his Garden of Eden over a period of twenty-eight years. As Leo explains, the garden is a crumbling curiosity that "everybody for a hundred miles knows about but for some reason never visits" (127). Spangler and his wife Opal, a kind of inverted version of Adam and Eve, tour the imaginary world Dinsmoor created, listening to the taped explanations the long-dead artist left among the vine and cement apparitions. Dinsmoor himself, a parodic creator, lies in a coffin made of concrete and glass, with a cement angel guard in case "The Boss" wants to take him up (128–30).

Their tour reflects the failure of the garden's promise. Dinsmoor's garden is not even a remnant of the raw material of the prairie past, but an imaginary collage of concrete forms rising, not from the land itself, but from the fertile mind of an eccentric literalist. Ironically, its existence in real space and time diminishes its mythic power: the garden is reduced to a cliché of a cliché.

At the end of the tour, Spangler and Opal emerge into a town of no color, only silhouettes, headed east of Eden, toward Kansas City and the Hall of Fame (132). Obstacles appear in the path at regular intervals, familiar shades of old stereotypes: the sheriff is a highway-patrol officer who is easily deflected by a threat, not of gunplay, but to "tell his wife about Hays" (122). When the herd is shot at, it is by camera-toting tourists, not ornery sodbusters (134). Not a band of Indians, but disgruntled townspeople, block their way outside of Lucas (125–26). Not buffalo, but a motor home, runs into the herd, killing five animals. The owner ignores the dead animals and expresses concern for his bumper. These days "the roads are for cars, fellow," he reminds Spangler (136).

Ironically, Leo imagines that he is reliving history, which is really what he is doing: "I could never get used to the idea that I was a real scout for a real cattle drive, and I'd find myself imagining doing pretty much what I was doing. There weren't any Indians, though. Only cars" (148). The hero-narrator acknowledges the irony of the situation when he is confronted by his Kansas City girlfriend, who has tracked him down by reading the newspapers and shows up driving his old MG: "I felt pretty silly when I realized I was stuck in a choice between a girl and a horse. It was getting hard to tell the movies from the life. A certain giddiness of absurdity rushed across me, like when you can't keep a straight face while you tell someone about a ridiculous tragedy." Of course, this being an authentic parody, Leo chooses the horse (153).

In Kansas City they are attacked by helicopters and police cars. In a final ironic twist, officials at the Agriculture Hall of Fame deny them permission to graze the herd on their "five acres of original prairie." As Spangler explains, "It seems the board read our letter and said that if my steers shit all over the original prairie, then it wouldn't be original anymore. 'Now if you'd been a buffalo herd, Mr. Tukel, we could accommodate you' " (221). When the cattle buyers deny Spangler choice grade for his road-weary herd, he stampedes the remaining herd through the city. Rounded up a final time, they bring appropriately high prices at auction. As Opal explains, "[E]very B-B-Q owner in Johnson County thinks Spangler is a big hero" (250).

The West has met the industrial East one last time. The garden is a concrete maze, or a patch of pristine prairie, without people working the land or cows grazing on new grass. *The Last Cattle Drive* is an ironic account of the end of the great prairie garden.

In his collection of stories *Nebraska* (1989), Ron Hansen inverts the Great Plains myth in "Red Letter Days" and "Playland." In these stories the land has been transformed into a nonproductive golf course or an amusement park, places of leisure, of work time wasted. "Red Letter Days" is the diary of Cecil, a retired lawyer living in a small northwest Nebraska town along Mari Sandoz's Niobrara River. The old man putters at repairing golf equipment. His wife wraps pennies and watches soap operas. Amid comments on daily chores, the weather, reading, eating, cemetery plots, and retirement in Arizona, Cecil reveals his attachment to high-school golfer "Wild Bill," a straight shooter on the golf course. Where Old Jules and Mary worked to establish orchards and homes on the stubborn land, Cecil tries desperately to fill his days with coffee chats, reading law and golf books, and running errands. He even strikes up a conversation with a magazine telephone solicitor (176). His golfing buddy dies of a heart attack; his wife is sixty-seven; he worries about his heart, his eyes (178–79).

To Cecil, golf is his work. When a friend figures out that Cecil has spent five years of his life on the golf course, he comments, "Five years, Cecil! You can't have 'em back. You could've accomplished something important. Ever feel guilt about that?" Cecil replies, "We're put here for pleasure, too" (184), a heresy on the Great Plains in Old Jules country. Cecil and his friends have given up on making something of their lives. At the end they are merely waiting. His friend Eugene has abandoned chemotherapy. "You gotta die of somethin'," he explains. "We have all this technology. . . . And the twentieth century is still unacceptable" (184).

Hansen's story "Playland" is one of the most elaborate inversions of the Great Plains myths. Playland is a 1918 agricultural exhibit that has been transformed into an amusement park, a wholly artificial and useless world. The architect, from Sardinia, "invented gardens as crammed as flower shops, glades that were like dark green parlors, ponds that gently over-lipped themselves so that water sheeted down to another pond, and trickle streams that issued from secret pipes sunk in the crannies of rocks" (25). Playland's centerpiece is a giant "swimming pool" nearly one mile long, more than half that in width, and thirty-six feet deep at the center, where the water is "so pellucid that a swimmer could see a nickel wink sunlight from the bottom" (27). Nothing – not cold weather, typhoid, poisonous snakes, the Depression, or war – can close Playland (27–28).

The story is about Gordon, a soldier nursing a war injury, his dazzling girlfriend Bijou, and her flashy Eastern cousin Frankie. When Frankie arrives in an airplane that sets him down in the middle of the swimming pool, things start to go awry in Playland. Gordon discovers a giant snapping turtle "as large as a manhole cover" in the pool (35). The possibility of conflict among these people, or with the potential forces of nature, symbolized by the giant turtle, is raised but not resolved.

Clearly, Hansen believes that something has happened to America's agricultural heartland. Playland is not a transformation but an aberration. The perfection of Playland is, quite literally, blinding. Lifeguards are blinded by the sand "as fine as that in hotel ashtrays" (27), and partygoers must wear green cellophane sunglasses to guard against the marquee's glare. "Playland was everywhere they looked, insisting on itself" (40). The prosaic agricultural exhibit has been turned into a garish parody of the original garden, the utopian dream.

Hansen warns us in all of the stories in this collection that at the right time and in the right place nature – the giant snapping turtle, the heart attack, the blizzard, the "wickedness" – can rise up from beneath the smooth calm surface. Cousin Frankie, symbol of the sophisticated, corrupt East, breezes in, spouts off, and breezes out, but he brings with him Hansen's point: "You and Bijou, you come to Playland, you dance to the music, swallow all this phonus-balonus, and you think you've experienced life to the hilt. Well, I got news for you, GI. You haven't even licked the spoon. You don't know what's out there, what's available" (39). Playland – America's Heartland – remains isolated, cut off by an innocent regard for the immediate need. The wider world and the demands of the land itself are unexplored.

Morris recombines the elements of Great Plains literature in his 1977 novel, *The Fork River Space Project*, which is perhaps his oddest Great Plains novel but also his clearest delineation of the multiple dimensions of the Great Plains. Ostensibly, the novel is about the narrator Kelcey's growing interest in the past and future of Fork River, Kansas, and its principal inhabitants, Harry Lorbeer and O. P. Dahlberg, who are waiting for the return of a spacecraft that may have landed in their town. But the novel is also, once again, about the raw material that stretches behind, beneath, and beyond plains dwellers in time and space.

From his vantage point on the eastern rim of the plains, Morris's Kelcey sees not only with his eyes but with his imagination. As in *Ceremony in Lone Tree*, the opening image is deliberately obscured. With slight pressure on his eyelids, Kelcey can magnify objects. If he is facing toward the light, motes flick and colors change "on the mind's eye, or on the balls of the eyes, or wherever it is we see what we imagine, or imagine what we see" (1–2). Morris, through Kelcey, explains what prairie and plains travelers and dwellers have known for generations: "[Y]ou have to know what you're seeing" (2). And what Kelcey sees is the continuum of the deep past stretching into the present and beyond, into orbit, escaping the boundaries of space and time:

What you see out here is from where you see it, and what you know. I see wagon tracks, covered wagons, hounded Indians, horse thieves, fur trappers and plagues of grasshoppers. My neighbor on the south sees only the weather. His eyes are faded and creased from sky gazing. His wife's people see corn, soybeans, and beef cattle, with the exception of her brother, an engineer, who sees freeways. I have an uncle who is big in center pivot irrigation. . . . An orbiting satellite might read them as a warning, or as a welcome. My friend Rainey, the weather man, sees prehistoric creatures waddling in a vast inland sea. He prefers what he sees to the missile silos that are actually there. My wife, Alice, sees the frost that will kill her garden. On my way to the market I often note a woman gazing over the half curtain at her kitchen window. Before her, westward, rolls the endless plains, but it is not what she sees. It could be that this is the right place for her, as it is for me. (3–4)

For Kelcey, seeing invokes time as well as space. Remembering that as a boy he viewed the plains and an apparently immovable train in the far distance, Kelcey explains, "If one was far enough from what was moving, the movement seemed to stop" (117). Kelcey's speculation shifts this movement into outer space: "If we are a few hundred miles in space, nothing visible moves on the surface of the planet" (117). Taken to its conclusion, this view from empty space freezes time, so that one might see a "huge leaf-eating monster," the land covered with ice, "Druids dragging their slabs of rock to Stonehenge." Kelcey envisions Plato's cave, with Lorbeer and Alice among those who have turned and seen the true reality (119–20).

On the plains, space persists, stretching horizontally, so that the motionless point on the horizon extends into the past, from the dinosaurs to the early settlers to Dahlberg, whose father collected meteorites and built a rocket on the plains (78), Lorbeer, whose mother was rendered speechless by the land, Kelcey himself, and his wife Alice, an imported forest child who, without the forest to impede her view, disappears into space with Dahlberg. The town of Fork River is a point in time and space between the present and the deep past: "Huge creatures once grazed here, tiny, dog-sized horses; saber-toothed tigers crouched on the rim rock. Red men speared their fish, white men set their traps, horse thieves, scoundrels, buffalo hunters looked up this ravine, screened by the willows, to the sanctuary of their imaginations" (184). In his pocket Kelcey carries a blackened penny, tactile proof of their presence in Fork River.

In Fork River, space extends vertically as well as horizontally. Like the Red Deer River in Kroetsch's novel, the town is beneath the surface of the plains, its trees appearing as scrub bushes from a distance. The force of something has blown the grass away from the roots, and seasonal flooding has left the buildings disconnected from the land and from time. Although he can find accounts of the town's history in the local library, it has been ignored by the present reality. Not even the looters have found it. The power and light company has no records after 1943 (182), although Kelcey talks by phone with residents Lorbeer and Dahlberg.

In the local library Kelcey discovers a book by Dahlberg, *A Hole in*

Space and Other Stories. An illustration for the title story – a wide stretch of the prairie with a small round hole, like an eye, in the overcast sky – reveals the controlling point of view in Morris's novel. Morris makes it clear that this vertical dimension arises naturally from our myths and historical concepts of the plains: "Think of it in 1840, unmapped and unknown, mountains alternating with burning deserts, . . . On the surface of the shrinking planet there would never again be a dream quite like it. . . . Next on the agenda loomed the sky" (54–55). The dreamer, the pioneer lured by the westering myths, has been awakened to historical reality but has not given up the myth of endless frontiers. In such circumstances, Kelcey, Dahlberg, Lorbeer, and Alice wait. Anticipation links the future to the past. Since the 1940s Lorbeer and Dahlberg have been waiting for the future.

Kelcey is reluctant to take over their role as one who anticipates the unexpected. A pragmatic plains dweller (but also a writer of humorous fantasy fiction under a pen name) for whom seeing what is on the surface is believing, Kelcey initially finds it difficult to see what is in his imagination. But when he does accept his waiting role, anticipating the future, faith in the myths is restored and history can begin again. Kelcey contemplates the past as his wife takes off for the future.

Morris draws on the Great Plains myths, especially Manifest Destiny and the theories of the westward course of civilization, to frame Kelcey's vision of plains history: "From the bluffs of the Missouri, looking west, the plains had once been an inland sea. Somehow they looked inviting. An illusion. All of that waving grass was nothing but a beachhead to the towering Rockies, and beyond the Rockies the infernos of sea-level valleys. Hell on earth. Why do so many dreams come out of such places?" (54). Transforming space into place, putting it on a map, constitutes the beginning of history and society. Plains people find that the land overwhelms them into speechlessness or inspires them to build rockets. Has it been worth it? In an article entitled "Time Warp" that Kelcey discovers in the library, Dahlberg wonders:

Everything in the state, once it became a state, or in the unmapped regions west of the Missouri, had a beginning as clearly defined as the heavens and the earth in scripture. One day it wasn't there at all: the next day it was "discovered." The writer asks in passing, "Was the discovery of America a mistake?" The systematic looting, polluting, exploiting, followed on the "discovery" as night follows day. That marked the beginning. The trapper and his traps, the wagon trains headed for the goldfields. Was it a beginning to be celebrated or an ending to be mourned? (87–88)

It is a question we will always ask about the Great Plains.

CHAPTER SEVEN

The Unifying Thread:
Connecting Place and Language

Leonard Lutwack, in his study *The Role of Place in Literature*, points out that, like sounds in poetry, the physical qualities of place must be made to seem appropriate and symbolic. The writer uses language to establish the meaning of place. Even the most ordinary places take on symbolic meaning when they become associated with themes and tones (34). Although the relationship between land and language is not unique to Great Plains fiction, the vast plains' expanses force writers to create meaning from an apparent void. What one writer "sees" and what another says may not always seem congruent. As John Milton points out, "Preconditioning, memory, temporary frame of mind, the attitude brought to the landscape, the degree of comfort of the observer, the point of view or position within the landscape – these are factors in the observation and interpretation of landscape and what it evokes" (56). For Willa Cather, these factors coalesced, and she made her own unique connection between words and place as she wrote her second novel, *O Pioneers!* "Here there was no arranging or inventing; everything was spontaneous and took its own place, right or wrong. This was like taking a ride through a familiar country on a horse that knew the way, on a fine morning when you felt like riding" (*Willa Cather On Writing* 91).

In their comments on the writer's craft Cather and Morris address the unique challenge Great Plains authors face. Cather expresses her frustration over the problem of control in her introduction to *The Song of the Lark*. Cather felt that her prose got out of control in the later parts of the novel – when Thea, who has succeeded as an opera star, is in the richer world of art and culture, far from simple Moonstone – and that she overwrote the novel (it grew to almost six hundred pages). She explains her purpose and, by implication, her problem: *The Song of the Lark* "set out to tell of an artist's awakening and struggle; . . . it should have been content to do that. I should have disregarded conventional design and stopped where my first conception stopped. . . . What I cared about, and still care about, was the girl's escape; the play of blind chance, the way in which commonplace occurrences fell together to liberate her from commonness" (ix). In a sense, Cather is admitting that she, like Thea, cannot wholly rid herself of Moonstone, Colorado, or Red Cloud, Nebraska. It is the common place that she wants to convey in her prose.

In Morris's *The Home Place*, Clyde Muncy explains the plainsman's focus on the deceptively simple surface: "I tell you, these crude looking people are delicate. They're soft when it comes to real vulgarity. I'd say the whole myth of the city slicker is built around that softness, and the fear they have of this complicated kind of indecency. They take a man at his face value, as they figure it's his own face, a fairly private affair, and the only one he has" (35). Morris is saying here that this focus on the surface is not a fault or a frivolous literary convention but a deliberate result of the sparse nature of what he calls the raw material. Nor does this emphasis on the surface of things spring from an ignorance of their deeper significance, as Morris says near the end of *The Home Place*, when Clyde tries to connect things and their meanings:

For thirty years I've had a clear idea of what the home place lacked, and why the old man pained me, but I've never really known what they had. I know now. But I haven't the word for it. The word beauty is not a Protestant thing. It doesn't describe what there is about an old man's shoes. The Protestant word for that is character. . . . Perhaps all I'm saying is that character can be a form of passion, and that some things, these things, have that kind of character. (141–43)

Morris's careful choice of common words and familiar clichés underlines his point: these qualities of frugality, these time-worn things, are symbols, not of poverty or hardship, banal materialism or a mean existence, but of deep-rooted character traits.[1]

Not surprisingly, writers return again and again to the same images and metaphors. One of the most pervasive of these prairie metaphors, that of the prairie as ocean, can illustrate this relationship between place and prose. It is a rare plains writer who does not invoke the image of the sea of grass, and a rare critic or observer who does not comment upon its ubiquity.[2] Why this recurring comparison? One obvious factor is the space itself. Milton points out that while the initial perception of a landscape is a simple visual act, it is often followed by a complex of reactions, including the remembrance of previously seen landscapes (56). The undulating, palpable emptiness and the absence of landmarks force observers to describe the vast spaces before them in the only terms they know. There are more important symbolic similarities: both the prairie and the ocean can give a bountiful harvest of fish or grain, and both can destroy tiny ships and towns with capricious storms. Both present a featureless face of indifference, a sense of eternal possibility, or annihilating isolation that can lead to madness. In yet another sense the image is ironic. The prairie begs for water: the life-giving element that threatens to destroy men at sea is withheld on the prairie, with the same ultimate possibility. As a result, both voyagers and settlers must come to terms with water on the ocean or the prairie: the resulting layers have become not merely metaphors but archetypal symbols.

By the time men and women began to write fictional accounts of the Great Plains, the image had become a conscious metaphor. Rølvaag, drawing on his years as a fisherman in his native land, weaves the familiar images into the opening pages of *Giants in the Earth:* "The track that [the caravan] left behind was like the wake of a boat – except that instead of widening out astern it closed in again" (3). The cow at the end of the wagon is "the rudder of the caravan" (5). They are advancing "deeper and deeper into a bluish-green infinity" (16). Per Hansa uses his watch, the sun, and the stars – mariners' tools – to take his bearings (7).

The symbol persists in contemporary plains fiction. For example, in *Beyond the Bedroom Wall*, Woiwode uses the image to describe the immigrant Otto Neumiller's first reaction to the "virgin Dakota plain, as limitless as the sea to look upon. . . . 'At first I didn't think there was such a place, seeing so much timber in Minnesota, but once I came across the Red River, I could feel the current of its waves' " (26). Dan O'Brien suggests that the ocean of grass gives Europeans "the feeling they are floating, unable to reach anything familiar" and that the feeling "tends to drive people crazy" (3).

On the Great Plains the land is full of sharp contrasts: sudden changes in weather, from hot to cold, wet to dry; a flat horizon cut by vertical grain elevators or isolated trees; bustling towns, isolated farms. The region's most persistent metaphors – the garden and the desert – reflect these climatic extremes. The first impression is often of the desert, ironically reflected in the ocean metaphor: a treeless, arid land, inhabited by dull people who live isolated lives on scattered farms or in sterile small-town societies. The garden, a metaphor that recurs even more frequently than the ocean motif, is an image of the future, the promise of the soil's hidden fertility, the gradual appreciation of a simple life on the land. These contraries exist together in both time and space and so provide the symbols and a frequent source of conflict in Great Plains fiction.

While the influence of place upon metaphor and symbol is obvious, the relationship between place and language is more difficult to establish. When writers use words to evoke images of space and climate, the words accumulate connotations and patterns that help to define a specific place. The way an author views the reality of place will control the language he or she uses. When a writer tries to describe a place with only two seasons and no rain, even the words dry up. Most Great Plains writing is direct and plain, and thus it is often dismissed as facile or simple-minded. The reasons for this plain style are in part historical, in part the result of literary tradition. Yankee and European immigrants who settled on open land – where, as Morris says, the sky's the limit – believed that a person could succeed no matter what the speaker's linguistic sophistication. Although settlers valued learning, out of necessity their schools emphasized essentials. It was important to understand and to be understood, especially for the immigrant, but learning for the sake of grace or style took workers away from more important tasks. They valued and encouraged concise, direct prose. The style of Great Plains writing reflects this conservatism as well as the writers' visions of plains space. Where the emphasis is on physical labor, words must be chosen carefully, even as physical energy, time, and money must be conserved. No need for three words when one will suffice.

Passages from works by three writers who were separated by time and by place can serve as models for analysis of some essential stylistic features of Great Plains fiction. These novels focus on the artist, the sensitive individual who is isolated from the commonplace. Like other isolates in Great Plains literature, Cather's Thea Kronborg, Ross's Mrs. Bentley, and Morris's Clyde Muncy symbolize the authors' awareness of the struggle to reconcile place and character. All three novelists establish their characters' separation through lengthy descriptions of towns that reveal some of the essential qualities of the language of Great Plains fiction.

The first passage is from *The Song of the Lark*. In the first section,

"Friends of Childhood," Cather uses the omniscient narrator to recount Thea's childhood in Moonstone, Colorado:

Seen from a balloon, Moonstone would have looked like a Noah's Ark town set out in the sand and lightly shaded by grey-green tamarisks and cotton-woods. A few people were trying to make soft maples grow in their turfed lawns, but the fashion of planting incongruous trees from the North Atlantic States had not become general then, and the frail, brightly painted desert town was shaded by the light-reflecting, wind-loving trees of the desert, whose roots are always seeking water and whose leaves are always talking about it, making the sound of rain. The long, porous roots of the cottonwood are irrepressible. They break into the well as rats do into granaries, and thieve the water. The long street which connected Moonstone with the depot settlement traversed in its course a considerable stretch of rough open country staked out in lots, but not built up at all, a weedy hiatus between the town and the railroad. When you set out along this street to go to the station, you noticed that the houses became smaller and farther apart, until they ceased altogether, and the board sidewalk continued its uneven course through sunflower patches, until you reached the solitary, new brick Catholic Church. The Church stood there because the land was given to the parish by the man who owned the adjoining waste lots, in the hope of making them more saleable – "Farrier's Addition," this patch of prairie was called in the clerk's office. An eighth of a mile beyond the church was a washout, a deep sand gully, where the board sidewalk became a bridge for per-haps fifty feet. (46–47)

In this passage Cather invites the reader into the story, to walk down the board sidewalk. Seen from above, Moonstone is a toy town on the vast landscape. Between the main town and the railroad, the link to the world, the town almost melts into the land, a "weedy hiatus." At the washout, the gully, someone has had to build a bridge in order to force a connection that will maintain the link between community and the outside world. Arklike in the painted desert, the town is protected by the shade of native trees.

This natural landscape invigorates Thea, who finds the society of Moonstone, in contrast, as shriveled and dry as the desert winds (32–40).

The second passage is from Ross's novel *As for Me and My House*. Here there is not an omniscient narrator but Mrs. Bentley, a lonely and frustrated minister's wife, and the form is a diary in which she records the failure of her marriage, a result of her frustrations with her role in the small prairie town of Horizon and with her husband's religious hypocrisy and hidden artistic nature. The passage occurs early in the novel, so that despite the undercurrent of fear that reflects her disaffection with her physical and social situations, her bitterness has not yet clouded her objectivity entirely:

I turned and looked back at Horizon, the huddled little clutter of houses and stores, the five grain elevators, aloof and imperturbable, like ancient obelisks, and behind, the dust clouds, lapping at the sky.

It was like one of Philip's drawings. There was the same tension, the same vivid immobility, and behind it all somewhere the same sense of transience.

I walked on, remembering how I used to think that only a great artist could ever paint the prairie, the vacancy and stillness of it, the bare essentials of a landscape, sky and earth, and how I used to look at Philip's work, and think to myself that the world would some day know of him.

I turned for home at the ravine where we sat in the snowstorm just a month ago. A freight train overtook me, and someone waved a towel from the caboose. When the clatter died away I sat down on a pile of ties to rest a few minutes. . . . The dust clouds behind the town kept darkening and thinning and swaying, a furtive tirelessness about the way they wavered and merged with one another that reminded me of northern lights in winter. It was like a quivering backdrop, before which was about to be enacted some grim, primeval tragedy. The little town cowered close to earth as if to hide itself. The elevators stood up, passive, stoical. All around me ran a hurrying little whisper through the grass. I waited there till nearly suppertime. (59)

Like Cather's Moonstone, Ross's town is a "huddled little clutter"; in fact Ross uses the word *transience*, the feeling that many Great Plains authors attempt to evoke in their descriptions of place. Ross's description is harsher than Cather's, where the town is replaced for a distance by colorful sunflower patches. Ross uses the image of dust clouds "like a quivering backdrop" to convey the vacancy and stillness, the bare essentials of sky and earth, that threaten to engulf the town. Where other writers use metaphors of the sea to symbolize the uncertain continuation of human existence, Ross uses dust.

In Ross's work, space is quite literally nothing. The passing train is only a freight carrying things, not people. There is no ark to shelter the town that huddles and cowers. In Mrs. Bentley's eyes, the false fronts are symbols of the residents of Horizon, who present a hypocritical façade to the town, especially to the preacher and his wife, which they reciprocate. The dust clouds not only forebode physical tragedy but reflect the narrator's state of mind as well: the land is largely the source of her depression and impending personal tragedy. In this passage Mrs. Bentley is talking to herself, unconscious of her reader-listener. The focus is on her, and on her indifferent husband, Philip. She is alone physically and emotionally with her inner thoughts, and the heavy use of first-person pronouns reflects this self-absorption.

The final passage is from *The Home Place*, narrated by Clyde Muncy, one of Morris's self-effacing narrators. Like Morris himself, Clyde views the plains with a trace of irony that gives emphasis to his literal and metaphorical images:

When the old man first came to the plains there was a rolling sea of grass, and a lone tree, so the story goes, where they settled the town. They put up a few stores, facing the west and the setting sun like so many tombstones, which is quite a bit what a country store has in mind. You have the high, flat slab at the front, with a few lines of fading inscription, and then the sagging mound of these stores, the contents, in the shadow behind. Later, if the town lasts, they put through some tracks, with a water tank for the whistle stop, and if it rained, now and then, they'd put up the monument. That's the way these elevators,

these great plains monoliths, strike me. There's a simple reason for grain elevators, as there is for everything, but the force behind the reason, the reason for
the reason, is the land and the sky. There's too much sky out here, for one
thing, too much horizontal, too many lines without stops, so that the exclamation, the perpendicular, had to come. Anyone who was born and raised on the
plains knows that the high false front on the Feed Store, and the white water
tower, are not a question of vanity. It's a problem of being. Of knowing you are
there. On a good day, with a slanting sun, a man can walk to the edge of his
town and see the light on the next town, ten miles away. In the sea of corn, that
flash of light is like a sail. It reminds a man the place is still inhabited. I know
what it is Ishmael felt, or Ahab, for that matter – these are the whales of the
great sea of grass. (76)

Morris, like Cather, addresses the reader directly, inviting the reader to
view the slab front of the country store. He wants the reader to know what
is on the surface.

Ironically, the town is created in images of death. The stores of the new
town look like tombstones; the country store, like the slab and mound of a
grave. But Morris also points up the striking contrast of nature's horizontal
and man-made vertical: The false fronts and the water tower are proofs of
being. The elevator provides an exclamation point: we are here. This is not
a mere gesture, a casual wave of a towel from a train, but an attempt to
change space: "[I]t reminds a man that the place is still inhabited." Morris
directly asserts the influence of the land: humans invent vertical lines to
counteract horizontal space. Without such symbols, Morris believes, man
would be lost in the flat, unshaded landscape. The passage ends with yet
another variation on the ocean metaphor, evoking specifically the nameless
terror of the great white whale that threatens to surface not only in seas of
water but in seas of grass as well; the sail or the elevator signifies the failure
to completely engulf humanity.

The images in these passages, described in deceptively simple words, reveal an important element of Great Plains prose: like dust, they accumu-

late. Even in these three brief passages images recur: the sea, the town, the elevator, the train, the store, the trees. One might assume that in a landscape supposedly bereft of concrete detail authors would merely describe again and again what *is* there, and yet it is clear that Cather, Ross, and Morris mean for these objects to represent more than what is on the surface. Their images are of fragile, transient human existence. The familiar ocean metaphor serves two of them, and in all three the depot and the train symbolize a weak link to civilization. But the human connection to space is the focus of these descriptions. In Great Plains fiction, men and women must first come to terms with the land.

In all three passages these tenuous clusters are tied to civilization by the slim thread of the railroad. The depot at the edge of Cather's town, the casual wave of greeting to Ross's Mrs. Bentley from a passing caboose, the tracks, tank, and whistle stop that signal permanence in Morris's Lone Tree – all affirm the existence of these places engulfed in space. For these novelists and other Great Plains writers, the train is a recurring symbol. It is a link to the outside, a provider of goods and employment, proof that the town itself has a reason to be, and, perhaps most important, a means of leaving the dust, the wind, and the horizontal. In *The Song of the Lark*, Thea's friend Ray Kennedy, a railroad man, is killed in a train wreck, and his insurance policy, naming Thea as beneficiary, ironically provides the means for her to leave Moonstone – by train. In Morris's fiction, the depot, the track, and the sometimes violent collision between man and machine are persistent symbols of the sharp distinctions between the bucolic plains town frozen in the past and the intrusive modern machine.[3] To Ross's Mrs. Bentley, trains that come and go represent an escape, however brief, from the stifling town society. In another incident in *As for Me and My House*, Mrs. Bentley and a friend hitch a ride on a handcar and pull up at the station just as the ladies are leaving the tea from which she has excused herself, feigning illness. The scene is a brief instance of comic relief in Ross's grim novel.

The transient train is not the symbolic center of these and other Great

Plains novels. The raw material is the land, the source of the most persistent symbols in Great Plains fiction, and, more specifically, the life-giving water. In Cather's description, the cottonwoods boring deep into the soil symbolize what man must do to persevere. If he insists on transplanting not only trees but also attitudes about what is appropriate for this land, he will shrivel and die as surely as the turfed lawns and incongruous trees will die in summer's heat. Like cottonwoods and thieving rats, plains inhabitants must learn to derive their subsistence from the land's hidden resources. For Morris, the water tower and the elevator, symbols of life-giving water and food, remind man that he is there, existing. In Ross's novel, the dust, a result of the absence of water, threatens to obliterate everything as surely as a storm at sea would sink a ship.

Great Plains writers draw upon other distinctive characteristics of the plains and prairies. They create isolated, barren farmyards, sod houses buried in the ground, and flat towns hidden by trees or lost in space to contrast small man with the immensity of nature. Ross and Morris use the grain elevator, and Cather the church, as indicators of human presence. While Cather's church, new and solitary, provides a simple note of optimism, the elevator is more problematic. In Ross's passage, the elevator, aloof and impenetrable, rises like an obelisk to a faded civilization. To Morris, it is a monolith that symbolizes human presence. Only a passing reference in Ross's novel, it is a persistent symbol for Morris, just as the cottonwood is for Cather. In Morris's view, the elevator symbolizes human attempts to control the horizontal, which threatens to flatten not only the horizon but men and women as well.

To evoke these images and describe this featureless landscape, a Great Plains style has developed, a subset of the plain prose style that is evident throughout American literature. Although other writers are just as adept at creating scenes with a minimum of words, Great Plains novelists consciously, and perhaps ironically, focus on the minimum to reveal the deeper significance of the apparently empty setting. In her essay "The Novel Démeublé," Cather spoke of her attempt to write the "unfurnished novel." As

Morris has explained, in Lone Tree the appropriate details "settled into their places, their roles, as icons: a hotel, a lone tree, a railroad, a cattle loader. These artifacts constituted 'the scene' in the way movable props located a Western movie. . . . It is the emotion that is strong, not the details" (Knoll 154–55). Bird points out that Morris's plain prose style and his use of clichés parallel his use of the commonplace and the past: "[I]t is a self-conscious struggle to transform the raw materials of experience through the power of imagination. Unavoidably, one distorts the experience by attempting to render it in words" (Bird 64–65).[4]

Word choice and sentence structure in the three passages quoted above are remarkably similar. Cather's images of trees and street are sustained by simple, concrete words – strings of adjectives ("the frail, brightly painted desert town . . . shaded by the light-reflecting, wind-loving trees"), appositives ("a washout, a deep sand gully"), restrictive phrases ("the long street which connected Moonstone with the depot settlement"), and concrete subjects and verbs ("moonstone looked," "people were trying," "the town was shaded," "the church stood").

Ross's prose reflects the narrator's journal form. Some paragraphs are only one sentence long. He uses parallel structure ("the same tension, the same vivid immobility . . . the same sense of transience"), clauses ("remembering how I used to think . . . and how I used to look"), and appositives ("Horizon, the huddled little clutter of houses and stores") to draw out sentences that reflect the narrator's meditations on the town and her husband. He ties the short paragraphs together by repeating the same subject-verb pattern in five sentences – "I turned and looked," "I walked on," "I turned for home," "I sat down," "I waited." Ross's sentences start abruptly and focus on the narrator, *I*. Oxymorons such as "vivid invisibility" underline the narrator's embittered statements and contradictory emotions. Even single words can pile up meaning in Ross's prose. The word *behind* gains force with repetition and near references. The dust clouds are behind: they obscure the town, the people, the land, and ultimately life itself. Repeated twice, this image of dust behind the village adds to the portrait of the cowering, stoical town.

Morris's description of Lone Tree seems more loosely written than the other two examples. He begins six sentences with *there, that,* or *it,* words that have no clear antecedents. Four sentences begin with introductory clauses or phrases – "In the sea of corn," "On a good day." He interrupts his sentences with conversational tags – "now and then," "as there is for everything" – and with other devices that separate subject and verb or delay both until the end of the sentence. The effect of all this is that when the parts come together, they have greater weight. The first sentence in the passage illustrates all these devices. There is an introductory clause ("When the old man first came to the plains"), an expletive and verb ("there was"), and a conversational interrupter ("so the story goes") before the long-delayed point of the sentence, namely, "where they settled the town." He repeats this rambling pattern in other sentences: "Anyone who was born and raised on the plains knows that the high false front on the Feed Store, and the white water tower, are not a question of vanity." Morris uses these devices repeatedly, just as Cather gathers layers of long descriptions into her orderly sentences.

Great Plains writers draw most of their images and symbols from what is there – lone trees, trains, towns, elevators, water towers, windmills, houses, barns, and the patchwork of farm fields. Images are held together by comparisons and allusions. Ross uses similes to compare grain elevators to obelisks, the town to a painting, the dust to the northern lights. Cather's similes are of Noah's Ark and trees that are thieving rats. Morris compares stores to tombstones and elevators to monuments, sails on the sea, or whales in a sea of grass. The vast emptiness moves Cather to personify the trees, with talking leaves and robber roots, and Ross to give human qualities to the ironically named town of Horizon itself, as it huddles and cowers, and to the passive, stoical grain elevators.

Sparse conversational language reveals the author's democratic view of society. Simple, concrete language unifies a society, because it is accessible to everyone. We know how Mrs. Bentley, Clyde Muncy, and Cather the narrator feel about their towns and about their place in society. Although Morris's narrator, writer Clyde Muncy, has been living in New York, he can converse with his Aunt Clara and the codgers in the barber shop with an easy familiarity because he was born in Lone Tree. As long as he speaks plainly, how long he has been gone and where he has been are immaterial in the town. Individuals, whether in conversation or narration, focus on the scene before them or the task to be completed. Philosophical speculations on good and evil, social niceties, and class distinctions are insignificant against the reality of a landscape created from space.

The deceptively simple prose gathers emotional power from accumulated detail until the image, the attending metaphor, and the deeper symbol become apparent. This language is an especially fitting vehicle for expressing values. In Great Plains fiction, work is the primary purpose, and the source of one's reward is satisfaction with the effort, not in material gain. Work leaves little time for idle chatter or rambling tales. To underline this fundamental Great Plains attitude, characters are often suspicious of words or ideas that do not reflect practical reality.

The image of space scarcely touched by natural or man-made landmarks often becomes a part of the motivation in Great Plains novels. Characters are drawn to the open spaces or repelled by them. The resulting conflict causes events to occur or not occur. *Things* take on significance beyond their actual value for the characters because they bring relief from the stifling, concrete town and annihilating, abstract space. In *The Song of the Lark*, Thea values the German tailor Fritz Kohler's tapestry as a representation of a fantastic world of color unimaginable in Moonstone. While Thea realizes fulfillment in music, Mrs. Bentley in *As for Me and My House* finds in music a retreat that symbolizes her unfulfilled sexual desire, just as her husband's bleak drawings reveal his deep aversion to the town and to his wife. In *The Home Place* and *The World in the Attic*, Clyde Muncy searches for symbols of the past that he is trying to recreate for his children. But simple things – a rug, a rocker, a pair of overalls – have collected smells and shapes that cannot be lightly cast aside. All of these images that become symbols are drawn from the surface of the world, an empty space that men and women fill with objects that reveal intricate relationships and conflicts.

The important point, finally, is not the simple language or the stark prairie landscape. Nor is it merely the recognition that commonalities exist. Similarities could arise from an endless stream of imitation. Certainly, literary tradition influences these writers even as they work to create language from what they *see*. But in Great Plains fiction the common elements that inform symbols and images, language, attitudes, and values arise from the land itself and from the emotional significance that people assign to place. As Wright Morris has said, it is emotion that generates image-making, it is emotion that processes memory of place and experience. The language of a prairie or plains novel springs from that memory of the region, not from imitation or convention. Like the land itself, the intricate design seems too simple even to be noticed, but each tiny detail reaches into the past to reveal the common design. Taken as a whole, Great Plains fiction is a web of intricate connections of land, society, myth, and reality.

Notes

INTRODUCTION

1. For discussions of early mythic conceptions of the West, see Baritz; and Vigil.

2. Scholars have used a variety of terms to refer to this mythic sense. Marx uses the term *cultural symbol* (4). Kolodny uses *fantasy* (*The Land before Her* 10). Smith uses the terms *myth* and *symbol* to designate, respectively, the larger and smaller intellectual constructions. Here *myth* refers to the intellectual context of experience and is not a cultural descriptor but a prescriptor that may influence one's perception of reality.

3. Smith's work drew together scholarship on the American West from the first half of the twentieth century and spurred scholarly interest in the Great Plains. See Bucco 1304–5; and Erisman 312–15.

4. Dorothy Dondore's pioneering study, *The Prairie and the Making of Middle America* (1926), is the earliest and still a most thorough survey of early Great Plains literature. See also Marx; Meyer; Smith; and Thacker.

1. For the cultural geographer's delineation of the region, see Shortridge, *The Middle West* 16–24, 124–33; idem, "Vernacular Middle West"; and idem, "Vernacular Regions in Kansas" 73–79.

2. For a discussion of the early European mythic images, see Jones, chaps. 1 and 2; Nash, chap. 1; and Thacker 38–39.

3. Dates in the text refer to the original publication date. All page references are to the edition cited in the bibliography unless otherwise noted.

4. Kollmorgen uses *woodsman* and Webb uses *timber dwellers* to refer to these migrants. See Hudson, "Who Was 'Forest Man'?" 70.

5. Stouck points out that Grove evidently read both *Giants in the Earth* and *Peder Victorious* (*Major Canadian Authors* 61).

6. Kolodny explores the virginal, pastoral myth and the sexual implications of the effort to cultivate the land in *The Lay of the Land* (1975). Although for the most part she discusses literature that predates most Great Plains fiction, her theories have implications for any discussion of landscape in American literature.

7. A number of critics have examined the mythic and psychological implications of Alexandra's dream. See Daiches 27; Moseley, "Dual Nature" 96; Motley, "The Unfinished Self"; and Murphy.

8. See Luebke; and Shortridge, "Heart of the Prairie" 206–21 for extended discussions of these cultural patterns.

9. For discussions of the small town, see Atherton, *Main Street on the Middle Border;* Emmons; and Hine, *Community on the American Frontier.*

10. In the 1870s, writers such as Joseph Kirkland and Edward Eggleston codified some of the themes that Garland, Howe, and later Great Plains writers use. See Quantic.

11. This theme is especially evident in *The Song of the Lark, One of Ours, Lucy Gayheart*, and "The Sculptor's Funeral."

12. For a study of the railroad's influence on town building, see Hudson's *Plains Country Towns*, esp. chaps. 5 and 6; and Miller.

13. For discussions of the relationships among the women that surround Cora and Sharon Rose, see Bird; and Waldeland.

2 THE LURE OF THE WEST

1. In the early 1980s, speculation and inflation increased prices of Great Plains farmland to record highs, and there was a predictable increase in farm foreclosures. The situation resulted in Farm Aid concerts and movies such as *Country* and the nostalgic Depression-era *Places in the Heart.* Jane Smiley's Iowa tragedy, *A Thousand Acres,* is set in this period of deceptive prosperity.

2. Other scholars have commented on this relationship between seeing and expectation. See Lamar; and Lowenthal.

3. The range of responses to the wilderness in Canadian plains fiction is similar in many respects to American reactions. See Francis, esp. chaps. 1 and 2, esp. 9–11, 32–35, 42–44, 57–58; and Owram.

4. For a thorough discussion of Boone, see Slotkin.

5. For a discussion of Jefferson's motivation, see DeVoto xxix–xxxiii; and Moulton, Introduction 2–3.

6. For a summary of the historical background and significance of the journey, see Moulton, Introduction 1–48; and DeVoto.

7. Unless stated otherwise, quotations are from Moulton's edition of *The Journals of Lewis and Clark.*

8. See Allen for a summary of the impact of Lewis and Clark on America's conception of the Great Plains.

9. For discussion of Cooper's use of landscape, see esp. Elliott; McWilliams; Mitchell, *Witnesses to a Vanishing America,* esp. 43–47; Motley, *The American Abraham* 108; Suderman; and Thacker, esp. 105–15.

10. Most critics see this question of law and society as the primary theme in *The Prairie.* See Adams; Elliott; Kelly; McWilliams; and Motley, *The American Abraham.*

11. Numerous scholars have analyzed the legal implications of *The Prairie.* See Adams; Kelly; and Motley, *The American Abraham.*

12. For an account of the party, see McDermott, "Washington Irving as Western Traveler."

13. Unless stated otherwise, quotations from *A Tour on the Prairies* and other references to it are to *The Crayon Miscellany*.

14. The rough country and the lateness of the season defeats Irving's party in their effort to reach the Great Western Prairie and the Texas border (80–81).

3 LEARNING TO LIVE ON THE LAND

1. The frontiersman myth is male-dominant. When the focus shifts from the frontier to permanent settlements, the female experience becomes more important.

2. Here and below, unbracketed ellipses are Rølvaag's.

3. The title is taken from Genesis 6:4: "The Nephilim [giants] were on the earth in those days; and also after that, when the sons of God came in to the daughters of men, and they bore children to them. These were the mighty men that were of old, the men of renown" (Revised Standard Version). The title and the biblical reference are ambiguous enough to refer either to the forces in the earth itself or to the "mighty men" who challenged those forces. The implication is that physical union will create a new superhuman race.

4. The tone of White's sentimental tale "The Homecoming of Colonel Hucks" approaches Garland's bucolic tone in this story. Cather's "Neighbour Rosicky," while it echoes Garland's hope, originates in very different themes and circumstances. Rosicky contemplates the end of a full life, while Rob looks ahead.

5. Recent critics have demonstrated that the garden is an integral part of Cather's intention. See Bailey; Baker; and Rosowski, "Willa Cather and the Fatality of Place."

6. Recent research among orphan-train survivors points up the persistence of this myth. See Jackson.

7. It is this Eastern point of view and set of explanations that control the women's accounts of the West that Kolodny examines in *The Land before Her*.

8. Rosowski believes that these pictures represent a "passage from brute to human sensibility" and that the context is "richly symbolic of the immigrant's spiritual confrontation with the plains" ("Willa Cather's Plains Legacy" 61).

9. In another context, Simonson suggests that for Beret the frontier is where "human beings faced unknown things about themselves" and where the "inner landscape of the mind" requires a different courage (*Prairies Within* 7). See also Farmer 186, 191; and Reigstad, esp. 65, 74–75, 87, 117–19.

4 THE DREAM DEFERRED

1. For a comment on the apparent inconsistencies in Caleb's death, see Keith.

2. In *A Thousand Acres*, Jane Smiley creates the patriarch Larry Cook, a Lear-like man who, like Caleb Gare, tyrannizes his family and isolates them from their community. Larry Cook lacks Caleb's fanatical commitment to the land itself.

3. Stauffer points out that Sandoz wrote *Slogum House* as "an allegorical study of a domineering nation using force to overcome opposition" (112; see also Rippey).

4. Woodress (*Willa Cather: Her Life and Art* 435) and Stouck (*Willa Cather's Imagination* 213) point out that Rosicky is modeled after the husband of Annie Pavelka, the model for Ántonia. Writing soon after her father's death, when her mother's health was declining, Cather was looking back with some nostalgia (Rowsowski, *Voyage Perilous* 438; Woodress, *Willa Cather: A Literary Life* 438. See also Arnold 135).

5. Harrison points out that what attracts Gander is work and machines, not any romantic sensitivity for the land (104), and that it is the machine that emasculates him (105–7). It is not by accident that he leaves the farm to work in a garage.

6. Many novels that have been mentioned in other contexts explore this melting-pot myth, among them Bojer, *The Emigrants;* Cather, *My Ántonia* and *The Song of the Lark;* Lindsay, *Shukar Balan: The White Lamb;* Moberg, *Unto a Good Land* (1954), *The Settlers* (1961), and *Last Letter Home* (1961); Rølvaag, *Giants in the Earth, Peder Victorious*, and *Their Father's God;* Sykes, *Second Hoeing;* Wiebe, *Peace Shall Destroy Many;* and Winther, *Take All to Nebraska* and *Mortgage Your Heart*. Erdrich's stories of Indians and whites, *Love Medicine, Beet Queen* (1986), and *Tracks* (1988), add another element to the ethnic mix trying to adapt to each other and to the plains.

7. Publishers' readers objected to Sandoz's unsympathetic portrait of her father. Furthermore, as Sandoz pointed out, critics and readers, reacting to the violence

and harshness of the story, "didn't believe that a frontier still existed fifty years ago" (quoted in Stauffer 98).

8. Morten Kvidal carries a similar image of a European ideal with him in Bojer's *The Emigrants*.

9. This longing for home seems to be most apparent in the Scandinavian novels of Rølvaag, Bojer, and Moberg. Lindsay's and Wiebe's German-Russians, who had remained separate from Russian society for a hundred years, have little nostalgia for the bleak land and society they abandoned. Moreover, members of these communities emigrated in large numbers, leaving few behind to mourn, and created close communities on the plains of Kansas or Saskatchewan.

10. This same mix of people – a new society – gathers at Ruedy Slogum's refuge in Sandoz's *Slogum House*.

5 THE ENCLOSED GARDEN

1. See Bredahl for a thorough analysis of "surface" and enclosure in Western literature.

2. The six original stories in *Main-Travelled Roads* are "A Branch Road," "Up the Coolly," "Among the Corn Rows," "The Return of a Private," "Under the Lion's Paw," and "Mrs. Ripley's Trip."

3. Garland blamed the unchecked rise of capitalism for many of the farmer's problems. He wrote the first stories in *Main Travelled Roads* at the height of his advocacy of the philosophy of Herbert Spencer as articulated by Henry George, who advocated a single tax that would discourage speculation by taxing land not on the basis of improvements but on the basis of the value of the surrounding land. See Pizer, *Hamlin Garland's Early Work*, esp. 37–41, or idem, "Herbert Spencer and the Genesis of Hamlin Garland's Critical System."

4. Stouck points out that Hagar is the captive exile, blind to herself and to the needs of others (*Major Canadian Authors* 245); Harrison agrees (194). See also Hales; Rooke; and Williams.

5. In *Peder Victorious*, Rølvaag focuses on the developing community. Without the force of myth and fairy tale behind the epic struggle, this novel and the final novel in the trilogy, *Their Fathers' God*, lack the classic proportions of *Giants in the*

Earth. Still, these two volumes offer one of the most complete accounts in American literature of the immigrants' struggle to establish farms and a viable society on the Great Plains.

6. For widely varying views of Beret, see Blegen; Reigstad; and Simonson, *Prairies Within*.

7. Gabrielsen is one of Rølvaag's "false ministers"; he advocates abandoning the past without replacing it with firmly rooted goals and virtues. In *Their Fathers' God*, Gabrielsen's opposite is Reverend Kaldahl, who stoutly defends everything Norwegian. If Norwegians are to prosper in America, he says, "we must do it as Norwegians" (209).

8. In the novel this quote is set in Old English script.

9. For a discussion of Ibsen's influence on Rølvaag, see Reigstad 33; and Simonson, *Prairies Within* 34–35, 46.

10. A number of critics have analyzed St. Peter's multiple houses, both real and symbolic. See esp. Edel; for an analysis of Edel's criticism, see Gleason, esp. sec. 2, 281–88; and Woodress, *Willa Cather: A Literary Life* 369–70.

11. Stegner and his critics point out the autobiographical nature of *The Big Rock Candy Mountain*. See esp. Baurrecht; Robinson and Robinson 20–37; and Stegner and Etulain 41–63. In this sense, *Wolf Willow* complements the earlier novel. As other critics point out, both the novel and the memoir are about Western history and westering myths as well. See esp. Hudson, "*The Big Rock Candy Mountain*: No Roots – and No Frontier"; and Singer.

12. Most critics focus on Stegner's conscious effort in *Wolf Willow* to come to terms with time and space on the high plains. See Lois Phillips Hudson, "*The Big Rock Candy Mountain*: No Roots – No Frontier"; and Robertson.

6 AFLOAT ON THE SEA OF GRASS

1. Hazard's work, *The Frontier in American Literature*, and Dorothy Dondore's *The Prairie and the Making of Middle America* (1926) are the pioneering historical surveys of frontier literature. Less analytical than later studies, they nevertheless established a canon of frontier literature. See Etulain.

2. Worster shares this view. See *The Dust Bowl* and *Under Western Skies*, esp. chap. 1, "Beyond the Agrarian Myth."

3. See Bird for analysis of Morris's concept of this transformation.

4. Critics generally agree that the theme of *A Lost Lady* is this loss of the past. For an overview of the standard readings, see Love 150–59; Rosowski, "Willa Cather's *A Lost Lady*"; Stouck, *Willa Cather's Imagination;* and Woodress, *Willa Cather: A Literary Life*, esp. 348–51.

5. For an analysis of Marian Forrester's historical and symbolic significance, see Love; and Rosowski, "Willa Cather's *A Lost Lady*."

6. There is a specific tie between Fitzgerald and Cather's Great Plains novels. See Quirk; and Woodress, *Willa Cather: A Literary Life* 351–52.

7. The sequel, *Born Brothers* (1988), parallels and expands Charles's memoir, focusing on the contrast between his childhood memories and his adult relations with his more successful brother, Jerome. The novel ends with Charles's suicide.

8. Bird points out that by the time Morris wrote *Ceremony in Lone Tree* his "raw material" had sustained him through twenty-one novels and almost a dozen other books, all processing the same material in different contexts, from different points of view. For example, *Field of Vision* (1956) concerns most of the same characters and some of their same memories that we encounter in *Ceremony*.

9. For a discussion of the Wild West in *Ceremony in Lone Tree*, see Crump 146–47; and Hafer.

10. In December 1957 and January 1958 Starkweather left nine dead across Nebraska. The case forced Morris to reevaluate some of his raw material. In a conversation with John W. Aldridge, Morris commented, "[T]he Starkweather case occurred in a place and among people where it was almost pointless to use facile psychological explanations. It forced a reexamination of the clichés associated with violence. . . . What had been easily accepted became a problem" (Knoll 28–29).

11. Another reworking of his raw material, the character Jennings is the son of Will Brady, the central character in Morris's novel *The Works of Love.*

12. Critics see Boyd as a pivotal figure in the novel. See Bird; Crump; and Hafer.

7 THE UNIFYING THREAD

1. For a thorough analysis of Morris's use of cliché, see Bird, esp. 10–18.

2. In *The Great Prairie Fact*, Thacker traces this metaphor throughout his discussion. His index contains twenty citations under the entry "Prairie, likened to ocean" (297).

3. The death of Emil Bickel, who is struck by a train, recurs in three of Morris's novels – *The World in the Attic, Field of Vision,* and *Ceremony in Lone Tree*. Hafer points out that his obsessive use of this image is typical of events that "on the lonely Plains assume more than normal importance and are milked for any possible meaning or emotion." Violent events, Hafer points out, "are a form of continuity between past and present" (15).

4. For an analysis of the relationship between language and reality in Morris's fiction, see Bird, chap. 3.

Bibliography

The primary works listed below are intended as a complete list of the Great Plains fiction and nonfiction works that were significant to this study. The secondary works are limited to works cited in the text.

PRIMARY WORKS

Aldrich, Bess Streeter. *A Lantern in Her Hand*. New York: Appleton-Century, 1928.

——— *The Rim of the Prairie*. 1925. Reprint. Lincoln: U of Nebraska P, 1966.

——— *Spring Came On Forever*. 1935. Reprint. Lincoln: U of Nebraska P, 1985.

——— *A White Bird Flying*. 1931. Reprint. Lincoln: U of Nebraska P, 1988.

Averill, Thomas, ed. *What Kansas Means to Me: Twentieth-Century Writers on the Sunflower State*. Lawrence: UP of Kansas, 1991.

Berglund, Martha. *A Farm under a Lake*. St. Paul MN: Graywolf, 1989.

Bojer, Johan. *The Emigrants*. 1925. Reprint. Lincoln: U of Nebraska P, 1978.

Cather, Willa. *Collected Short Fiction, 1892–1912*. Lincoln: U of Nebraska P, 1965.

———— *A Lost Lady*. New York: Knopf, 1923.

———— *Lucy Gayheart*. 1935. Reprint. New York: Random House, 1976.

———— *My Ántonia*. Boston: Houghton Mifflin, 1918.

———— *Obscure Destinies*. 1932. Reprint. New York: Random House, 1974.

———— *One of Ours*. New York: Knopf, 1922.

———— *O Pioneers!* Boston: Houghton Mifflin, 1913.

———— *The Professor's House*. 1925. Reprint. New York: Random House, 1973.

———— *The Song of the Lark*. 1915. Reprint. Boston: Houghton Mifflin, 1963.

———— *Willa Cather on Writing*. New York: Knopf, 1940.

———— *Youth and the Bright Medusa*. 1920. Reprint. New York: Vintage, 1975.

Chandler, Edna Walker. *Chaff in the Wind*. WaKeeney KS: Harold Chandler, 1964.

Cooper, James Fenimore. *The Prairie*. 1827. Reprint. Edited by James Elliott. Albany: SUNY P, 1985.

Day, Robert. *Four Wheel Drive Quartet*. Sparks MD: Galileo, 1986.

———— *The Last Cattle Drive*. New York: Avon, 1977.

Erdrich, Louise. *The Beet Queen*. New York: Bantam, 1986.

———— *Love Medicine*. New York: Bantam, 1984.

———— *Tracks*. New York: Henry Holt, 1988.

Fitzgerald, F. Scott. *The Great Gatsby*. New York: Scribners, 1925.

Flint, Timothy. *Recollections of the Last Ten Years*. 1826. Reprint. New York: Da Capo, 1968.

Garland, Hamlin. *Boy Life on the Prairie*. New York: Macmillan, 1899.

———— *Daughter of the Middle Border*. New York: Macmillan, 1921.

———— *Jason Edwards*. Boston: Arena, 1892.

———— *Main-Travelled Roads*. 1891. Reprint. New York: Harper & Row, 1956.

———— *The Moccasin Ranch*. New York: Harper & Bros., 1909.

———— *Other Main-Travelled Roads*. New York: Harper & Bros., 1910.

———— *Rose of Dutcher's Coolly*. 1895. Reprint. Lincoln: U of Nebraska P, 1969.

———— *Son of the Middle Border*. New York: Macmillan, 1917.

———— *Wayside Courtships*. New York: Appleton, 1897.

Gregg, Josiah. *Commerce of the Prairies: A Selection.* Edited by David Freeman Hawke. New York: Bobbs-Merrill, 1970.

Grove, Frederick Philip. *Fruits of the Earth.* Toronto: J. M. Dent, 1933.

———*Settlers of the Marsh.* Toronto: Ryerson, 1925.

Haldeman-Julius, Mr., and Mrs. E. Haldeman-Julius. *Dust.* New York: Brentano's, 1921.

Hall, James. *Letters from the West.* 1828. Reprint. Gainesville FL: Scholars Facsimiles & Reprints, 1967.

Hansen, Ron. *Nebraska: Stories.* New York: Atlantic Monthly, 1989.

Haruf, Kent. *The Tie That Binds.* New York: Penguin, 1984.

Hasselstrom, Linda. *Going over East: Reflections of a Woman Rancher.* Golden CO: Fulcrum, 1987.

——— *Land Circle: Writings Collected from the Land.* Golden CO: Fulcrum, 1991.

——— *Windbreak: A Woman Rancher on the Northern Plains.* Berkeley: Barn Owl Books, 1987.

Heat-Moon, William Least. *Prairyerth.* New York: Houghton Mifflin, 1991.

Howe, Edgar Watson. *Plain People.* New York: Dodd, Mead, 1929.

——— *The Story of a Country Town.* 1883. Reprint. Cambridge: Harvard UP, 1961.

Hudson, Lois Phillips. *The Bones of Plenty.* 1962. Reprint. St. Paul: Minnesota Historical Society Press, 1984.

——— *Reapers of the Dust.* 1965. Reprint. St. Paul: Minnesota Historical Society Press, 1984.

Irving, Washington. *The Crayon Miscellany.* 1849. Reprint. Edited by Dahlia Kirby Terrell. Boston: Twayne, 1979.

——— *Letters.* Vol. 2, *1823–1838.* Edited by Ralph M. Aderman, Herbert L. Kleinfield, and Jenifer S. Banks. Boston: Twayne, 1979.

——— *The Western Journals of Washington Irving.* Edited by John F. McDermott. Norman: U of Oklahoma P, 1944.

Ise, John. *Sod and Stubble.* 1936. Reprint. Lincoln: U of Nebraska P, 1967.

Kimball, Phillip. *Harvesting Ballads.* New York: E. P. Dutton, 1984.

Kirkland, Caroline. *A New Home—Who'll Follow?* 1839. Reprint. Edited by William S. Osborne. New Haven CT: College & University Press, 1965.

Kroetsch, Robert. *Badlands*. 1975. Reprint. Toronto: General Publishing, 1982.

——— *The Studhorse Man*. New York: Simon & Schuster, 1969.

Larsen, Eric. *An American Memory*. Chapel Hill NC: Algonquin Books, 1988.

Laurence, Margaret. *A Bird in the House*. Toronto: McClelland & Stewart–Bantam, Seal Books, 1970.

——— *The Diviners*. 1974. Reprint. Toronto: McClelland & Stewart–Bantam, Seal Books, 1990.

——— *The Fire Dwellers*. 1969. Reprint. Toronto: McClelland & Stewart, 1990.

——— *A Jest of God*. 1966. Reprint. Toronto: McClelland & Stewart–Bantam, Seal Books, 1977.

——— *The Stone Angel*. 1964. Reprint. Toronto: McClelland & Stewart-Bantam, Seal Books, 1978.

Lewis, Meriwether, and William Clark. *The Journals of the Lewis and Clark Expedition*. Edited by Gary E. Moulton. 8 vols. to date. Lincoln: U of Nebraska P, 1983–.

Lewis, Sinclair. *Main Street*. New York: Harcourt Brace, 1921.

Lindsay, Mela Meisner. *Shukar Balan: The White Lamb*. Lincoln NE: American Historical Society of Germans from Russia, 1976.

Low, Ann Marie. *Dust Bowl Diary*. Lincoln: U of Nebraska P, 1984.

Manfred, Frederick. *Apples of Paradise*. New York: Trident, 1967.

——— *The Chokecherry Tree*. 1948. Reprint. Albuquerque: U of New Mexico P, 1975.

——— *The Golden Bowl*. 1944. Reprint. Albuquerque: U of New Mexico P, 1976.

——— *Of Lizards and Angels: A Saga of Siouxland*. Norman: U of Oklahoma P, 1992.

——— *This Is the Year*. Garden City NY: Doubleday, 1947.

McMurtry, Larry. *The Last Picture Show*. New York: Penguin, 1966.

Mitchell, W. O. *Who Has Seen the Wind?* Toronto: Macmillan of Canada, 1947.

Moberg, Vilhelm. *Last Letter Home: The Emigrants, Part IV*. Translated by Gustaf Lannestock. New York: Popular Library, 1961.

——— *The Settlers: The Emigrants, Part III*. Translated by Gustaf Lannestock. New York: Popular Library, 1961.

———— *Unto a Good Land: The Emigrants, Part II*. Translated by Gustaf Lannestock. New York: Popular Library, 1954.

Morris, Wright. *Ceremony in Lone Tree*. 1959. Reprint. Lincoln: U of Nebraska P, 1973.

———— *Collected Stories: 1948–1986*. New York: Harper & Row, 1986.

———— *Field of Vision*. 1956. Reprint. Lincoln: U of Nebraska P, 1974.

———— *Fire Sermon*. 1971. Reprint. Lincoln: U of Nebraska P, 1979.

———— *The Fork River Space Project*. 1977. Reprint. Lincoln: U of Nebraska P, 1981.

———— *God's Country and My People*. New York: Harper & Row, 1968.

———— *The Home Place*. 1948. Reprint. Lincoln: U of Nebraska P, 1968.

———— *A Life*. 1973. Lincoln: U of Nebraska P, 1980.

———— *Plains Song for Female Voices*. New York: Harper & Row, 1980.

———— *The Territory Ahead*. 1957. Reprint. Lincoln: U of Nebraska P, 1978.

———— *Will's Boy: A Memoir*. New York: Harper & Row, 1981.

———— *The Works of Love*. 1949. Reprint. Lincoln: U of Nebraska P, 1972.

———— *The World in the Attic*. 1949. Reprint. Lincoln: U of Nebraska P, 1971.

Moses, Edwin. *Astonishment of Heart*. New York: Macmillan, 1984.

Norris, Kathleen. *Dakota: A Spiritual Geography*. New York: Ticknor & Fields, 1993.

O'Brien, Dan. *In the Center of the Nation*. New York: Avon, 1991.

Ostenso, Martha. *Wild Geese*. New York: Dodd, Mead, 1920.

Parkman, Francis. *The Oregon Trail: Sketches of Prairie and Rocky Mountain Life*. 1847. Reprint. Boston: Little, Brown, 1906.

Pike, Zebulon Montgomery. *Zebulon Pike's Arkansaw Journal: In Search of the Southern Louisiana Purchase Boundary Line*. 1932. Reprint. Edited by Stephen H. Hart and Archer B. Hulbert. Westport CT: Greenwood, 1972.

Quick, Herbert. *Vandemark's Folly*. New York: A. L. Burt, 1922.

Richter, Conrad. *The Sea of Grass*. 1936. Reprint. New York: Ballantine, 1984.

Rølvaag, O. E. *Giants in the Earth*. 1927. Reprint. New York: Harper & Row, 1965.

———— *Peder Victorious*. 1929. Reprint. Lincoln: U of Nebraska P, 1982.

———— *Their Fathers' God*. 1931. Reprint. Lincoln: U of Nebraska P, 1983.

Ross, Sinclair. *As for Me and My House*. 1941. Reprint. Lincoln: U of Nebraska P, 1978.

———— *The Lamp at Noon and Other Stories*. Toronto: McClelland & Stewart, 1968.

Sandemose, Aksel. *Ross Dane*. 1928. Reprint. Winnepeg: Gunnars & Campbell, 1989.

Sandoz, Mari. *Capital City*. 1939. Reprint. Lincoln: U of Nebraska P, 1982.

———— *Love Song to the Plains*. 1961. Reprint. Lincoln: U of Nebraska P, 1966.

———— *Miss Morissa*. 1955. Reprint. Lincoln: U of Nebraska P, 1980.

———— *Old Jules*. 1935. Reprint. Lincoln: U of Nebraska P, 1962.

———— *Old Jules Country*. New York: Hastings House, 1965.

———— *Sandhill Sundays and Other Recollections*. 1930. Reprint. Lincoln: U of Nebraska P, 1970.

———— *Slogum House*. 1937. Reprint. Lincoln: U of Nebraska P, 1981.

———— *The Tom Walker*. 1947. Reprint. Lincoln: U of Nebraska P, 1984.

Scarborough, Dorothy. *The Wind*. 1925. Reprint. Austin: U of Texas P, 1979.

Smiley, Jane. *A Thousand Acres*. New York: Knopf, 1991.

Stead, Robert. *Grain*. Toronto: McClelland & Stewart, 1926.

———— *The Homesteaders*. 1916. Reprint. Toronto: U of Toronto P, 1973.

Stegner, Wallace. *The Big Rock Candy Mountain*. New York: Duell, Sloan & Pearce, 1943.

———— *Wolf Willow*. New York: Viking, 1962.

Sykes, Hope Williams. *Second Hoeing*. 1935. Reprint. Lincoln: U of Nebraska P, 1982.

Thomas, Dorothy. *The Home Place*. 1934. Reprint. Lincoln: U of Nebraska P, 1966.

Unger, Douglas. *Leaving the Land*. New York: Harper & Row, 1984.

Vinz, Mark, and Thom Tammaro, eds. *Inheriting the Land: Contemporary Voices from the Midwest*. Minneapolis: U of Minnesota P, 1992.

Walker, Mildred. *Winter Wheat*. 1944. Reprint. Lincoln: U of Nebraska P, 1992.

Weaver, Will. *A Gravestone Made of Wheat*. St. Paul MN: Graywolf, 1989.

White, William Allen. *The Autobiography of William Allen White*. New York: Macmillan, 1946.

―――― *A Certain Rich Man*. New York: Macmillan, 1909.

―――― *The Court of Boyville*. New York: Doubleday & McClure, 1899.

―――― *In Our Town*. New York: McClure Phillips, 1906.

―――― *In the Heart of a Fool*. New York: Macmillan, 1918.

―――― *The Real Issue: A Book of Kansas Stories*. Chicago: Way & Williams, 1897.

Whitman, Walt. *Complete Poetry and Selected Prose*. Edited by James E. Miller Jr. New York: Houghton Mifflin, 1959.

Wiebe, Rudy Henry. *Peace Shall Destroy Many*. Toronto: McClelland & Stewart, 1962.

Wilder, Laura Ingalls. *By the Shores of Silver Lake*. 1939. Reprint. New York: Harper & Row, 1953.

―――― *Farmer Boy*. 1933. Reprint. New York: Harper & Row, 1953.

―――― *The First Four Years*. New York: Harper & Row, 1971.

―――― *Little House in the Big Woods*. 1932. Reprint. New York: Harper & Row, 1953.

―――― *Little House on the Prairie*. 1935. Reprint. New York: Harper & Row, 1953.

―――― *Little Town on the Prairie*. 1941. Reprint. New York: Harper & Row, 1953.

―――― *The Long Winter*. 1940. Reprint. New York: Harper & Row, 1953.

―――― *On the Banks of Plum Creek*. 1937. Reprint. New York: Harper & Row, 1953.

―――― *These Happy Golden Years*. 1943. Reprint. New York: Harper & Row, 1953.

Winther, Sophus Keith. *Mortgage Your Heart*. New York: Macmillan, 1937.

―――― *Take All to Nebraska*. New York: Macmillan, 1936.

Woiwode, Larry. *Beyond the Bedroom Wall*. New York: Farrar, Straus & Giroux, 1975.

―――― *Born Brothers*. New York: Viking Penguin, 1988.

―――― *The Neumiller Stories*. New York: Farrar, Straus & Giroux, 1989.

Young, Carrie. *Nothing to Do But Stay: My Pioneer Mother*. New York: Dell, 1991.

———— *The Wedding Dress: Stories from the Dakota Plains*. New York: Dell, 1992.

SECONDARY WORKS

Adams, Charles Hansford. *"The Guardian of the Law": Authority and Identity in J. F. Cooper*. University Park: Pennsylvania State UP, 1990.

Allen, John Logan. *Passage through the Garden: Lewis and Clark and the Image of the American Northwest*. Urbana: U of Illinois P, 1975.

Arnold, Marilyn. *Willa Cather's Short Fiction*. Athens: Ohio UP, 1984.

Atherton, Lewis. *Main Street on the Middle Border*. 1954. Reprint. Bloomington: Indiana UP, 1984.

Bailey, Jennifer. "The Dangers of Femininity in Willa Cather's Fiction." *Journal of American Studies* 16 (1982): 391–406.

Baker, Bruce P. "*O Pioneers!* The Problem of Structure." *Great Plains Quarterly* 2 (1982): 218–23.

Baritz, Loren. "The Idea of the West." *American Historical Review* 66 (1961): 618–40.

Baurrecht, William C. "Within a Continuous Frame: Stegner's Family Album in *The Big Rock Candy Mountain*." In *Critical Essays on Wallace Stegner*, edited by Anthony Arthur, 98–108. Boston: G. K. Hall, 1982.

Billington, Ray Allen. *Land of Savagery, Land of Promise: The European Image of the American Frontier*. Norman: U of Oklahoma P, 1981.

Bird, Roy. *Wright Morris: Memory and Imagination*. New York: Peter Land, 1985.

Blegen, Helmer M. "Ole E. Rølvaag: A Reminiscence." In *The Prairie Frontier*, edited by Sandra Looney, Arthur Huseboe, and Geoffrey Hunt, 94–109. Sioux Falls SD: Nordland Heritage Foundation, 1984.

Boorstin, Daniel J. *The Americans: The National Experience*. New York: Random House, 1965.

Bredahl, Carl. *New Ground: Western American Narrative and the Literary Canon*. Chapel Hill: U of North Carolina P, 1989.

Bucco, Martin. "Epilogue: The Development of Western Literary Criticism." In *A Literary History of the American West*, edited by J. Golden Taylor and Thomas J. Lyon, 1283–1316. Fort Worth: Texas Christian UP, 1987.

Bukoski, Anthony. "Grandeur in Washington Irving's *A Tour on the Prairies.*" *Illinois Quarterly* 43.4 (1981): 5–15.

Center for the New West. *Overview of Change in America's New Economy*. Denver, 1992.

Crump, G. B. *The Novels of Wright Morris: A Critical Interpretation*. Lincoln: U of Nebraska P, 1978.

Cutright, Paul Russell. *Lewis and Clark: Pioneering Naturalists*. 1969. Reprint, Lincoln: U of Nebraska P, 1989.

Daiches, David. *Willa Cather: A Critical Introduction*. 1951. Reprint. New York: Collier, 1962.

Davis, Kenneth. *Kansas: A Bicentennial History*. New York: W. W. Norton, 1976.

DeVoto, Bernard. Introduction to *The Journals of Lewis and Clark*. Edited by Bernard DeVoto. Boston: Houghton Mifflin, 1953.

Dick, Everett. *The Sod House Frontier, 1854–1890*. Lincoln: U of Nebraska P, 1937.

Dodge, Richard Irving. *The Plains of North America and Their Inhabitants*. 1876. Edited by Wayne R. Kime. Newark DE: U of Delaware P, 1989.

Dondore, Dorothy. *The Prairie and the Making of Middle America: Four Centuries of Description*. 1926. New York: Antiquarian, 1961.

Eckstein, Neil T. "*Giants in the Earth* as Saga." In *Where the West Begins*, edited by Arthur Huseboe, 34–41. Sioux Falls SD: Center for Western Studies, 1978.

Edel, Leon. "A Cave of One's Own." In *Sleep and Dreams: Experiments in Literary Psychology*, 216–40. New York: Harper & Row, 1982.

Elliott, James P. Historical introduction to *The Prairie*. Albany: SUNY P, 1985.

Emmons, David M. *Garden in the Grasslands: Boomer Literature of the Central Great Plains*. Lincoln: U of Nebraska P, 1971.

Erisman, Fred. "Early Western Literary Scholars." In *A Literary History of the American West*, edited by J. Golden Taylor and Thomas J. Lyon, 303–16. Fort Worth: Texas Christian UP, 1987.

Etulain, Richard. "Shifting Interpretations of Western Cultural History." In *Historians and the American West*, edited by Michael P. Malone, 414–32. Lincoln: U of Nebraska P, 1983.

Farmer, Catherine D. "Beret as the Norse Mythological Goddess Freya/Gurthr." In *Women and Western American Literature*, edited by Helen Stauffer and Susan Rosowski, 179–93. Troy NY: Whitson, 1982.

Francis, R. Donald. *Images of the West: Perceptions of the Prairies, 1690–1960*. Saskatoon: Western Producer Prairie Books, 1989.

Gleason, John B. "The Case of Willa Cather." *Western American Literature* 20 (1986): 275–99.

Goetzmann, William H., and William N. Goetzmann. *The West of the Imagination*. New York: W. W. Norton, 1986.

Hafer, Jack. "Setting and Theme in Morris' *Ceremony in Lone Tree*." *Heritage of Kansas* 10.3 (1977): 10–20.

Hales, Leslie Ann. "Spiritual Longing in Laurence's Manawaka Women." *English Studies in Canada* 11 (1985): 82–90.

Harrison, Dick. *Unnamed Country: The Struggle for a Canadian Prairie Fiction*. Edmonton: U of Alberta P, 1977.

Hazard, Lucy Lockwood. *The Frontier in American Literature*. 1927. Reprint. New York: Frederick Ungar, 1961.

Hudson, John C. *Plains Country Towns*. Minneapolis: U of Minnesota P, 1985.

——— "Towns of the Western Railroads." *Great Plains Quarterly* 2 (1982): 41–54.

——— "Who Was 'Forest Man'? Sources of Migration to the Plains." *Great Plains Quarterly* 6 (1986): 69–83.

Hudson, Lois Phillips. "*The Big Rock Candy Mountain:* No Roots—and No Frontier." In *Critical Essays on Wallace Stegner*, edited by Anthony Arthur, 137–45. Boston: G. K. Hall, 1982.

Hulbert, Archer Butler. *Soil: Its Influence on the History of the United States*. New Haven: Yale UP, 1930.

Jackson, Donald Dale. "It Took Trains to Put Street Kids on the Right Track out of the Slums." *Smithsonian* 17.5 (1986): 94–103.

James, Edwin. *Account of an Expedition from Pittsburgh to the Rocky Mountains.* 1823. Vol. 2. Ann Arbor: University Microfilms, 1966.

Jones, Howard Mumford. *O Strange New World.* New York: Viking, 1952.

Keith, W. J. *"Wild Geese:* The Death of Caleb Gare." *Studies in Canadian Literature* 3 (1978): 274–76.

Kelly, William P. *Plotting America's Past: Fenimore Cooper's Leatherstocking Tales.* Carbondale: Southern Illinois UP, 1983.

Knoll, Robert C., ed. *Conversations with Wright Morris.* Lincoln: U of Nebraska P, 1977.

Kollmorgen, Walter. "The Woodsman's Assault on the Domain of the Cattlemen." *Annals of the American Association of Geographers* 59 (1969): 215–39.

Kolodny, Annette. *The Land before Her: Fantasy and Experience of the American Frontiers, 1630–1860.* Chapel Hill: U of North Carolina P, 1984.

——— *The Lay of the Land: Metaphor as Experience and History in American Life and Letters.* Chapel Hill: U of North Carolina P, 1975.

Kraenzel, Carl Frederick. *The Great Plains in Transition.* Norman: U of Oklahoma P, 1955.

Kreisel, Henry. "The Prairie: A State of Mind." In *Trace: Prairie Writers on Writing,* edited by Birk Sproxton, 3–17. Winnipeg: Turnstone, 1986.

Lamar, Howard Roberts. "Seeing More Than Earth and Sky: The Rise of a Great Plains Aesthetic." *Great Plains Quarterly* 9 (1989): 69–77.

Love, Glen A. *The New Americans: The Westerner and the Modern Experience in the American Novel.* London: Bucknell UP, 1982.

Lowenthal, David. "The Pioneer Landscape: An American Dream." *Great Plains Quarterly* 2 (1982): 5–19.

Luebke, Frederick C., ed. *Ethnicity on the Great Plains.* Lincoln: U of Nebraska P, 1980.

Lutwack, Leonard. *The Role of Place in Literature.* Syracuse: Syracuse UP, 1984.

Malin, James C. *The Grassland of North America: Prolegomena to Its History, with Addenda and Postscript.* Gloucester MA: Peter Smith, 1967.

Marx, Leo. *The Machine in the Garden: Technology and the Pastoral Idea in America.* New York: Oxford UP, 1964.

Maxfield, James R. "Strategies of Self-Deception in Willa Cather's *The Professor's House.*" *Studies in the Novel* 16 (1984): 72–86.

McDermott, John Francis. Introduction to *A Tour on the Prairies*, by Washington Irving. Norman: U of Oklahoma P, 1956.

——— "Washington Irving as Western Traveler: Editor's Introduction." In *The Western Journals of Washington Irving*, edited by John Francis McDermott, 3–66. Norman: U of Oklahoma P, 1944.

McWilliams, John P., Jr. *Political Justice in a Republic: James Fenimore Cooper's America.* Berkeley and Los Angeles: U of California P, 1972.

Meyer, Roy W. *The Middle Western Farm Novel in the Twentieth Century.* Lincoln: U of Nebraska P, 1965.

Miller, John. "Place and Community in *Little Town on the Prairie:* DeSmet in 1883." *South Dakota History* 16 (1986): 351–72.

Milton, John. "Plains Landscapes and Changing Visions." *Great Plains Quarterly* 2 (1982): 55–62.

Mitchell, Lee Clark. *Witnesses to a Vanishing America.* Princeton: Princeton UP, 1981.

Moseley, Ann. "The Dual Nature in Art in *The Song of the Lark.*" *Western American Literature* 14 (1979): 19–32.

——— *Ole Edvart Rølvaag.* Boise ID: Boise State University, 1987.

Motley, Warren. *The American Abraham: J. F. Cooper and the Frontier Patriarch.* New York: Cambridge UP, 1987.

——— "The Unfinished Self: Willa Cather's *O Pioneers!* and the Psychic Cost of Woman's Success." *Women's Studies* 12 (1986): 149–65.

Moulton, Gary E. Introduction to vol. 2 of *The Journals of the Lewis and Clark Expedition*, edited by Gary E. Moulton and Thomas Dunlay. Lincoln: U of Nebraska P, 1986.

Murphy, John J. "A Comprehensive View of Cather's *O Pioneers!*" In *Critical Essays on Willa Cather*, edited by John J. Murphy, 113–27. Boston: G. K. Hall, 1984.

Nash, Roderick. *Wilderness and the American Mind.* New Haven: Yale UP, 1973.

Opie, John. "Learning to Read the Pioneer Landscape: Braudel, Eliade, Turner and Benton." *Great Plains Quarterly* 2 (1982): 20–30.

Owram, Doug. *The Promise of Eden: The Canadian Expansionist Movement and the Idea of the West.* Toronto: U of Toronto P, 1980.

Parrington, Vernon Louis. *Main Currents in American Thought: The Beginnings of Critical Realism in America, 1860–1920.* New York: Harcourt, Brace, World, 1930.

Pizer, Donald. *Hamlin Garland's Early Work and Career.* Berkeley and Los Angeles: U of California P, 1960.

——— "Herbert Spencer and the Genesis of Hamlin Garland's Critical System." *Tulane Studies in English* 7 (1957): 153–68.

Quantic, Diane D. "The Revolt from the Village and Middle Western Fiction, 1870–1915." *Kansas Quarterly* 5.4 (1973): 5–16.

Quirk, Tom. "Fitzgerald and Cather: *The Great Gatsby.*" *American Literature* 54 (1982): 576–91.

Reigstad, Paul. *Ole Rølvaag: His Life and Art.* Lincoln: U of Nebraska P, 1972.

Relph, Edward C. *Place and Placelessness.* Minneapolis: U of Minnesota P, 1977.

Richtik, James M. "Competition for Settlers: The Canadian Viewpoint." *Great Plains Quarterly* 3 (1983): 39–49.

Rippey, Barbara. "Mari Sandoz' Historical Perspective: Linking Past and Present." *Platte Valley Review* 17 (1989): 60–68.

Robertson, Jamie. "Henry Adams, Wallace Stegner, and the Search for a Sense of Place in the West." In *Critical Essays on Wallace Stegner,* edited by Anthony Arthur, 90–97. Boston: G. K. Hall, 1982.

Robinson, Forrest Glenn, and Margaret G. Robinson. *Wallace Stegner.* Boston: Twayne, 1977.

Ronda, James P. *Lewis and Clark among the Indians.* Lincoln: U of Nebraska P, 1984.

Rooke, Constance. "Hagar's Old Age: *The Stone Angel* as *Vollendungsroman.*" In *Crossing the River: Essays in Honor of Margaret Laurence,* edited by Kristjana Gunnars, 25–42. Toronto: U of Toronto P, 1988.

Rooney, John F., Wilbur Zelinsky, and Dean Louder, eds. *This Remarkable Continent: An Atlas of the United States and Canadian Society.* College Station: Texas A&M UP, 1982.

Rosowski, Susan. "The Pattern of Willa Cather's Novels." *Western American Literature* 15 (1981): 243–63.

—— *The Voyage Perilous: Willa Cather's Romanticism.* Lincoln: U of Nebraska P, 1986.

—— "Willa Cather and the Fatality of Place: O, Pioneers! My Ántonia, and A Lost Lady." In *Geography and Literature: A Meeting of the Disciplines,* edited by William Mallory and Paul Simpson-Housley, 81–94. Syracuse: Syracuse UP, 1987.

—— "Willa Cather's A Lost Lady: Art versus the Closing Frontier." *Great Plains Quarterly* 2 (1982): 239–48.

—— "Willa Cather's Plains Legacy: The Early Nebraska Stories." *Nebraska Humanist* 6 (1983): 48–52.

Ruud, Curtis. "Rølvaag, the Ash Lad, and New and Old World Values." In *Big Sioux Pioneers: Essays about the Settlement of the Dakota Prairie Frontier,* edited by Arthur Huseboe, 63–78. Sioux Falls SD: Nordland Heritage Foundation, 1982.

Shortridge, James. "The Heart of the Prairie: Culture Areas of the Central and Northern Great Plains." *Great Plains Quarterly* 8 (1988): 206–22.

—— *The Middle West: Its Meaning in American Culture.* Lawrence: UP of Kansas, 1989.

—— "The Vernacular Middle West." *Annals of the American Association of Geographers* 75 (1985): 48–57.

—— "Vernacular Regions in Kansas." *American Scholar* 21 (1980): 73–91.

Simonson, Harold. "Beret's Ineffable West." Paper presented at the annual meeting of the Western Literature Association, Denton TX, October 1990.

—— *Beyond the Frontier: Writers, Western Regionalism, and a Sense of Place.* Fort Worth: Texas Christian UP, 1989.

—— *The Closed Frontier: Studies in American Literary Tragedy.* New York: Holt, Rinehart, Winston, 1970.

———— *Prairies Within: The Tragic Trilogy of Ole Rølvaag*. Seattle: U of Washington P, 1987.

Singer, Barnett. "The Historical Ideal in Wallace Stegner's Fiction." In *Critical Essays on Wallace Stegner*, edited by Anthony Arthur, 124–36. Boston: G. K. Hall, 1982.

Slotkin, Richard. *Regeneration through Violence: The Mythology of the American Frontier*. Middleton CT: Wesleyan UP, 1973.

Smith, Henry Nash. *Virgin Land: The American West as Symbol and Myth*. 1950. Reprint. Cambridge: Harvard UP, 1970.

Stauffer, Helen. *Mari Sandoz: Story Catcher of the Plains*. Lincoln: U of Nebraska P, 1982.

Stegner, Wallace. *Beyond the Hundredth Meridian: John Wesley Powell and the Second Opening of the West*. 1953. Reprint. Lincoln: U of Nebraska P, 1982.

Stegner, Wallace, and Richard Etulain. *Conversations with Wallace Stegner on Western History and Literature*. Salt Lake City: U of Utah P, 1983.

Stouck, David. *Major Canadian Authors: A Critical Introduction to Canadian Literature in English*. Lincoln: U of Nebraska P, 1984.

———— *Willa Cather's Imagination*. Lincoln: U of Nebraska P, 1975.

Sturges, Hollister, ed. *The Rural Vision: France and America in the Late Nineteenth Century*. Lincoln: U of Nebraska P, 1987.

Suderman, Elmer F. "Cooper's Sense of Place in *The Prairie*." *North Dakota Quarterly* 55 (1987): 159–64.

Taylor, J. Golden, and Thomas J. Lyon, eds. *A Literary History of the American West*. Fort Worth: Texas Christian UP, 1987.

Thacker, Robert. *The Great Prairie Fact and Literary Imagination*. Albuquerque: U of New Mexico P, 1989.

Tuan, Yi-Fu. *Space and Place: The Perspective of Experience*. Minneapolis: U of Minnesota P, 1977.

Turner, Frederick Jackson. *The Frontier in American History*. 1920. Reprint. Tucson: U of Arizona P, 1986.

Unruh, John D., Jr. *The Plains Across: The Overland Emigrants and the Trans-Mississippi West*. Urbana: U of Illinois P, 1979.

Vigil, Ralph H. "Spanish Exploration and the Great Plains in the Age of Discovery." *Great Plains Quarterly* 10 (1990): 3–17.

Waldeland, Lynne. "Plains Song: Women's Voices in the Fiction of Wright Morris." *Critique* 24 (1982): 7–20.

Webb, Walter Prescott. *The Great Plains*. 1931. Reprint. Lincoln: U of Nebraska P, 1981.

Williams, David. "Jacob and the Demon: Hagar as Storyteller in *The Stone Angel*." In *Crossing the River: Essays in Honor of Margaret Laurence*, edited by Kristjana Gunnars, 81–98. Toronto: U of Toronto P, 1988.

Woodress, James. *Willa Cather: A Literary Life*. Lincoln: U of Nebraska P, 1987.

———— *Willa Cather: Her Life and Art*. Lincoln: U of Nebraska P, 1970.

Worster, Donald. *The Dust Bowl*. New York: Oxford UP, 1979.

———— *Under Western Skies: Nature and History in the American West*. New York: Oxford UP, 1992.

Yongue, Patricia Lee. "*The Professor's House* and 'Rip Van Winkle.'" *Western American Literature* 18 (1984): 281–97.

Zelinsky, Wilbur. *The Cultural Geography of the United States*. Englewood Cliffs NJ: Prentice Hall, 1973.

Index

Lion's Paw," 67; "Up the Coolly," 100–101

geographic determinism, xvii, 4, 11, 21

George Willard (character), 70

Great American Desert. *See* myths

Great Plains, xv–xvi, 4; as barrier in Cooper, 39; concepts of, 5–8; culture, 17; economics, 5, 30, 126; flora and fauna, 35–37; in Unger, 126

Great Plains fiction, xv–xviii, xix, xx, 4, 5, 7, 23, 53, 68, 76–77, 87, 96–97, 99, 101, 112, 116, 138, 145, 164, 169; early examples, 60. *See also* land; past; society

Great Plains language, 155–57, 159, 167; images and metaphors, xx, 163–65; ocean metaphor, 46, 105, 110, 139, 157–58, 162, 163, 164; style, 159–69; symbols, 157–59, 163, 164, 165, 167–69. *See also* society

Gregg, Josiah, 11

Grove, Frederick Philip, 3, 33; *Fruits of the Earth*, 14–15

Hall, James, 60

Hansen, Ron: *Nebraska Stories*, 148–50; "Playland," 149–50; "Red Letter Days," 149

Harrison, Dick, 83

Haruf, Kent, 9, 115; *The Tie That Binds*, 75, 111

Hazard, Lucy Lockwood, 125

Hill, James J., 135

homestead, 69, 71, 123, 136. *See also* settlers

Homestead Act, 8, 20, 65, 72. *See also* timber claim

house: as entrapment, 15, 97; —, in Haruf, 111–12; —, in Laurence, 106; as home, 2–3; as link to past, in Cather, 119; —, in Laurence, 106–7; —, in Morris, 110; as refuge, in Laurence, 105–8; —, in Manfred, 109; —, in Morris, 110–11; in Sandoz, 79, 80. *See also* refuge

house, dugout, 73

house, sod, 2, 53, 165

Howe, Edgar Watson: *The Story of a Country Town*, 24

Hudson, Lois Philips: *The Bones of Plenty*, 6, 19, 74–75, 127–28; "Water Witch," 52

Hugh Glass legend, 45

Hulbert, Archer B., 7, 10

Ibsen, Henrik, 118

Illinois, 105

immigrants, 26, 33, 62–64, 68, 82, 90, 98, 159; Bohemian, 91; Catholic, 72; Czech, 81; English, 72; German, 91; Irish, 113; Mennonite, 90; Norwegian, 91, 123; in Rølvaag, 112; Russian, 32; in Sandoz, 91–94; separation from home, 22; in society, 62; Swedish, 91; Swiss, 92, 93. *See also* society

Indiana, 110

Indians, 33, 34, 51, 115, 119, 120; in Cooper, 41; in Day, 146, 147, 148; in Erdrich, 138; in Irving, 43, 45; in Kroetsch, 128; in Morris, 128, 141, 151; in Rølvaag, 114; in Stegner, 123; in Unger, 89

industrial revolution. *See* capitalism

insanity, 23–24. *See also* society; women

Iowa, 35–36, 50, 67, 97, 111

Irving, Washington, xix; *A Tour on the Prairie*, 43–47

Ise, John: *Sod and Stubble*, 2, 9, 25, 73–74

Ishmael, 163

isolation. *See* society

Jake Barnes (character), 70

Jefferson, Thomas, 5, 8, 30, 33, 51

Job, 99, 100

Kansas, xix, 4, 5, 10, 13, 21, 23, 24, 50, 65, 67, 69, 120, 145; in Day, 146, 147

CPSIA information can be obtained
at www.ICGtesting.com
Printed in the USA
LVHW041457041221
705284LV00015B/882